THE DIMINISHING PARADISE

Changing Literary Perceptions of Australia

Ross Gibson

A SIRIUS BOOK

SIRIUS BOOKS
an imprint of Angus & Robertson Publishers

First published in Australia by Angus & Robertson Publishers in 1984
First published in the United Kingdom by Angus & Robertson (UK) Ltd in 1984

National Library of Australia
Cataloguing-in-publication data.

Gibson, Ross, 1956- .
The diminishing paradise.

Bibliography.
Includes index.
ISBN 0 207 14926 7.

1. *English literature — 18th century — History and criticism.*
2. *English literature — 19th century — History and criticism.*
3. *Australia in literature. I. Title.*

820′.9′3294

Typeset in 11pt Paladium by Setrite Typesetters, Hong Kong
Printed in Hong Kong

THE DIMINISHING PARADISE

For
E.A.G and E.M.G.

Contents

in this best of all possible worlds,
and the last he found —

a land of ochre red and courtesy,
of sheep that will cross the horizon,
a large English gaol, a meet Purgatory
& a strange Hell and Heaven of no limits.

Larry Buttrose,
"Doctor Pangloss in Pitt Street, 1788"

Introduction

> But the spirits have to be recognized to become real. They are not outside us, nor even entirely within, but flow back and forth between us and the objects we have made, the landscape we have shaped and move in. We have dreamed all these things in our deepest lives and they are ourselves. It is our self we are making out there . . .
>
> David Malouf, *An Imaginary Life* (1978)

It is generally agreed that the 1850s and the 1890s are crucial periods in the history of Australian culture. The "roaring days" of the goldrushes are perceived as the era when many elements of a future national ethos arose during a turbulent period of increased population and economic expansion. In their turn the "legendary" nineties are traditionally regarded as the years in which a national character began to develop out of the pell-mell of attitudes and experiences which had arisen during the colony's first hundred years.

There are, however, periods other than the 1850s and 1890s which cannot be ignored in an assessment of the nation's conception and development. The miserable years of the gaol-colony, and the hopeful times of the emancipations and early emigrations between 1810 and 1830 all left their mark on a burgeoning society. Also, the decades of the great inland explorations — the 1830s and 1840s — figure significantly in the colonial history. During this period, Thomas Mitchell, Edward Eyre and Charles Sturt probed the mysterious centre of the continent and returned with knowledge in journals which would eventually influence the way people regarded Australia.

There has been a need to re-examine the earliest times (colonial and pre-colonial) since authors such as Patrick White, Francis Webb and Thomas Keneally, to name but three, demonstrated that the colonial past is still a goldmine of inadequately assessed myth, inspiration and insight about the Australian ethos. White, for example, drew on the deeds and journals of the explorers when writing *Voss*, in which he shifted the focus of attention back past the 1890s and 1850s as he presented an imaginative history of the pursuit and resolution of Australian dreams. Similarly, in poems such as "Eyre All Alone", "Leichhardt in Theatre" and "Sturt and the Vultures", Francis Webb has concentrated on the themes which arise from these questers' writings. Thomas Keneally, on the other hand, has taken the First Fleet journals (particularly those by Watkin Tench) as the bases for his examination of Australian history and myth in *Bring Larks and Heroes*. Further examples include Kenneth Slessor, who examined Australian themes by looking through the "Five Visions of Captain Cook" (1932); and James McAuley, who was inspired by the "Memorials" of Pedro Fernandez de Quiros to contemplate the south land and the days when its existence was not even positively verified, when an enduring image of *Terra Australis* arose, an image which I have chosen to call the "diminishing paradise". (See McAuley's "Terra Australis" and "Captain Quiros".)

Such achievements compel students of Australian culture to examine the earliest published literature about the country, to analyse it as serious writing which has played a perhaps unrecognised role in the development of Australian literature.

Of course, a reader in the 1980s, coming to the pre-1850 literature after the modern interpretations, encounters difficulties in gaining a clear perspective on the original works. For example, an awareness of White's and Webb's mythologising of figures such as Eyre, Leichhardt and Sturt inevitably shapes —

perhaps distorts — a modern reader's understanding of the early writings. As T. S. Eliot has explained in "Tradition and the Individual Talent", the past can be "altered by the present" when a new work of art is added to the traditional canon.[1]

However, despite these problems of perspective, now that modern authors have indicated that there may be a key to some Australian mythologies concealed in the earliest literature about the country, critics must attempt to peel back the layers of new readings which have accrued to the original writings. There is a need to examine the works in their earliest setting, to ascertain what the authors were thinking about Australia at the time of their experience. While never denying that the modern consciousness has been formulated after the work of writers such as White, Webb and Keneally, a critic must adopt a degree of distance from the modern world in order to embrace the issues which the original writers (and not their more recent interpreters) sought to elucidate.

The arguments in this book culminate in examinations of the published journals of Mitchell, Sturt and Eyre. There are two points about this literature which, salient as they are, must be established at the outset. First, the explorers' literature belongs to the initial stage of Anglo-Saxon society in Australia, to the era when the society was an outpost of England and owed its population and its economic well-being almost entirely to the cooperation of authorities in England. This is the parochial, colonial phase before the goldrushes. Secondly and concomitantly, the explorers (with the exception of Leichhardt, whose nationality places him outside the terms of reference of this work) were British men whose literary sensibilities derived from British literary traditions. The explorers were investigating, describing and interpreting a continent which was not yet populated with a "native" white society. As a result, their contributions to the development of a literary consciousness in Australia must be construed as "external" in influence at a time when alienated English minds were attempting to formulate an image of the land and its society. This English vision of the country predominated throughout the first era of white Australian history, until the 1850s when influences on the image of Australia were to switch from external to internal.

After 1850 the first sizeable generation of native-born white Australians was coming to maturity. Also, the goldrushes were in progress, and Australia quite suddenly developed a sense of self-sufficiency resulting from the growth of a population large enough and prosperous enough to begin to support its own economy and its own culture. The emergence about this time of an Australian-born poet as talented and as concerned with national identity as Charles Harpur is indicative of a change in the influences on Australia's image, as responsibility for the national ethos began to be handed over from English to Australian authors.

Students of Australian culture have been thorough in their coverage of the goldrushes and the 1890s. The representations of the country prior to 1850, however, have received insufficient attention. Admittedly, Russel Ward selects the sixty years before the goldrushes as the period when "a specifically Australian outlook grew up first and most clearly among the bush workers in the Australian pastoral industry".[2] Ward may be correct in all that he claims within the scope of *The Australian Legend*, but even when examining the earliest years of the colony, he does not account for the significance of English authors' views about the country at this time when the image of Australia was most in need of formation and when the culture of the colony was necessarily still predominantly English.

Ward is right to select the era before the goldrushes as the time when a "national mystique" began to develop. However, because of his "internal" approach he cannot claim to be comprehensive in scope. Coral Lansbury's *Arcady in Australia*, might be thought to complement *The Australian Legend*. Invoking Ernst Cassirer's pertinent opinions about the primacy of a nation's myths over its history, she adopts an "external" perspective in studying "The Evocation of Australia in Nineteenth-Century English Literature". However, Dr Lansbury's book is deficient because, in her zeal to concentrate on major writers of the 1850s (Dickens, Reade, Bulwer Lytton and Sydney), she underemphasises the writings from the earlier years. To similar effect, Richard White's *Inventing Australia* devotes only twenty pages to the era prior to 1850.

Other critical works impinge on, without addressing themselves directly to, the questions which I propose to cover in this study. Bernard Smith's *European Vision and the South Pacific 1768-1850* is an outstanding history of art and ideas, but it is concerned with the visual arts and encompasses far more than

Australia in its "external" approach to the representations of a new world. Brian Elliott's *The Landscape of Australian Poetry* is predominantly "internal" in approach and does not concentrate on the period before 1850. (Elliott's "Antipodes: An Essay in Attitudes", *Australian Letters* 7, 1966, pp.51-75, does consider some writing by English authors prior to 1850, and the article is valuable as a background to chapter one of this book.) W. P. Friederich's *Australia in Western Imaginative Prose Writings* is very wide-ranging in the nationalities of the writers who are anthologised and does not cover the specific questions of English views in great depth. V. T. Harlow's monumental *The Founding of the Second British Empire* provides valuable background material on Pedro Fernandez de Quiros and the English anthologists, but the particular question of a mythic image of Australia is not crucial to his project. And Sidney Rosenberg's unpublished Ph.D. thesis, *Black Sheep and Golden Fleece. A Study of Nineteenth Century English Attitudes toward Australian Colonials*, focuses on character-types rather than the image of a nascent nation, and also it emphasises the latter half of the nineteenth century.

There is a need therefore to understand better the nature of the literary heritage bequeathed to Australian writers at the conclusion of the first, colonial (or "external") period of Australian culture. The image which was handed over at this stage was something which Australians were free to accept, reject, modify or embellish, but because it entailed Australia's earliest means of identifying itself it would figure largely in the country's systems of myth. The way that Australians (and the rest of the world) regarded themselves would always be influenced to some extent by the way the country was first interpreted.

Writings such as Sturt's, Mitchell's and Eyre's, for example, could be described as "quasi-myths", or perhaps more accurately, "proto-myths". Certainly they have influenced the formation of a national sense of identity, but they have become truly mythic only at second-hand and retroactively because their stories have penetrated the "collective consciousness" through imaginative interpretations by modern writers. The original writings which contained the elements of myth were submerged for almost a century before their significance emerged. They were covered over, not so much in the obscuration of a palimpsest, but rather in the manner of a skeleton which is a structuring influence despite its invisibility at the surface level.

It will be necessary to consider, in due course, the reasons for the submergence, but the first point to be made at this stage is that the pre-1850 writings do warrant analysis as serious literature concerned with national identity.

The second point is that an examination of the English influence on the image of Australia prior to 1850 cannot focus solely on any one phase of the early colonial experience. Certainly the work should culminate with the writings of Mitchell, Sturt and Eyre, but these works can be appreciated only as part of a larger corpus — a tradition perhaps — of previous attempts by English authors to understand and evoke the southern continent. The explorers' visions cannot be comprehended as separate from the attitudes espoused by writers who dreamt of *Terra Australis* even before its discovery, or from the observations recorded by the writers during the "hungry years" of the original convict settlement, or from the fantasies which coloured so much of the emigrants' propaganda of the 1820s and 1830s. Also it must be emphasised that the English writing from the period before 1850 deserves to be treated as creative literature rather than as dead source material which has been vivified by twentieth-century historical novelists and poets. The works arose from the struggles of alienated people to make sense of a new and seemingly normless environment. Any literature which deals with something as mutable as the perceived characteristics of a new society and its habitat must be construed as creative. Impressions, observations and fantasies regarding the country are filtered through a writer's personality, prejudices and language, so that any image which ensues must be treated as a constructed entity created by a mind which applies some order to the profusion of initial sensations. In this respect a marine officer's detailed and speciously objective description of, say, a surveying trip in the environs of Port Jackson can be counted just as creative as, for example, Erasmus Darwin's allegory illustrating Josiah Wedgewood's medallion depicting Hope's visit to Botany Bay. This is not to say that the two pieces of writing are to be treated as generically identical. A recognition of the different intentions of authors is necessary in an assessment of the works, as is an awareness of the degree of fictive impulse or of first-hand observation informing each particular representation. Erasmus

Darwin's poem and the marine officer's description may both contribute to an image of Australia, but because the two pieces use different methods and draw on different degrees of Australian experience to reach that common end, they should not be analysed as if they were similar in style and purpose.

Even so, all of the writing prior to 1850 can be perceived as united in one particular process: the attempt to make sense of an English colony's existence in the Australian environment as English writers endeavour to define themselves and their fellows in terms of the new habitat so that two previously disparate entities — the new land and the Anglo-Saxon writer's self — become united in expression of new experience. It is a process which involves initially a description of the new country, and later, an evocation of the land and the new society in more abstract, almost symbolic terms. Or, as Hegel wrote pertaining to human expression:

> Man realizes himself through *practical* activity, since he has the impulse to express himself, and so again to recognize himself, in things that are at first simply presented to him as externally existent. He attains this end by altering external things and impressing on them the stamp of his own inner nature, so that he rediscovers his own character in them. Man does this in order that he may profit by his freedom to break down the stubborn indifference of the external world to himself, and may enjoy in the countenance of nature only an outward embodiment of himself.[3]

All of the writing about Australia prior to 1850 is concerned with attaining some integration between the mere description of an alienating world and the impression of character on an environment as the self "absorbs" the new land through experience. After the centuries of speculation which led up to the discovery of the southern continent, English literature concerned with Australia progressed, generally speaking, through three stages: (a) 1770-1800: the descriptive journals of the *Endeavour* writers, the First Fleet annalists and the earliest colonists, when scientists and government officials produced speciously objective accounts of the environment and of the events which occurred within it; (b) 1800-1835: the more "imaginative" literature up to the mid-1830s in which inexperienced writers sought to impress their own natures on the new colony by evoking it in terms of a terrestrial paradise, using metaphors and motifs which derived from their English literary heritage; and (c) 1835-1850: the explorers' literature created by writers whose "practical activity" enabled them to produce more enduring and convincing interpretations of Australian experience, interpretations which are at once descriptive and symbolic.

In setting up these three stages, with their arbitrary chronological divisions, I am not asserting that certain attitudes belong exclusively to certain periods. However, I do maintain, with fidelity to overwhelming evidence, that the shifts of popular opinion can be delineated according to the three designated phases. As this work examines the stages, two questions ought to be answered. Firstly, what was the English image of Australia prior to 1850? Secondly, what caused the image, in its varying forms, to appear as it did?

In order to formulate some answers, one must trace the image right back to the beginnings of white society in Australia. Indeed, to make a start, it is necessary to go back even further, to before Captain Cook's voyage along the Australian east coast in 1770.

CHAPTER ONE

A Diminishing Paradise:

AN IMAGE OF *TERRA AUSTRALIS* PRIOR TO 1770

Voyage within you, on the fabled ocean,
And you will find that Southern Continent,
Quiros' vision — his hidalgo heart
And mythical Australia, where reside
All things in their imagined counterpart.

James McAuley, "Terra Australis" (1946)

This land always gives me the feeling that it doesn't *want* to be touched, it doesn't *want* men to get hold of it.

D. H. Lawrence, *Kangaroo* (1923)

Long before Captain James Cook discovered and surveyed the east coast of New Holland, dreamers had postulated the existence of *Terra Australis Incognita*. For centuries, before errant traders and buccaneers stood on the arid western coastlines and shook their heads while gazing inland, a wondrous south land had been virtually willed into existence. In the tradition of Hesiod's Blessed Isles which lay beckoning at the navigable extremity of the world, *Terra Australis* was as alluring as it was distant. And so long as the south land was not discovered, fancy could invest it with all the characteristics which might satisfy Utopian yearnings. The southern continent glowed in the imagination, a region far away in time and space, where a newly implanted society could flourish in freedom and plenty.

In many respects, from the Middle Ages onwards, people were justified in crediting the existence of *Terra Australis*. Rumours persisted over centuries until they were difficult to ignore. Apart from the tall tales of Sinbad the Sailor in the *Arabian Nights*, there were Marco Polo's seemingly more authentic claims (which actually derived from garbled translations and misreadings of Marco's original writings) about the existence of a rich southern continent. And after Marco Polo, the reports of travellers such as Friar Odoric in the fourteenth century and Nicolo de Conti in the fifteenth all rendered the existence of extensive southern lands more credible.

Moreover, the great exploratory exploits of Polo and, later, of Columbus, da Gama and Magellan all suggested that if one travels far enough and intrepidly enough in a new direction one establishes a new landfall. Such an expectation seemed all the more legitimate in the light of ancient geographical theory, dating back to Ptolemy in the second century A.D. Applying deceptively scientific thinking, geographers for centuries likened the globe to any gravity-governed body: stability being dependent on balance, and the earth being constant in its rotation, the distribution of mass above and below the equator was assumed to be equable. Therefore the expected southern continent would be a concrete "reflection" of the Eurasian land-mass, located behind the "mirror" of the equator. A precise and representative example of the balance theory occurs in an "Appendix" concerning *Terra Australis Incognita* (dated 1656) bound into the British Museum's second edition (1657) of Peter Heylyn's *Cosmographie in foure Bookes Contayning the Chorographie and Historie of the whole World* (first published in 1652):

> It is clearly known, that in the other two Continents, the land which lyeth on the North-side of that Line [the equator], is four times at the least as large as that which lies South thereof; and therefore since the earth is equally poized on both sides of the *Center*, it must needs be that the earth in answerable measure

> and proportion must advance it self in some places above the Sea, on the South-side of the Line, as it doth in others on the North. [p.1901 (*sic*), misprint for p.1091)]

By popular and enduring consensus the south land was to be expansive, located for the most part "under the first meridian; that is, betwixt 180 and 230 degrees of longitude".[1] It was not originally imagined to be specifically in the region of what is now known as Australia. The *Terra Australis* of dreamers' imaginations was a much grander realm than that of later actuality.

In this fact lies the essence of an image of Australia which has remained influential until the present day. This is the image which I have chosen to call the "diminishing paradise". In people's imaginations the southern continent had always been a large and various land catering for El Doradoan fantasies. For example, circa 1620 Robert Burton wondered:

> Whether *Guinea* be an Island or part of the Continent, or that hungry Spaniard's [that is, Quiros's] discovery of *Terra Australis Incognita*, or *Magellanica*, be as true as that of *Mercurius Britannicus*, or his of *Utopia*, or his *Lucinia*. And yet in likelihood it may be so, for without all question it being extended from the Tropick of *Capricorn* to the circle *Antarctick*, and lying as it doth in the temperate *Zone*, cannot choose but yield in time some flourishing Kingdoms to succeeding ages, as *America* did unto the *Spaniards*.[2]

Unfortunately, in *actuality* such a felicitous realm could never be located. As the historical experience gradually put speculation to the test, the southern continent proved elusive and increasingly diminutive while its ideal remained alluring.

Magellan had provoked optimism with his discovery of Tierra del Fuego, but too soon writers had to admit that these were "Islands that depend rather upon America than Australia".[3] Furthermore, exploration of the Indian and Pacific Oceans by the Dutch (Tasman, Jansz, Pelsaert), the Portuguese and Spanish (Mendana, Quiros and Torres) and the French (de Gonneville) had continually restricted the range within which the undiscovered continent might have been lying.

By the middle of the seventeenth century the enormity of the anticipated south land had diminished on all four sides. The

Indian Ocean had been comprehensively traversed, and it had to be conceded that the western extremity of *Terra Australis* must be the New Holland coastline (nowadays known as Western Australia). To the east, the New Hebrides (now Vanuatu) and the inadequately surveyed New Zealand (discovered in 1642 by Abel Tasman) marked the most generous possible margin. Van Diemen's Land was thought to be part of the southern coast, but the continent could conceivably trail off into the vast uncharted regions of the Antarctic, the icy uninhabitability of which was notorious. To the north were the coastline of the Gulf of Carpentaria and the separate islands of New Britain and the East Indies.

Over a period of centuries, therefore, expectations about *Terra Australis* were continually compromised as the extent of the unknown regions of the southern hemisphere diminished each time an explorer returned from there. Anti-climax followed anti-climax as the peripheries of the known world were gradually extended. Moreover, the sense of bathos about the south land seemed appropriate in the light of previous experience in America. Once colonists had begun to test their fantasies and aspirations against the actual problems of living and working in that New World, they had been obliged to reassess their original optimism. After America, it became apparent that any Utopian realm would be extremely difficult to locate.

However, in spite of the ever-diminishing region in which *Terra Australis* might exist, speculation still surrounded it. For a tradition of literature had been preparing people for encounters with something wondrous on the other side of the equator. Medieval thinking had contended that any inhabitants of the antipodes could not have descended from the First Parents in Eden (in the east of the northern hemisphere) because they could not have survived the crossing of the infernal equatorial seas. As G. A. Wood has observed, there was a reason to anticipate "the existence of a race of men that had not died in Adam, and that had not in Christ been made alive".[4]

Writers recurrently depicted a wondrous and topsy-turvy world in the great south land. As early as the third century A.D., Lactantius felt compelled to refute an established belief: "About the antipodes also one can neither hear or speak without laughter. It is asserted as something serious, that we should believe that there are men who have feet opposite to ours".[5]

And in the Middle Ages Saint Augustine scoffed at "that fabulous hypothesis", obviously still in popular circulation, "of men who walk a part of the earth opposite to our own, whose feet are in a position contrary to ours, and where the sun rises when it sets with us".[6] Against such a background Andrew Marvell ("Upon Appleton House", LXXXVII, ll.769-72) could later invoke a literary commonplace when describing fishermen with their coracles:

> But now the *Salmon-Fishers* moist
> Their *Leathern Boats* begin to hoist;
> And, like *Antipodes* in Shoes,
> Have shod their *Heads* in their *Canoos*.

And, relishing the popular joke, Richard Brome, the Jacobean dramatist, wrote *The Antipodes* in which he depicts a land where the swans are black, the ravens white, and parrots teach their mistresses to talk; it is a land indeed that "is th' Antipodes of England". The people there "are contrary to us,/ As thus: here (heaven be prais'd) the magistrates/ Govern the people; there the people rule/ The magistrates".[7]

Whether patently comic, as here, or in earnest, the tradition of bizarre life in the antipodes complemented voyagers' euphuistic reports about the East Indies and the South Sea Islands. By 1670 expectations of wonders in the southern regions were prevalent enough to make Peter Heylyn's speculations seem reasonable:

> The country [*Terra Australis*] being so large, so free from the Incumbrances of Frosts and Ice, and endless Winters; I have oft marvelled with my self that no further progress hath been made in Discovery of it: considering chiefly by the site and position of the Country, especially in those parts which lie nearest *Asia*, that there is nothing to be looked for elsewhere, either of profit or of pleasures, but may there be found.[8]

Examined in overview, therefore, the image of *Terra Australis* during the years before Captain Cook's voyage along the eastern coast of Australia is curiously paradoxical. On the one hand, people had come to accept that the grandeur of a great south land would amount to appreciably less in actuality than had been anticipated in their imaginations. On the other hand, fantasy prevailed insofar as people still expected wonders to abound in the ever-decreasing ambit in which a south land might exist.

As a result of this pattern of alternating optimism and bathos, the image of *Terra Australis* as a diminishing paradise became well established. At each disappointment writers concentrated their hopes on a region on the far side of what was known about the southern hemisphere. Once the Pacific and Indian Oceans had been adequately explored, and it became increasingly obvious that New Holland was actually the closest that questers would ever come to locating the legendary *Terra Australis*, writers began to concentrate on the unknown regions of the continent. In time, even after the circumnavigation and settlement of Australia, a "centripetal" impetus of hopeful interest in a great south land would continue to compel dreamers toward the very centre of the land.

The Observations of William Dampier

The image of the diminishing paradise featured in the work of the first English writer to experience Australia at first-hand. William Dampier, appositely dubbed "that cool observant pirate"[9] by James McAuley, ranged far from his Somerset birthplace to circle the world eventually and to return to English publishers with journals which, in terms of both style and content, were to prove extraordinarily influential. The first English travel-writer to present his personal impressions of Australia, Dampier became something of a celebrity and an occasional member of London's literary coterie, counting Samuel Pepys and John Evelyn among his acquaintances. (Evelyn notes in his diary that Dampier and Pepys dined with him on 6 August 1698.) His *A New Voyage Round the World*, first published in 1697, went through three editions in just over a year, was in its sixth edition in 1717, and has been widely read ever since. The two-part *A Voyage to New Holland*, published progressively in 1703 and 1709, enjoyed comparable success.

The two works constitute the first English literature to deal with the theme of *actual* Australia. Whereas *Terra Australis* had long been the subject of obfuscating legend, Dampier's seemingly accurate and uncompromising renditions of what he saw in New Holland served to locate the south land very much in the "real world". The most distinctive aspect of Dampier's writing is his determination to describe all that he saw in as dispassionate a manner as possible. In this respect the two *Voyage* works ought to be regarded as seminal in naturalistic literature.

His writing is derived not from imaginative contemplation but from lived experience of unfamiliar regions. He writes of lands which he could know only externally because of his itinerancy and his sense of alienation in unexplored territory. Accordingly his language is descriptive as he adopts an outsider's perspective and concentrates on recording empirical detail. In turn, the images presented in that language appear as somewhat distanced or "unknowable" on any level deeper than simple description of external detail. There is little evocation of spirit of place in Dampier's writing about New Holland, because his sea-traveller's experience did not allow him to communicate any. Dampier undertakes to describe only what he knows from experience, and he often deals with completely new sights and sensations by comparing them with what is already familiar to him and his readers. For example, Australian trees are rendered more comprehensible by a comparison with the English apple tree; and when something is outside Dampier's ken, he admits it readily instead of speculating or concocting spurious facts — he simply records the mysteries and lack of information as features of the land as he has experienced it:

> The Land is of a dry sandy soil, destitute of Water, except you make Wells: yet producing divers sorts of Trees: but the Woods are not thick, nor the Trees very big. Most of the Trees that we saw are Dragon-Trees as we supposed; and these too are the largest Trees of any there. They are about the bigness of our large Apple Trees, and about the same heighth: and the rind is blackish, and somewhat rough. The Leaves are of a dark colour; the Gum distils out of the knots or cracks that are in the bodies of the Trees. We compared it with some Gum Dragon or Dragon's Blood that was aboard; and it was of the same colour and taste. The other sorts of Trees were not known by any of us. There was pretty long grass growing under the Trees; but it was very thin. We saw no Trees that bore Fruit or Berries.
>
> We saw no sort of Animal, nor any Track of Beast, but once,

> and that seemed to be the Tread of a Beast as big as a great Mastiff Dog. Here are a few small Land-birds, but none bigger than a Black-bird; and but few sea-fowls. Neither is the sea very plentifully stored with fish, unless you reckon the Manatee and Turtle as such.[10]

Dampier's first encounter with New Holland had occurred while he was circumnavigating the globe during the travels which form the basis of *A New Voyage*. He had landed on the north-western coast and gazed on a scorched land whose most obvious characteristic was its absence of virtually all encouraging features: "There is neither Herb, Root, Pulse, nor any sort of Grain, for them [the Aborigines] to eat, that we saw: nor any sort of Bird, or Beast that they can catch, having no Instruments wherewithal to do so. I did not perceive that they did worship any thing". Dampier could best describe the region in terms of negation: "We searched afterwards 3 days, in hopes to find their Houses; but found none"; "In all our search we found no water, but old Wells on the sandy Bays" (*A New Voyage Round the World*, pp.466-67).

However, despite these disappointments, and true to the tradition of interest in a diminishing paradise Dampier returned to Australia during the discovery-project which he commanded aboard the *Roebuck* between 1699 and 1701. Out of this expedition came *A Voyage to New Holland*.

Dampier held out great hope for the then unknown east coast of the continent, cancelling his disappointment with known Australia by projecting his dreams onto its uncharted areas. When the *Roebuck* anchored off Shark Bay on the forbidding west coast of New Holland, it was only as a stock-taking and re-provisioning exercise that the voyagers tarried en route to the opposite side of the continent, which Dampier intended to map out by running south to the bottom of the west coast then heading east until the coastline veered off into promising new regions. At Shark Bay Dampier saw nothing to invalidate his earlier opinion of the Aborigines as the most miserable people in existence: "all of them of the most unpleasant looks and worst Features of any People that ever I saw, tho' I have seen great variety of Savages".[11]

The outsider's vision and writing style obtain as Dampier's sea-traveller's perspective enables him to observe only the peripheries of the continent for the briefest time:

> The Land hereabouts was much like the part of *New Holland* that I formerly described . . . 'tis low, but seemingly barricado'd with a long Chain of Sandhills to the Sea, that let's [*sic*] nothing be seen of what is farther within Land. At high Water the Tides rising so high as they do, the Coast shews very low; but when 'tis low Water it seems to be of an indifferent heighth. At low Water-Mark, the Shore is all Rocky, so that then there is no Landing with a Boat; but at high Water a Boat may come in over those rocks to the Sandy Bay, which runs all along on this Coast. The Land by the Sea for about 5 or 600 yards is a dry Sandy Soil, bearing only Shrubs and Bushes of divers sorts. [*A Voyage to New Holland,* p.151]

Even when he was able to venture inland, Dampier allowed himself only to record empirical details of the region instead of attempting, say, a qualitative assessment of the mood or atmosphere:

> The Land farther in, that is lower than what borders on the Sea, was, so much as we saw of it, very plain and even; partly Savannahs, and partly Woodland. The Savannahs bear a sort of thin coarse Grass. The Mould is also a coarser Sand than that by the Seaside, and in some places 'tis Clay. Here are a great many Rocks in the large Savannah we were in, which are 5 or 6 Foot high, and round at the top like a Hay-cock, very remarkable; some red, and some white. The Woodland lies farther in still; where there were divers sorts of small Trees, scarce any three-Foot in circumference. [*A Voyage to New Holland,* p.152]

Dampier eschews the literary realms of metaphor or symbol and concentrates on presenting the results of his practical activities in this new world.

While in the vicinity of Shark Bay Dampier decided that the proposed southern route would be dangerous with the winter approaching, and mindful of the deteriorating condition of the *Roebuck* and disquieted by the waning fresh water supplies, he decided to steer north with the option of circumnavigating clockwise and sailing home via the south coast. Had things gone according to plan, Dampier would have left Shark Bay, traced the coastline north-east, and then sailed across the Gulf of Carpentaria and rediscovered Torres Strait (whose existence the

Spanish had managed to keep a secret for almost a century); and he would have eventually discovered and described the lush tropics of what is now known as North Queensland. However, water levels were still causing anxiety, and the *Roebuck* was an even greater problem, as it was disintegrating into the Indian Ocean faster than carpenters and caulkers could gum it back together. Finally, with the ship lurching along the north-west coast, "Tornadoes, violent Gusts, etc." blew up, and Dampier prudently "resolv'd to steer away for the Island *Timor*"[12], never to revisit any region of New Holland. (Fifteen months after this change of course, the *Roebuck*, after several attempted restorations in various ports of call, crumbled into the sea in sight of Ascension Island in February 1701.)

Despite the frustrations, Dampier does not leave his descriptions of the arid coastline to stand as his final image of the south land. He declares that Shark Bay is not representative of all of the *Terra Australis* which he believes to exist and which he expects to be discovered eventually:

> I had spent about five Weeks in ranging off and on the Coast of *New Holland*, a Length of about three hundred Leagues; and had put in at three several places, to see what there might be thereabouts worth discovering; and at the same time to recruit my stock of fresh Water and Provisions for the further Discoveries I purposed to attempt on the *Terra Australis*. This large and hitherto almost unknown Tract of Land, is situated so very advantageously in the richest Climates of the World, the *Torrid* and *Temperate Zones*. . .I could not but hope to meet with some fruitful Lands, Continent or Islands, or both, productive of any of the rich Fruits, Drugs, or Spices, (perhaps Minerals also, etc.) that are in the other Parts of the *Torrid Zone*, under equal Parallels of Latitude; at least a Soil and Air capable of such, upon transplanting them hither, and Cultivation. . .though as to the *New Hollanders* hereabouts, by the Experience I had had of their Neighbours formerly, I expected no great matters from them. [*A Continuation of a Voyage to New Holland*, pp.2-4]

The regions which Dampier saw and described were disillusioning in the extreme. However, as soon as he ceases to deal with the evidence before his eyes, the idea of the south land appeals to his imagination, and his speculations turn to a splendid region just outside the limits of his experience. By thus rekindling hope about the unknown areas of the country, Dampier contributes to, at the same time as he is influenced by, the image of the diminishing paradise.

As a result of Dampier's writings this image was given a locus — New Holland — which was firmly situated in actuality. The *Terra Australis* of longstanding dream was now linked to a world of historical experience. After Dampier the south land became, to British sensibility, a place of daunting fact at the same time as it was paradoxically a site for hopeful fiction. Sobering reality and optimistic fantasy were represented in the one image. This duality of attitude toward Australia would linger for centuries.

Daniel Defoe's New Voyage Round the World

Closer to his own time Dampier's impact on literature concerning Australia was emphatic. No travel-writer in the early eighteenth century could escape the influence of Dampier's *Voyage* works. Daniel Defoe is a case in point. At the very least, Dampier's works provided Defoe with a wealth of geographical and nautical information. And as W. H. Bonner has demonstrated in *Captain William Dampier: Buccaneer-Author*, the connection between Defoe and Dampier is strengthened by the fact that Alexander Selkirk, the historical model for Robinson Crusoe, was marooned on Juan Fernandez when serving as sailing master on a privateering adventure commanded by Dampier.[13]

On the subject of New Holland, Dampier's *Voyage* works prompted Defoe to think of *Terra Australis* as a literary setting. When Defoe came to write his own fictional *A New Voyage Round the World*, a south land was featured strategically in the narrative. It is an alluring region — mysterious, exotic, daunting, but potentially rewarding — which draws the characters onward to action (and dispute) throughout most of the novel.

The narrator and crew set out on a privateering adventure, with the resolution "to make some Attempts for new Discoveries, as Opportunity offered".[14] More specifically they are looking to make "Discoveries towards the South Pole" (Part I, p.7). On reaching the Philippines they head east to the Ladrones (or

Marianas Islands) from which they sail east-south-east and then south-east-by-south until, sixteen days later, in latitude 17° south, they sight land:

> A vast Tract of Land, extended, as we had Reason to believe, from the Side of *Gilolo*, and the Spice Islands, or that which we call *Nova Guinea*, and never yet fully discovered. The land lying away from the *West N.W.* to the *S.E.* by *South*, still *Southerly*. [Part I, p.121]

Here is a region similar to Dampier's land of daunting actuality. The party "found the Country look'd wild and savage", and they "could find no Houses, [nor] speak with the Inhabitants" (Part I, p.122). Then the echoes from Dampier continue when the crew also encounter an adjacent south land of fantastic promise. Following the coastline of the "savage" country they soon arrive at a fertile land uncorrupted by civilisation:

> I take the more Notice of these People's [*sic*] not having convers'd, as I say, with the World, because of the Innocence of their Behaviour, their peaceable Disposition, and their Way of living upon the Fruits and Produce of the Earth. [Part I, p.133]

The narrator continues his praise of these blessed isles, where the "climate seemed to be very hot, and yet the country very fruitful", where "Cocoa Nuts, Plantains, Oranges, Lemons, etc., and Maiz" all grow in abundance (Part I, p.133) and where even human nature seems entirely benevolent:

> The natives went indeed naked, some of them stark naked, both Men and Women; but I thought, they differ'd in their Countenances, from all the wild People I ever saw; that they had something singularly honest, and sincere in their Faces, nor did we find any Thing of Falsehood or Treachery among them. [Part I, p.133]

The ship continues its southerly course, losing sight of land for a time until at 27°13′ latitude south and about 16° east of the Ladrones (i.e. about eight hundred kilometres east of latter-day Brisbane) the crew encounter a region with all the attractions of the previous port of call and with the added advantage that the natives here are generous with their gold (Part I, p.137)!

In *Captain Singleton* (1720) Defoe describes a similar discovery of land in southern latitudes (17° south), but this time the ship sails westward, away from the locality of any promising land postulated by Dampier, towards a region in the Indian Ocean. Here they find territory whose salient features resemble the known areas of New Holland as described by Dampier: it was an inhospitable land where "for living Creatures we could find none; for the People, if they had any Cattle, drove them all away, and shew'd us nothing but themselves".[15]

As Defoe gradually filled in his image of the austral land, he drew on and developed Dampier's image of New Holland. He complied with Dampier's negative naturalistic account of the continent at first sighting; and then, persevering into the unknown regions which Dampier speculatively praised but could not investigate, Defoe's fictional characters found at last a type of paradise just inside the ever-decreasing circle of the unknown territory in the southern hemisphere. By locating attractive dominions in the vicinity of New Holland, Defoe contributed to the image of the diminishing paradise. He implied that the disappointments traditionally associated with the quest for *Terra Australis* need not be perennial.

Moreover, in creating this alluring image of a south land Defoe also deliberately directed readers' attention towards the undiscovered east coast of New Holland. When assessing his discoveries in the Pacific he avers that all that he found was satisfactory, but even so, he admits making a mistake inasmuch as "I stood away east from the Philippines to the Ladrones, before I had gone any length to the south" (*A New Voyage*, Part I, p.181). Had he investigated the vicinity of eastern New Holland the rewards would have been even greater:

> So had we gone the best Way, and taken a Course more to the *South* from *Manilla*, not going away E. to the *Ladrones*, we should certainly have fallen in with a Country, from the Coast of *New Guinea*, where we might have found Plenty of Spices, as well as of Gold. [Part I, p.198]

Before Defoe's voyagers head eastward to encounter a land inhabited by fierce and intractable natives whose description resembles that of the New Zealand Maoris, he emphasises his optimism about the unsurveyed areas of the south:

> I lay it down as a Foundation; that whoever, Sailing over the *South-Seas*, keeps a stated Distance from the Tropick to the

> Latitude of fifty six to sixty Degrees, and steers Eastward towards the *Straits of Magellan*, shall never fail to discover new Worlds, new Nations, and the new inexhaustible Funds of Wealth and Commerce, such as never were yet known to the Merchants of *Europe*. [Part I, p.178]

While there is mystery in the southern hemisphere there are still hopes and dreams which persist despite the disappointments of previous discoveries.

Jonathan Swift's Lands of Fact and Fantasy

Defoe's interest in the southern continent did not discredit the image of the diminishing paradise which Dampier had helped to validate. Indeed, this interpretation of Australia remained current during the 1720s. In *Travels Into Several Remote Nations of the World in Four Parts. By Lemuel Gulliver* (1726), for example, Defoe's great contemporary, Jonathan Swift, manipulated an image of New Holland which, like Defoe's, is derived at least partially from Dampier, and which emphasises both the disappointments and the hopes associated with the land. In the 1735 edition of *Gulliver's Travels*, Swift appended "A Letter from Capt. Gulliver to his Cousin Sympson", in which the Captain acknowledges the worth of *A New Voyage Round the World* by "my cousin Dampier" and in which Swift tips his hat to a mentor. As Harold Williams has affirmed, Swift possessed at least one copy of Dampier's *A New Voyage* and was doubtless impressed by the "matter-of-fact narrative style" which Dampier employed so successfully.[16]

Swift's interest in New Holland is reinforced by his knowledge of Dampier, and he wastes no time in introducing the reader to the south land early in Part One of *Gulliver's Travels*. He begins to utilise the image of New Holland at the same time as he manages a joke about the putative lascivious propensities of the South Seas natives:

> It would not be proper, for some Reasons, to trouble the Reader with the Particulars of our Adventures in those Seas: Let it suffice to inform him, that in our Passage from thence to the

> *East Indies*, we were driven by a violent Storm to the North-West of *Van Diemen's Land*.[17]

In this region Gulliver was marooned, and he awoke, fettered and minutely scrutinised, on the shore of Lilliput.

The south land reappears throughout *Gulliver's Travels*. Ever mindful of the connotations pertaining to the continent, Swift utilises both aspects — the known facts and the fantastic speculations — of the contemporary English image of New Holland. In Part Two, when Gulliver is voyaging back from Brobdingnag, he specifically mentions following the coastline of New Holland and then keeping the course "West-south-west, and then South-south-west till we doubled the *Cape of Good Hope*" (vol.I, Part 2, p.162). In Part Four, having left Houyhnhnm-Land, Gulliver "arrives at *New-Holland*, hoping to settle there" (vol.2, Part 4, p.164); this being, by Gulliver's estimation, the south-west of the continent, it is located generally in that area already encountered by genuine historical figures such as Pelsaert, Hartog and Houtman. Accordingly, although his version of this region is appreciably less hostile than those areas of New Holland which were described by Dampier, Swift takes care to employ a "responsibly" naturalistic style when depicting this *known* sector of the country:

> I saw no Inhabitants in the Place where I landed,. . .I found some Shell-fish on the Shore, and eat them raw. . .and I fortunately found a Brook of excellent Water, which gave me great Relief. . .
>
> On the Fourth Day, venturing out early a little too far, I saw twenty or thirty Natives upon a Height, not above five hundred Yards from me. They were stark naked, Men, Women, and Children round a Fire, as I could discover by the Smoak. One of them spied me, and gave notice to the rest; five of them advanced towards me leaving the Women and Children at the Fire. . .The Savages observing me retreat ran after me; and before I could get far enough into the Sea, discharged an Arrow, which wounded me deeply. . .I apprehended the Arrow might be poisoned, and. . .I made a shift to suck the Wound, and dress it as well as I could. [vol.2, Part 4, pp.168-69]

The attention to external detail and physical activity rather than to Gulliver's inner psychological complexities while in danger,

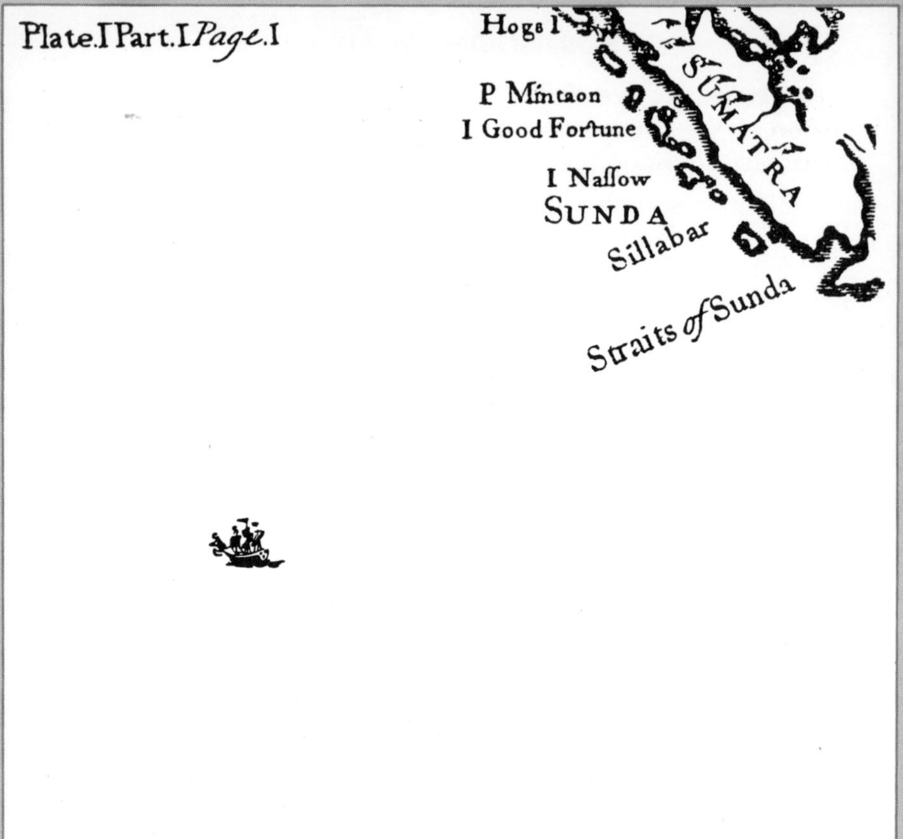

Map of Blefuscu and Lilliput, in Jonathan Swift's **Gulliver's Travels.**
By permission of the British Library.

serves to reinforce the sense that Swift is representing an *actual* region. It is a style very much in the manner of Dampier's naturalistic descriptions of his experiences at Shark Bay. In preference to pursuing the possibilities of the fictional narrative or character development, Swift is concerned here to enhance the sense of his writing's veracity by seeming to present a description of a real territory and its inhabitants — as if he had actually visited New Holland instead of experiencing it vicariously through books like those of Dampier.

Yet in this same work where he draws attention to the historically verifiable regions of New Holland, Swift also exploits the sense of mystery and unassessed potential pertaining to the south land. To this end he deliberately locates the fantasy-worlds of Lilliput, Blefuscu and Houyhnhnm-Land within the outlines of the known dimensions of New Holland. Lilliput and Blefuscu are said, with log-book detail, to be "North-West of *Van Diemen's Land*. . .in the Latitude of 30 Degrees 2 Minutes South" (vol.I, Part 1, p.5); and according to the map included in the 1726 edition, and in concurrence with the fact that Gulliver sailed from there to the south-west coast of New Holland, Houyhnhnm-Land is situated near Nuyt's Land in the Great Australian Bight.[18]

It may be amusing to realise that according to Gulliver's navigational directions, Lilliput lies in the vicinity of Lake Torrens in latter-day Australia. But the crucial point is that Swift deliberately chooses the known areas of New Holland and Van Diemen's Land as reference points from which he can draw up a society of wonders and radically altered perspectives.

The geography of *Gulliver's Travels* has long been a subject of debate. A. E. Case and W. P. Friederich have argued that typographical errors in the first edition are responsible for seeming anomalies such as the fact that the island of Lilliput is actually situated within the bounds of New Holland. However, these critics overlook or dismiss the point made by J. R. Moore that the geographical directions are part of Swift's scheme for presenting a burlesque of travel literature. Also with regard to Lilliput, Houyhnhnm-Land and New Holland, account has not been taken of Swift's use of the image of *Terra Australis* as a land which was simultaneously connotative of optimistic fantasy and well-testified actual experience.

Swift utilises the paradoxes inherent in the contemporary

image of the diminishing paradise in order to produce specific effects. His exploitation of and contribution to the image of *Terra Australis* is best considered in the light of what he is trying to achieve in *Gulliver's Travels*. Swift's disgust with the baser aspects of humanity in Europe provides much of the impetus for the depiction of his fantasy-worlds. He is not conjuring a nebulous Utopian vision. Rather he is attempting to emphasise, by a process of point and counterpoint, the follies of European civilisation. With Lilliput, Blefuscu and Houyhnhnm-Land Swift provides a mirror and a magnifying-glass to be held to the reader's own world. By utilising the image of the south land and all its connotations, and by drawing on the specious empiricism of geography and cartography, he could strike a balance between experience and imagination. *Gulliver's Travels* is therefore a work of fiction about places of fantasy which are inextricably linked to the real world. Within the New Holland which is portrayed in this work the two worlds of beckoning fantasy and discouraging actuality still co-exist.

The English Anthologists: John Campbell and John Callander

In 1726 *Gulliver's Travels* was the most recent in a line of accounts, such as Dampier's and Defoe's respective *New Voyage* works, which served to consolidate the image of Australia as a diminishing paradise. After the 1720s interest in the elusive south land increased, slowly but steadily. In 1744, for example, there appeared John Cambell's revised edition of the travel literature anthology, *Navigantium atque Itinerantium Bibliotheca* (first published 1705), in which significant additions on the subject of the southern continent were included. The first edition, edited by John Harris, contains only passing references to *Terra Australis*. There is a brief reference to *Van Diemen's Land* in Harris's paraphrase of part of the journal of Abel Tasman, and some description of New Holland can be found in the forty-one page extract from Dampier's *A New Voyage Round the World*, which Harris quotes with very little editorial comment. Clearly the south land was not one of Harris's focuses of interest in 1705. In Campbell's 1744 edition of *Navigantium*, however, the *Terra Australis* content has been increased con-

Map of Houyhnhnms Land, in Jonathan Swift's **Gulliver's Travels.**
By permission of the British Library.

siderably, and it is "showcased" in the anthology's new first section entitled "The History of the Circumnavigators". In a lengthy editorial comment Campbell proclaims that the search for the great south land must continue despite past disappointments:

> It is very certain, that the Discovery of *Terra Australis incognita* is considered, by many wise and knowing People, as a kind of Philosophers-stone, perpetual Motion, or, in plain *English*, as a Chimera, fit only to take up the empty Brains of wild Projectors. Yet this seems to be no sufficient Reason, why such as are competent Judges of the Matter in Dispute, should decide, peremptorily, that there is no such Country; or, if there be, that it is not worth the finding. These sort of hasty Conclusions are extremely fatal to Science in general, and to the Art of Navigation in particular. To say the Truth, all Notions built upon Conjectures only, however beautifully ranged in a System, serve only to puzzle and mislead People. The Discovery of all Parts of the World seems to be, at once, the Business and the Glory of Man.[19]

In this edition of *Navigantium*, Campbell gradually builds up to an emphatic recommendation that the English nation should intensify its exploration of the southern hemisphere. He commences his argument by referring to the voyages and the writings of Pedro Fernandez de Quiros, the Portuguese-Spanish sea-captain who, during the initial years of the seventeenth century, ranged the South Seas and became acquainted and then obsessed with the islands which he christened Austrialia [*sic*] del Espiritu Santo, and which are now more commonly known as the New Hebrides. Quiros convinced himself that he had discovered the best of all possible worlds and that this region formed either the eastern coastline or the offshore fragments of the southern continent. Accordingly, he spent the rest of his life petitioning the King of Spain to annex this South Land of the Holy Spirit.

There is more than one reason for Quiros's choice of the name Austrialia del Espiritu Santo. "Austrialia" was coined to draw attention to the southerly aspect of the new lands at the same time as Quiros paid homage to his sovereign's Austrian lineage. With regard to the "Espiritu Santo" part of the name, Celsus Kelly offers two explanations: (a) one of the main purposes of the voyages had been the "conversion of the natives of *La Austrialia* to Christianity through the operation of the Holy Spirit"; and (b) the possession ceremony on *La Austrialia* took place on Pentecost Sunday.[20]

Also with reference to "Espiritu Santo", Quiros may have been implying, consciously or unconsciously, that his Austrialia was a land of the future, a paradise belonging to the final stage of history. Such an implication derives from a tradition of Spanish theology which can be traced back to Joachim, Abbot of Fiore. Late in the twelfth century Joachim was prophesying a third and final era of history, the time of the Holy Spirit, when the church would reign in peace and contentment and when an *ordo novus* or "new people of God" would rise to dominance.

Joachim's ideas figure in the history of Spanish exploration insofar as Christopher Columbus was familiar with the Abbot's writings and justified his American explorations by proclaiming that he was acting under the influence of the Holy Spirit. As Bernard McGinn explains, "Columbus was the first, but by no means the last to interpret the discovery of the New World in the light of an optimistic Joachite vision of a more perfect age".[21]

A spirit of Joachite optimism still animated Spanish imperialism when Quiros sailed the South Seas. Like Columbus, Quiros was dedicated to the Franciscan missionary order, and he sought to lead the natives of the lands he discovered into the kingdom of the Catholic god. By invoking Columbus as his spiritual predecessor he emphasised his exhortations to King Philip III to colonise this newest New World. Furthermore there are distinct echoes of the Joachite *ordo novus* in Quiros's investiture of his officers as "Knights of the Holy Spirit" ("Caballeros del Espiritu Santo") during the sojourn at Austrialia.

Short of discovering a written affirmation by Quiros himself, there is no way of establishing that the visionary captain was drawing explicitly on the Joachite tradition in naming the south land. But it is incontestable that Quiros did regard his Austrialia del Espiritu Santo as a land with a glorious future and as a potential site for the development of a new, divinely sanctioned social order. This notion served to reinforce the image of *Terra Australis* as a paradoxical paradise where difficulties can be transcended in attendance of future felicity.

Quiros and his obsession first became widely known in

England through the work of the prolific travel-anthologist Samuel Purchas. In *Purchas His Pilgrimes* of 1625 there are two of Quiros's exhortations to King Philip. The first, known as the "Eighth Memorial", is in English translation; the second is in Spanish. The editorial preface in *Purchas His Pilgrimes* (signed "Walsingham Gresley") places the petitions in a context by emphasising the more alluring aspects of Quiros's conjectures:

> He did discover a mayne Land, and sayled eight hundred leagues upon the Coast, untill he came to the height of fifteen degrees to the Southward of the Equinoctiall Line where hee found a very fruitful and pleasant Countrey and well peopled, abounding with Pearles, Gold and Silver, great store of Limons; Orenges and other Fruites excellent good, and in great quantitie: great store of Goats, Hogges, Geese, Partridges, Conies and Fowle, Pepper and Spices. The Country is very temperate and healthfull, great store of fish of many different sorts; full of wood and goodly high Trees for shipping; very good pasture, ground for Corne and Cattell.[22]

Aptly described by Celsus Kelly as a "prose-poem narrative"[23], the "Eighth Memorial" lists Austrialia's advantages in an inspired and unremitting compendium of social and material desiderata. Quiros claims to have discovered a "fat and fertile Land" (vol.XVII, p.225) populated by a peaceable race who existed contentedly in a balmy atmosphere smelling of herbs and flowers while at the dawning of each day "a sweet and various harmonie of a thousand Birds of all sorts" commenced a musical accompaniment to a life in paradise (vol.XVII, pp. 226-27). The country was rich in silver, pearls and gold, (vol.XVII, p.223) and the natives were blessed with healthy longevity as they interacted in a prosperous and industrious society:

> Their houses are built of wood, covered with Palme-tree leaves; they have Pitchers and Vessels made of earth, they are not without the mysterie of weaving, and other curiosities of that kind. They worke on Marble, they have Flutes, Drummes and wooden Spoones, they set apart certaine places for Oratories and Prayers, and for buriall places. Their Gardens are artificially severed into beds, bordered and paled; Mother of Pearle and the shels which containe Pearle, they have in much use and estimation. [vol.XVII, p.221]

Moreover, they seemed amenable to colonisation:

> With the assistance of God, if they may be gently and amiably intreated, they will be found very docible and easie of mannage, and that we shall without much worke accommodate our selves unto them. [vol.XVII, p.220]

Quiros's euphuistic account of this new world with a glorious future focused optimistic attention on the regions to the east of what was already known of New Holland. The "Eighth Memorial" embellished the image of the diminishing paradise in the southern hemisphere, and Quiros and his vision became fundamental to the developing image of *Terra Australis*.

In Campbell's *Navigantium* the editor gives his own paraphrase of Quiros's image of the great south land. He, like Gresley, emphasises the putative mineral wealth and the exotic spices, and he also refers to the happy inter-racial society which would appear to be living there: "As to the People, [Quiros] reports, that they were of various Complexions; some white, some black, some tawny: But is positive [*sic*] that the Country he saw was very well peopled, and very well-cultivated; the Inhabitants generally of a quiet and peaceable Disposition" (Campbell, vol.I, p.64).

Campbell concludes his brief outline of Quiros's descriptions of Austrialia del Espiritu Santo by admitting that Quiros "speaks partly from his own Knowledge, but mostly from Conjecture, having discovered only that Part [of a potential southern continent], which lay in or near 15° South Latitude" (vol.I, pp.63-64). Even so, Campbell predisposes the reader to consider Quiros's speculations favourably, for in the rest of the "Circumnavigators" section, he selectively quotes from other southern hemisphere voyagers in order to convince his readers that the rich south land does in fact exist, even though it is still undiscovered. For example, Dampier's optimism about tropical territories to the east of Shark Bay is in no way discredited when Campbell quotes excerpts from the two *Voyage* works (see vol.I, p.130). Then the canny editor accounts for the unattractiveness of the Dutch Captain Pelsaert's reports of the west coast of New Holland by explaining that the Dutch have been reticent about the country's better features in order to discourage other powers such as England from investigating the south land.

Finally, after referring to Abel Tasman's voyage to Van Diemen's Land and New Zealand, Campbell feels he has evidence enough to speculate about a southern continent:

> In the first place, then, it is most evident, from Captain *Tasman's* Voyage, that *New Guiney, Carpentaria, New Holland, Antony Van Diemen's Land,* and the Countries discovered by *de Quiros,* make all one continent, from which *New Zealand* seems to be separated by a Streight. [vol.I, pp.330-31]

He goes on to assert that the location of the south land is "the happiest in the World", and that "Van Diemen's Land [resembles] in all respects the South of France" (vol.I, p.331). Indeed, as if to render his optimism more undeniable, he concedes that there must be one less than excellent area, just the one, in the undiscovered eastern sector of the Australian continent:

> As there are in all Countries some Parts more pleasant than others, so there seems good Reason to believe, that within two or three Degrees of the Tropic of Capricorn, which passes through the Midst of *New Holland,* is the most unwholesome and disagreeable Part of this Country. [vol.I, pp.331-32]

The exception proves the rule, and Campbell concludes the Australian part of his "Circumnavigators" section after having intensified interest in a southern paradise. Over the next two decades enthusiasm for a promised south land was not to wane. Campbell himself managed to republish much of the *Navigantium* material about the region, by inserting it into the mammoth *Universal History,* of which he was co-author. In volume five of the "Modern Part" of the *Universal History* (published in 1760) he includes a large chapter entitled "Terra Australis: Or a history of the Southern Continent" in which he reiterates his arguments from *Navigantium.*

Then, as public notice was being directed increasingly toward the southern hemisphere, the next embellishment of the English image of Australia occurred in 1766, when John Callander's *Terra Australis Cognita*[24] was published.

Callander, the son of a well-established Scottish family from the Craigforth area of Stirlingshire, was a qualified advocate of the Scottish bar, but he never went into practice. He preferred instead to become a man of letters, researching ancient Scottish poetry, editing Milton's *Paradise Lost*, and anthologising travel literature. His contribution, like Campbell's, to the development of the Australian image is not so much authorial as editorial. The selectiveness with which he accumulates and translates passages pertaining to his subject contributes as much as any imaginative writer's impulse to the formulation of the contemporary reader's vision of Australia. His editorial comments on the chosen tracts, and his prudent omission of passages which would contradict the image which he is framing, all serve to render Callander a considerable literary figure with regard to the south land.

Callander's work comes ten years after the publication in Paris of a voyage anthology edited by Charles de Brosses and entitled *Histoire des Navigations aux Terres Australes*. In his Preface Callander acknowledges a debt to "one of the members of the *French* Academy of Sciences" and an asterisked footnote refers to a publication date of 1756 (vol.I, p.i.). De Brosses's work forms the basis of Callander's anthology, but the Scotsman does not present a simple translation of the French text. Callander's work includes editorial passages of his own composition, as well as extracts and editorial comments from Campbell's *Navigantium* and excerpts from a collection of Dutch voyagers' accounts published in Amsterdam in 1753 by Nicholas Struyk. Of course he also had recourse to Dampier's original writings, whereas de Brosses had presented a French translation.

As *Terra Australis Cognita* was assembled it became a rather different book from de Brosses's *Histoire des Navigations*, which had been effectively an appeal for French colonial expansion in the South Pacific. By adding and subtracting sections in the framework of de Brosses's anthology the British editor formulated his own chauvinistic argument. For example, in his notice "To the Reader" Callander makes an assertion that has no direct parallel in de Brosses:

> The Editor flatters himself, that the following Journals, (many of which never appeared in *English* before) may be of Use to advance the Knowledge of Geography and Navigation; and thus tend to promote the Commercial Interests of *Great Britain*, and extend her Naval Power. [vol.I, "To the Reader"]

Then in the Preface he proclaims that although the "French Writer" was advocating settlement by his own nation, the

English claim to *Terra Australis* seems incontestable:

> And here it appears, to the honour of our country, that the best and surest accounts of the *Terra Australis* are deduced from our own navigators, Drake, Narborough, Cavendish, Dampier, and others. [vol.I, p.ii]

He pursues his theme:

> It may with reason be presumed, that, from the nature of our government, the genius of our people, the skill and acknowledged bravery of our navigators, the following Treatise may meet with superior attention from a nation, who, by the success of their maritime commerce, have raised themselves to the present distinguished rank they hold among the powers of *Europe*. [vol. I, p.ii]

In producing a three-volume anthology on the subject of *Terra Australis Cognita*, Callander deliberately sets out to appropriate for himself a "grand theme" concerning the land of untold riches which was lying fallow below the equator, providentially reserved for British annexation. He launches his literary campaign by formulating the definition of his subject: "the great southern continent may be commodiously divided into three parts, to which we have given the names of *Magellanica*, *Polynesia* and *Australasia*" (vol.III, p.716. "Magellanica" refers to South America. The three categories are de Brosses's). Of these three regions Callander is perhaps most enthusiastic about Australasia:

> Our best maps show us, to the south of *Asia*, the immense tracts that are found in these latitudes, under the several names of *Diemen's Land*, *New Holland*, *Carpentaria*, *New Guinea*, *New Britain*, and *New Zealand*. There is great reason to think, that this is not one continent, but divided by unknown Straits: Such is that island discovered by our navigator Dampier, to which he gave the name of *New Britain*. Be this as it may, who can doubt that this tract must furnish objects innumerable, both of commercial advantage and curiosity, equal to any that were found in America by the first discoverers? [vol.I. pp.10-11. The parallel passage in de Brosses's *Histoire* occurs in Tome I, pp.15-16. It is noteworthy that Callander has inserted the rather chauvinist observation about "our navigator Dampier" into an otherwise direct translation of de Brosses.]

Callander allows the readers no doubt that they are contemplating something of enormous significance:

> We have said before that this immense country makes a fifth quarter of our globe. But we may go further, and now divide the whole world into three great parts, each of them intirely [*sic*] surrounded by the ocean, *viz. The Old World, America* and *The Great Southern Continent*. [vol.I, p.48. De Brosses has a similar opinion, Tome I, pp.77-80]

He advises the readers that the book in front of them is entirely trustworthy because the unanimity of the cited authors is plainly convincing:

> For it cannot be supposed that all these different Writers should unite in a design to impose on the reader, especially if we consider how well their reports agree with the situation of the country, and that the trees on the land, and the fish on the coast, corresponding exactly with the trees and fishes of those countries where these commodities are known to abound within land, seem to intimate a perfect conformity throughout. [vol.I, p.48. There is no parallel passage in de Brosses, but this same paragraph occurs in Campbell's *Navigantium*, vol.I, p.332.]

The plain truth is that a uniting plan is applied by Callander as he edits and splices the tracts. Literary sleights of hand must be acknowledged as Callander's forté. Once he has accustomed his readers to great expectations he begins to show his cards. His hopes for the uncharted regions of New Holland are high indeed. By way of expressing his optimism he utilises Campbell's opinions both that the country's "situation . . . [is] the best in the world; the country called *Diemen's Land* resembling in all respects the south of *France*", and that the region around the Tropic of Capricorn would be the only unattractive area of the continent (vol.I, p.47).

The "promotion campaign" for Australasia receives further support when Callander features the petitions of Pedro Fernandez de Quiros. He cites (with acknowledgments) the translation of the "Eighth Memorial" which appeared in *Purchas His Pilgrimes* (1625) and he intensifies English attention on Quiros by presenting an English version of the previously untranslated second tract which had appeared in *Purchas His Pilgrimes*. Quiros's description of what he called the "terrestrial paradise" of Austrialia (vol.II, p.166) suits Callander's purposes

Map of New Holland and "Terre de S. Esprit", in John Callander's **Terra Australis Cog**

ermission of the Fisher Library, University of Sydney.

ideally. As the editor sees it, Quiros's discovery completes a picture of Australasia and verifies that New Holland is indeed a paradisaic great south land. Callander explains his vision in an introductory essay entitled "Of the Utility of Further Discoveries":

> As to the product and commodities of this country in general, there is the greatest reason to believe that they are extremely rich and valuable; because the richest and finest countries in the known world lie all within the same latitude. Thus the land discovered by Quiros makes a part of this great island, and forms the opposite coast to that of *Carpentaria*. This country the discoverer called La *Australia* [sic] *del Espiritu Santo*, in the latitude 15° 40′ South; and, as he reports, it abounds with gold, silver, pearl, nutmegs, mace, ginger, and sugar-canes of an extraordinary size. Dampier's account, though formed from a very slight view of the country he called *Cape St. George*, and *Port Montague*, agrees very well with the other. That region he visited lies within 9° of the country described by Quiros. Schouten also observed that they had ginger and other spices on this coast. So that, on the whole, there seems not the least reason to doubt, that if any part of this country was to be settled, it must be attended with a very rich commerce. [vol.I, pp.47-48. There is no parallel passage in de Brosses's *Histoire*.]

Callander's attractive image of Australasia is further embellished when he translates de Brosses's account of tales relating to Binot Paulmier de Gonneville. The de Gonneville story is as much legend as factual report, yet Callander is concerned to highlight the historical authenticity of his cited version as he explains the derivation of the tale:

> This voyage, which now makes its appearance in *English* for the first time, is extracted from a judicial declaration, made by Paulmier de Gonneville before the admiralty in *France*, July 19, 1505, and inserted in the *Memoires touchant l'Etablissement d'une Mission Chretienne dans la Terre Australe*...1663, and dedicated to Pope Alexander VII by an ecclesiastic, originally from the *Terra Australis*. He designs himself in no other way than by these initials, *J.P.D.C. Pretre Indien*. This priest, as well as his father and grandfather, was born in *France*; but his grandfather was one of the *Australians*, or natives of the Southern World, whom Gonneville had brought into *France* at his return from that country, and whom he afterwards married

> to one of his own relations there. . .Unfortunately Gonneville's journals, in his return, fell into the hands of the *English*, and were lost. However, our author collected his materials from the traditions and loose papers of his own family and the judicial declaration above-mentioned. [vol.I, p.63]

Then follows Callander's translation of de Brosses's rendition of the mysterious J.P.D.C.'s approximation of de Gonneville's confiscated story. (Truth at several removes!) The reader is told how de Gonneville "was thrown upon this great southern land. The natives of this unknown region received the *French* with the most cordial hospitality, and, during an abode of six months, did them every good office in their power" (vol.I, p.65). In his editorial comments Callander re-emphasises the congeniality of the natives, and he portrays the climate as particularly salubrious. It is generally agreed nowadays that if de Gonneville's tale is to be treated as factual, the southern land which he encountered must be interpreted as South America, but Callander seizes upon the account in order to corroborate his extremely high opinion about one of the three divisions of *Terra Australis*; he asserts that de Gonneville's land is located "to the south of the Little Moluccas, in that quarter which, according to our division, is called by us *Australasia*" (vol.I, p.64).

As a result of Callander's enthusiasm about Australasia, New Holland and its environs — about which more speculation than facts could be presented — remained attractive to the English imagination. There was no denying that reports such as Dampier's had described much desolation in the *known* regions of New Holland, but such discouraging reports could always be transcended by recourse to the speculations concerning splendid territories awaiting discovery just outside the extent of the actual Australasian experience.

At the same time as Callander was extolling the virtues of his imagined Australasia, pressure was mounting in England for an expedition to investigate *Terra Australis*. In 1767 Alexander Dalrymple published a pamphlet passionately asserting both that a wondrous south land existed and that he was the man to discover it: "The same motive which carried Columbus and Magellan into foreign countries, in some measure, induces the Author of the following sheets to publish them to the world".[25]

Dalrymple was adamant that the great south land would be discovered not in the region of New Holland but in the south-eastern Pacific, with New Zealand as the country's west coast and the Easter Islands and the Isle of Juan Fernandez as the eastern extremity. His theories were granted little credence, however, and attention continued to focus on the environs of New Holland.

In the course of events, Dalrymple was not taken as seriously as he yearned to be, and it was James Cook who was put in charge of the legendary expedition which led ultimately to the discovery and extensive surveying of the east coast of Australia in 1770. Yet, although Cook proved that the continent of New Holland was the closest approximation to the great south land that would ever be discovered, the quest for the diminishing paradise was by no means over. As much of the literature prior to 1770 implied, hopes were still running high for the discovery of a type of terrestrial paradise in the southern continent. Writers and dreamers would not be satisfied until some kind of haven was located somewhere within the ever-decreasing ambit of unsurveyed Australian territory.

The fact that for every Australian aspiration there always seemed to be a concomitant disillusionment could not permanently dispel the optimism associated with the idea of the southern continent. As the image of the diminishing paradise became established, people developed a paradoxical ability to tolerate disappointment while continuing to expect some Australian felicity. Indeed the frustrations might even have been interpreted as integral to, if not prerequisites of, the benefits which were attended.

It was the more sobering aspect of the image of the diminishing paradise which was to dominate the English interpretations of Australia for the remainder of the eighteenth century. Callander *et al* may have delighted in their fantasies of the temperate tropics, but the earliest actual experience of the land was to indicate that much of Australia ought to be depicted in terms which were far more daunting.

The southern paradise continued to diminish, even as it beckoned. The next important stage in the development of an image of Australia would be concerned with the very real disappointments and misery which prevailed in the known areas of a new gaol-colony.

CHAPTER TWO

Silence, Sin and Suffering (1770-1800)

From this remote, this melancholy shore;
Round whose bleak rocks incessant tempests roar;
Where sullen Convicts drag the clanking chain,
And desolation covers all the plain . . .

George Hamilton, "The Telegraph; A Consolatory Epistle" (ca 1796)

Only he and Halloran perhaps, in that whole town, did not resent the grotesque land, did not call it evil because it was weird. But the busy compilers of journals called it evil at some length.

Thomas Keneally, *Bring Larks and Heroes* (1967)

In 1770 James Cook discovered and surveyed most of the east coast of New Holland, thereby defining the geographical dimensions of *Terra Australis*. The south land could still be a region to dream of, but after Cook's voyage speculations about the diminishing paradise inevitably referred to a real world in which experience would sooner or later put expectations to the test. Now visions such as the luxuriant regions of eastern New

Holland anticipated by Quiros and Dampier had a specific setting and would eventually be verified or invalidated. The ambit in which paradisaic fantasies about *Terra Australis* could be located had diminished again, and in future the hopes and dreams about an idealised south land would be directed toward the centre of New Holland, toward that region which would retain its mystery longer than any other.

The two publications which resulted from Cook's voyage in the *Endeavour* conveyed a sense of the writers' alienation in confrontation with the new land. It is a sense similar to that found in Dampier's writing, as itinerant voyagers describe the land which they encounter only superficially while travelling along the coast. The major difference from Dampier's writing is that the *Endeavour* authors do not perceive the degree of desolation which Dampier described. Sydney Parkinson, in his *Journal of a Voyage to the South Seas, in his Majesty's Ship, The Endeavour*, presents an outsider's view as he records his passing impressions which arise from his necessarily limited experience of the country:

> On the 25th, we were in the latitude of 34°22′. The weather was very fine, but we were often becalmed. The land appeared still flat, remarkably level, and strait [*sic*] on the top. We saw several fires along the coast lit up one after another, which might have been designed as a signal for us[1];

but he also finds encouraging evidence as his ship continues its voyage north: "The country looked very pleasant and fertile; and the trees, quite free from underwood, appeared like plantations in a gentleman's park" (p.134).

Admittedly such descriptions are not very instructive because of their lack of detail. But this point in itself is informative because it highlights the fact that writers were now constrained to limit the flights of their fancy, constrained by the fact that the south land now had been located and that assertions about it were now liable to be tested against experience.

A similar tone of responsible and somewhat cautious observation suffuses the published version of Cook's *Endeavour* journal (edited by John Hawkesworth). Of the natives of New Holland, Cook observes:

> All the inhabitants that we saw were stark naked: they did not appear to be numerous, nor to live in societies, but like other

> animals were scattered about along the coast, and in the woods. Of their manner of life, however, we could know but little, as we were never able to form the least connection with them.[2]

Cook keeps speculation and explicit value judgments to a minimum, as he tries, simply, to render all this newness in a representation which is comprehensible and verifiable. Take for example the description of Point Hicks and its environs, the first land sighted on the east coast:

> The weather being clear, gave us a good view of the country, which has a very pleasing appearance: it is of a moderate height, diversified by hills and valleys, ridges and plains, interspersed with a few lawns of no great extent, but in general covered with wood: the assent of the hills and ridges is gentle, and the summits are not high. [vol.III, p.484]

As a result of the *Endeavour* voyage and because of Cook's and Parkinson's earliest and necessarily inconclusive attempts to describe the land, a new sense of reticence developed about New Holland. Now that the south land was located in actuality, writers were witholding their opinions and awaiting more verifiable evidence. Accordingly, little more was written of New Holland until after 1787 when the First Fleet, laden with convicts' chains and marines' muskets instead of ploughs and hoes, set off to found a new colony.

The objective style of rendering Australian experience, which was used by Dampier and also by Parkinson and Cook, was further utilised by the First Fleet writers who published their chronicles of the earliest extended English activity in Australia. This recourse to an observational mode of writing derives in part from the fact that Cook's discovery obliged all writers to curb their fictive imaginations in favour of a degree of empiricism. The style also arose from the authors' training and from the circumstances in which they were writing. The First Fleet authors were military officers and/or men of science whose educations had instilled in them a trust — indeed a reliance — in a direct, unadorned mode of expression such as was extolled by the Royal Society. As Bishop Sprat had proclaimed in his *History of the Royal Society of London*, this is a mode characterised by:

> a constant Resolution, to reject all the Amplifications, Digressions, and Swellings of Style; to return back to the

> primitive Purity and Shortness, when Men deliver'd so many *Things*, almost in an equal Number of *Words*.[3]

For writers using such a style, "Their Purpose is, in short, to make faithful *Records* of all the works of *Nature*, or *Art*, which can come within their Reach" (p.61). Because of their training and because of their situations as newcomers, the First Fleet writers were attempting to understand and describe new experience in empirical terms as the first step in a long process which might eventually lead to more evocative or symbolic treatment of the spirit of the land. Before interpretation there must be description.

This is not to say that the earliest writers were always entirely objective in their renditions of Australia. Inevitably their own personalities and private experiences were to colour the images which they perceived and communicated; inevitably they would project some of their own selves onto the scene in which they were now subsisting and writing, as the process of expression began in earnest, as they commenced "altering external things and impressing on them the stamp of [each writer's] own inner nature."[4] Now that a colony was establishing itself in Australia, English people's relationships to the country would have to change. Utter alienation like that experienced by Dampier at Shark Bay, and the unsubstantiated fantasies such as those in *Gulliver's Travels* would all have to give place to an "incorporation" of the country; the English culture and the Australian environment would have to work on each other to produce a white society which could feel that it belonged in the land.

Ordinarily, as Ellen Semple explains, in well-established societies "Man is a product of the earth's surface . . . the earth has mothered him, fed him, set him tasks, directed his thoughts, confronted him with difficulties that have strengthened his body and sharpened his wits . . . She has entered into his bone and tissue, into his mind and soul".[5] On the shorelines of Port Jackson in 1788 the motley assortment of outcasts and gaolers transported from comparatively verdant England had not yet so absorbed the land. But as soon as Governer Phillip had chosen a site for the settlement and had run the Union Jack up a make-shift flag-pole, the process had commenced. Writers such as John White, David Collins and Watkin Tench continued that process by presenting their impressions of life in the colony. At the outset the land and the new society cleaving to it had to be understood in their external details before writers could project their selves effectively onto the environment. Australian nature could not seem immediately to be a mother; and white Australian society could not appear immediately to be a natural outgrowth of the environment.

The English writer's sense of alienation would not be dispelled rapidly, and it is no surprise to find the First Fleet authors employing the objective style to describe a colonial experience which they found taxing, confusing and at times desperate. Nature in Australia could seem simply unnatural. Over the decades Australia would appear to be a land where "Nature (having made horses, oxen, ducks, geese, oaks, elms, and all the regular useful productions for the rest of the world) seems determined to have a bit of play"[6]; it was a land inhabited by creatures such as the kangaroo, "Joined by some divine mistake . . . /On Creation's holiday"[7], and the dingo, which was perceived to threaten all creatures with a sinisterly silent malevolence.[8] It was an environment in which birds might drop dead from torrid summer skies.[9] It was a disconcerting continent which more than one writer would find could give people a "sensation of loneliness, as though a cold gust from the open grave" had blown over them.[10] And in this environment a somewhat perverse society was being set up. The existence of the gaol-colony was to cast further gloom on the entire land as writers perceived it. It was a community aware of its exile and oppressed for the most part with a sense of either guilt or injustice. It could be seen as a fallen society, banished not just over hills east of Eden, but to the end of the world. As well as being strangers, the majority of the colonists were also branded as sinners in a strange land. And as Hayden White has observed, to people aware of their fall and exile, nature must assume "the aspect of a chaotic and violent enemy against which man must struggle to win back his proper humanity or godlike nature."[11]

The earliest colonial experience was certainly one which might force an individual to lose his or her humanity. As Governor Phillip observed:

> There were . . . many individuals whom neither lenity could touch, nor rigour terrify; who, with all sense of social duty, appeared to have lost all value for life itself, and with the same

> wantonness exposed themselves to the darts of the savages, and to the severe punishments which, however reluctantly, every society must inflict when milder methods have been tried without success.[12]

The newly established society which Phillip and his First Fleet colleagues describe was composed of bitter and ill-adapted people with "arts untaught, and fruits unknown", conveyed to Botany Bay in frigates "o'er burdened" and "fraught with guilt and woe".[13] It was a place of intense suffering and much cruelty; it was a place, for example, where convicts on the decks of transport ships sailing into Port Jackson harbour in 1800 could see the tar-daubed skeleton of a hanged malefactor swinging in warning from the gibbet on Pinchgut Island.[14] In short, a brutalised society was attempting to survive in an unfamiliar environment which could well be described as infernal.

It was First Fleeters John White and David Collins, and to a lesser extent Watkin Tench, who published the earliest works which seemed to ratify experientially the forbidding aspect of the image of the diminishing paradise. These writers, the first to live and work in the south land, could find little evidence of the dreamland conjured in the past by Quiros and Callander. The practical activity of growing into the land, of allowing the earth to enter into the colonists' bones and tissues, into their minds and souls had just commenced.

The First Fleet Annalists

Although it is historical rather than literary irony that the First Fleet writers mention how their convoy was escorted out of English waters by the frigate, the *Hyaena*, an apposite metaphor nevertheless presents itself, and the image of a hyaena trailing behind the group of initial Australian colonists seems appropriate. Had the frigate persisted all the way to Botany Bay instead of leaving the Fleet west of the Scilly Isles, writers would still be coining phrases about scavengers pursuing the afflicted to a land of carrion and bloodletting. In the eyes of more than one early chronicler Australia was a nightmarish realm of brutality and adversity.

In *A Journal of a Voyage to new* [sic] *South Wales*, John White, the surgeon-general of the First Fleet, attempts to describe the eeriness and inhumanity of the gaol-land. The *Journal* is a mixture of literary genres. It is loosely constructed around a chronological narrative of events which occur during the voyage to Botany Bay and during the first eight months of the settlement's existence. This format gives White scope to digress with anecdotes about the "social life" and the Aborigines in the colony and with descriptions of natural history. Interspersed in the narrative are scientific records of flora and fauna, many of which are illustrated by splendid colour plates. In addition to the corpus of the work, the "Natural History Appendix" is devoted exclusively to botanical and zoological descriptions and illustrations.

The reader is constantly aware of conflicts between aspects of White's authorial personality: the historian, the anecdotist, and the scientist. The scientist occasionally "usurps" the historian as the dominant voice in the book. For example, while White as narrative-historian is chronicling daily events, he records that a hunting-party returns to the garrison with a "cassowary" (emu). At this juncture White-the-scientist takes over and details the size and appearance of the bird, even accounting for the number of toes and dimensions of the internal organs. It is not until two pages and one colour plate later that the interrupted narrative is resumed.[15]

The seeming inconsistencies of tone in the *Journal* might be interpreted as evidence of White's inability to resolve the disparate elements in the subject of his narrative. However, the variations of tone — at one moment scientific, then diarist, then anecdotal — derive not only from the fact that White is, admittedly, not a great writer, but also from the nature of his task as he attempts to find the correct voice in which to describe, and perhaps to evoke, experiences in a region which is not yet served by a coherent literary tradition.

A man of science, White attempts to record all that comes within his ken. Citing as much "data" as possible, he represents Australian experience in a candid, simple prose, generally eschewing subjective judgments. Within the narrative which constitutes most of the *Journal* this is a style which facilitates a disconcertingly blasé depiction of the bleakness and menace which seem endemic to the Australian environment. Throughout the commentary White maintains an objectivity which most often simply imbues the narrative with verisimilitude, but which can also evoke a feeling of world-weariness or, most effectively, *sang froid*, as when he announces that yet another convict has been "launched into eternity" (p.128) at the gallows, or when he records that debility due to scurvy is preventing convicts from undergoing the entirety of their five hundred lashes of scourging punishment (p.159). Without registering any personal emotional reaction he reports that convicts on work detail are speared to death by the natives, for no apparent motive, and are found with shattered skulls and eyes picked out *possibly* by birds (p.160). And he reports the effects of Australian experience on the convicts who become "so hardened in weakness and depravity . . . that they seem insensible to the fear of corporal punishment, or even death itself" (pp.132-33).

White presents impressions of an environment where abnormality might be the norm; where, for example, " no wood in this country, though sawed ever so thin, and dried ever so well, will float" (p.133); or where solitary trees are encountered burning in deserted landscapes (p.150). Recorded with White's detachment, the bizarre becomes disturbingly quotidian. New South Wales is represented as a barren land indifferent to the new society. In such a disquieting habitat the English colony must begin to establish its own sense of identity. The most basic mundanities can become significant in this process, as is exemplified when White recounts the activities of his survey-team on the north-west shoreline of Port Jackson:

> About four o'clock in the afternoon we came to a steep valley, where the flowing of the tide ceased, and a fresh-water stream commenced. Here, in the most desert, wild, and solitary seclusion that the imagination can form any idea of, we took up our abode for the night, dressed our provisions, washed our shirts and stockings, and turned our inconvenient situation to the best advantage in our power. [p.142]

This sense of the English person's alienation in the environment is a dominant feature of White's *Journal*. In this respect there are resemblances between White's chronicle and Dampier's reports about the desolate regions of northern and western New Holland. In each case, knowing an area of the south land at first-hand entails disappointment. However, whereas Dampier could leave Shark Bay and speculate about luxuriant territory in uncharted southern latitudes, White and his "compatriots" were obliged to stay in New South Wales and face all the daunting realities which confronted them before any colonist could speculate about a possible paradise to be found either at Botany Bay or out past the western horizon. The First Fleet writers were constrained by everyday realities and they were not at liberty to describe Australian felicity, known or anticipated.

White's colleague, David Collins, the judge-advocate of the colony, produced a book which details graphically the earliest attempts of this new society to graft itself onto the seemingly indifferent Australian environment. In *An Account of the English Colony in New South Wales* Collins is a lawyer who is also his own witness, and he is especially concerned, in an advocate's fashion, to supply all the evidence possible in order to piece together a truthful version of the *events* which occur in the colony. In this sense he is preoccupied much more with Australian society than with nature, although he is well aware of the qualities of a land in which:

> The extreme danger attendant on a man's going beyond the bounds of his knowledge in the forests of an unsettled country could nowhere be more demonstrable than in this. To the westward was an immense open track before him, in which, if unbefriended by either sun or moon, he might wander until life were at an end.[16]

As social history Collins's journal is the most exhaustive of all the literature concerning the establishment of the colony. The two volumes of the *Account* comprise approximately one thousand pages of historical narrative which, as Collins himself affirms, has been recorded in a spirit of stringent objectivity:

> For his labours [the author] claims no credit beyond what may be due to the strictest fidelity in his narrative. It was not a romance that he had to give to the world; nor has he gone out of the track that actual circumstances prepared for him, to furnish food for sickly minds, by fictitious relations of adventures that never happened. [vol.I, p.vii]

Collins's scope is extremely broad because, like White before him, he does not want to miss a single aspect of the history which is unfolding around him; the events are so close to him that he cannot take the liberty of excluding too many occurrences as insignificant in this burgeoning society of little tradition and uncertain norms:

> If [the author] should be thought to have been sometimes too minute in his detail, he hopes it will be considered that the transactions here recorded were penned as they occurred, with the feelings that at the moment they naturally excited in the mind; and that circumstances which, to an indifferent reader, may appear trivial, to a spectator and a participant seem often of importance. [vol.I, p.vii]

Although the journals are actually a national history, they are also an intimate portrayal of an extraordinary "village life" in which no occurrence, under the circumstances, ought to go unnoticed.

In overview the most compelling impression arising from the *Account* is far from trivial, as death and suffering prevail implacably while Collins details continual ration cuts, disease, and soul-destroying labour in an unresponsive environment. To an extent which is almost obsessive he concludes his report on each year by tabulating the deaths which have occurred. For more than a decade he chronicles the misfortunes of a society where larceny seems a way of life, where venereal disease and scurvy are rife and "scorbutic patients. . . are daily seen creeping to and from the hospital tents" (vol.I, p.25), and where murders, suicides, and native attacks seem normal. He develops a chilling disinterest in his recording of the facts, as when he concludes a chapter with this simple statement: "From Parramatta two convicts were missing, and were said to be killed by the natives" (vol.I, p.184). Life is constantly threatened: "With a dreadful sick list, and with death making rapid strides upon us, the month of April commenced" (vol.I, p.204). Ultimately stoicism is the only benefit accruing to the survivors: "we had been well trained in New South Wales to meet and endure disappointment" (vol.I, p.286).

Certainly most of Collins's *Account* is imbued with the objective detachment which Sydney Smith praised as "candour" and "good, plain, common sense"[17], but H. M. Green's assessment of Collins's style as "dry as sawdust" is unfair.[18] Despite Collins's attempts to remain habitually disinterested, he is capable of evocative language and on more than one occasion he does project his personality onto the subject of his writing. His authoritarianism is manifest whenever he describes the "villany [*sic*] and idleness" (vol.I, p.47) of the "lower class of people" (vol.I, p.40) whom he must judge every day. He is self-righteous but not self-pitying, and there is a certain dignity in the way he continues to detail Botany Bay life with the worldliness of a man who has known hardship and is determined to outlast these special tribulations. His personal suffering was considerable: on top of the constant threat of starvation, disease and violent death, there were his daily encounters with crime and seemingly futile punishment; he was separated from his American wife, Maria, who was living sad and alone in London; and there was his sense of stagnation in his career as he was "trapped" with little hope of promotion in a far outpost. Collins emerges from the chronicle as a man of sensitivity who has been somewhat "cauterised" by his experience. It is to his credit that he could hope "to oppose [in his daily work and in his writing] the soft harmonising arts of peace and civilisation to the baneful influence of vice and immorality" (vol.I, p.6). Equally laudable in the light of his travails are his occasional (and successful) attempts to bring a scene to life against the background of prosaic reportage. Take for example his rendition of the Port Jackson site, in which the images of stillness are complemented by the leisurely but well-controlled drift of the long sentence which is eventually truncated by the description of the activity which dispels the pristine silence:

> The spot chosen for this purpose was at the head of the cove, near the run of fresh water, which stole silently through a very thick wood, the stillness of which had then, for the first time since the creation, been interrupted by the rude sound of the labourer's axe, and the downfall of its ancient inhabitants; a stillness and tranquillity which from that day were to give place to the voice of labour, the confusion of camps and towns, and "the busy hum of its new possessors". [vol.I, p.5]

Consider also his depiction of the scene during the disembarkation of the First Fleet, in which the somewhat chaotic activity is evoked well in the short phrases and in the rapid "cataloguing" of sights and sounds:

> The confusion that ensued will not be wondered at, when it is considered that every man stepped from the boat literally into a wood. Parties of people were every where heard and seen variously employed; some in clearing ground from different encampments; others in pitching tents, or bringing up such stores as were immediately wanted; and the spot which had so lately

> been the abode of silence and tranquillity was now changed to that of noise, clamour, and confusion: but after a time order gradually prevailed every where. As the woods were opened and the ground cleared, the various encampments were extended, and all wore the appearance of regularity. [vol.I, p.6]

In both of these passages Collins has sought to highlight one process in particular: the commencement of practical activity in the new land, the initial steps of an English colony as it seeks to adapt itself and the landscape to the task of survival and expansion. This is a process which writers must undergo also, as English people begin to interact with the land, so that culture and environment modify each other. An equilibrium between the two must be sought so that seeming chaos can give way to a new order. This applies to writing as much as to setting up a camp.

The First Fleet writer who was most aware of this developing need to shape the scene around him while still attempting to describe and understand the society and its environment was Lieutenant Watkin Tench. His two eye-witness accounts — *A Narrative of the Expedition to Botany Bay* and *A Complete Account of the Settlement at Port Jackson in New South Wales* — are chronicles of significant events. Within this framework, similar in structure to the works by White and Collins, Tench can expound on philosophical questions which arise from his experience and from his observations of the environment and the Aborigines. Like White and Collins he describes a tiny, vulnerable community of misfits struggling in an environment to which they have not yet adapted as effectively as the native inhabitants. In the *Complete Account*, for example, Tench describes the attempts by a detachment of marines to capture a group of Aborigines:

> We pursued; but a contest between heavy-armed Europeans, fettered by ligatures, and naked unencumbered Indians, was too unequal to last long. They darted into the wood and disappeared.[19]

Doggedly the marines continue the chase but they are not yet creatures fitted to their environment, as they "clamber" over a foreign terrain:

> The soil of every part of the peninsula, which we had traversed, is shallow and sandy, and its productions meagre and wretched.

> When forced to quit the sand, we were condemned to drag through morasses, or to clamber over rocks, unrefreshed by streams, and unmarked by diversity. [*Complete Account*, pp.97-8]

Tench is dealing obliquely here with the problem which confronted all English people — writers as well as soldiers and settlers — as they subsisted in the strange new country before they had managed to modify their Old World attitudes. Although it was not an English land, English writers were always liable to graft English expectations onto it. Or as Thomas Watling (whose work will be examined next) understood it, appreciation of a new region can be hindered by "those national prejudices every man imbibes, and perhaps cannot entirely divest himself of".[20]

Tench differs from White and Collins inasmuch as he is the first author who clearly moves past an attitude of objectivity towards taking account of his own yearnings, disappointments and biases as he begins to interpret what the land means to him at the same time as he attempts to describe what the land consists of objectively. The author's self looms larger in Tench's work than in White's and Collins's.

Tench was a career soldier whose background is obscure, although there is speculation that he was of Welsh descent and well connected with an aristocratic family. (See the familiar tone of respect and gratitude in the dedicatory epistle to Sir Watkin Williams Wynn in A *Complete Account*.) Certainly he appears a man of keen intellect and remarkable compassion, especially in the light of his role as an officer of the marines assigned to the colony as a peace-keeping and disciplinary force in charge of the convicts. (Tench occasionally sympathises with the convicts, and in one notable instance he cites a dolorous letter — possibly apocryphal — written by a prisoner condemned to be hanged, and addressed to the felon's mother who will have been bereaved for months before reading the dictated note.) He is well apprised of contemporary philosophical issues and is able to discuss and refute Jean-Jacques Rousseau and concepts from academies of European enlightenment as he sits writing in his tent on the shorelines of Port Jackson.

Tench is prepared to embellish the "feelingless" diction (which paradoxically becomes so emotionally effective) preferred by his colleagues. This is the first of two specific ways in which Tench adds to the image of Australia set up by the First Fleet authors. He addresses himself to the question of how a writer can make sense of new experiences encountered during colonisation. He is aware of the need to acknowledge the amount of creative editing that occurs in any apparently objective travel account, and he proclaims at the outset that "the utmost circumspection is necessary to prevent imposition, in those who give account of what they see in unknown countries" (*Complete Account*, p.6). He knows that the individual inevitably fulfils a subjective, creative function when synthesising confusing information — be it news from home, say, or disparate impressions of a new land — into a comprehensible overview.

Tench deals with this topic when he describes the scene after he and his marines have greeted the crew of HMS *Lady Juliana*, the first contact with the Old World in approximately three years:

> We continued to ask a thousand questions on a breath. Stimulated by curiosity, they inquired in turn; but the right of being first answered, we thought, lay on our side. "Letters! Letters!" was the cry. They were produced, and torn open in trembling agitation. News burst upon us like meridian splendor upon a blind man. We were overwhelmed with it; public, private, general, and particular. Nor was it until some days had elapsed, that we were able to methodize it, or reduce it into form. [*Complete Account*, p.46]

In this short excerpt Tench sums up the predicament of the colonists who are struggling in a lonely land, without encouragement and afflicted with a sense of normlessness and woeful homesickness. Like Alexander Pope before him[21], in very different circumstances, he is concerned with the process of "methodising", of finding order in diversity. Removed from the English society and environment the colonists are alienated from the assumptions, institutions and norms which have shaped their lives. "Methodising" must occur with their Australian experience, and with their English heritage as the two influences must be married.

Tench readily acknowledges that his emotions come into play when he considers the colony. As he affirms early in *A Narrative of the Expedition*, "Ithaca itself was scarcely more longed for by Ulysses, than Botany Bay by the adventurers who had traversed so many thousand miles to take possession of it."[22] Of course, when the voyagers arrived at Botany Bay there were no feasts in progress, and optimistic aspirations had to be compromised immediately at landfall in that region which Tench soon assesses as "this forlorn and distant circle" (*Narrative*, p.109). In this awareness lies the second of Tench's preoccupations (in addition to his concern for "methodising"). He comes to assess Australia as a strange land abounding with "perpetual disappointments" (*Complete Account*, p.6) which underlie attractive surfaces. For example, should a work-party travel a short distance from Botany Bay, they would pass "through the country, which the discoverers of Botany Bay extol as 'some of the finest meadows in the world'" only to find that these "meadows, instead of grass, are covered with high coarse rushes, in a rotten spungy bog" (*Complete Account*, pp.121-22). So much of the land is deceptively alluring:

> The first impression made on a stranger is certainly favourable. He sees gently swelling hills, connected by vales which possess every beauty that verdure of trees, and form, simply considered in itself, can produce: but he looks in vain for those murmuring rills and refreshing springs, which fructify and embellish more happy lands. [*Complete Account*, p.160]

The encouraging first impressions, similar to Sydney Parkinson's fleeting glimpses of tracts which appear "like plantations in a gentleman's park", do not withstand the test of experience. As far as Tench is concerned, disappointment is the inevitable subsequence of initial hope for some kind of traditional blessed land in Australia. And this personal sense of disillusionment must be taken into account if a writer is to become involved in the dual process of beginning to "methodise" some sense out of Australian experience at the same time as he or she attempts to record its disparate elements.

As Tench realised that paradise had not been found at Botany Bay and that the colonists had to strive to formulate a tolerable life on the periphery of the unknown continent, he emphasised the note of bathos in that continuing rhythm of optimism and disappointment which was essential to the developing image of Australia as a diminishing paradise. Because of the First Fleet annalists, the image of Australia darkened considerably. White,

Collins and Tench all described harrowing experience in a grim society and a daunting environment.

Even at this time, however, the alienating effects of the new land were being broken down, as the colony survived and gradually made a mark on the landscape. By his diligent recording for over a decade Collins showed that the society refused to perish and was slowly imposing some order on the Australian nature. At this same time Tench was indicating that mere detached observation was not sufficient to develop an understanding of Australian experience; he was aware of the need for a degree of "methodising", of projecting one's own vision onto a representation of life in the colony so that the people inhabiting the land might have some say in the type of spirit which arose in it as it became "civilised".

Tench's perspicacity led him further, to the realisation that "perpetual disappointment" was an essential aspect of this spirit. His interpretation of Australian experience was to be corroborated by Thomas Watling who was concerned with the interaction of the self and the Australian scene to the extent that he wrote of the country as a subject and a setting for artistic creativity. Watling was to continue with the "methodising" which concerned Tench, but there was to be little sense of optimism or progress behind the projection of his personality onto the environment.

Exiles and Martyrs

Thomas Watling was born in Dumfries, Scotland, where he was raised by his aunt Marion Kirkpatrick. During his youth he trained as an artist, and he eventually turned his skills to illicit ends until being sentenced in late 1788 to fourteen years' transportation for forgery. During his years in Australia he produced an extensive folio of paintings of landscapes and specimens of natural history, and he also wrote a series of short prose pieces which were published under the title of *Letters from an Exile at Botany Bay, to his Aunt in Dumfries*.

This publication presents an image of Australia through the eyes of a person on the wrong side of the military lines at Botany Bay, and while the bleakness of Watling's representations is comparable to that in White, Collins and Tench, the manner of his writing is quite different. Watling has been unfairly judged by posterity. Generally he has been described as unintelligent and inept in both his chosen crafts of painting and writing. Certainly his work is flawed, but the deficiencies derive from the special difficulties of the task that he set himself. He was probably the first white person to attempt, in paint and in words, to test and extend a symbolic use of landscape in the Australian setting, thereby overreaching the merely descriptive practices which had previously predominated. (Apropos of this apologia, art historians would be rewarded in re-examining Watling's paintings.)

Watling had served his artistic apprenticeship in Scotland at a time when theories of the picturesque and Macpherson's *Ossian* were prevalent influences, and they show through in his writing; he fits precisely Bernard Smith's pen-picture of him as a "wayward child, not of the Enlightenment but of early Romanticism in Scotland with its cult of sentiment, rhetoric and the picturesque".[23] Given Watling's background, given his situation as a convict whose only chance of autonomy in the circumstances lay in his imaginative response to the environment, and given also his psychological susceptibility to what he calls an "*il pensoroso* [*sic*] gloom" (*Letters from an Exile* p.28), it is not surprising that he eschews objectivity in his verbal depictions of Australian experience. The expressive projection of personality, which can be seen to a limited extent in Tench's work, is the essence of Watling's writing. *Letters from an Exile*, written in "much indigence, sickness, and indescribable sorrow" (p.22), details Watling's attempts to come to terms with his existence in the colony. It is a struggle which usually defeats him, as he confides to his aunt:

> In my saddest hours, and God knows there are many of them, I have observed you are then most busy with my memory. Melancholy's sombre shadow louring over my soul, endears the fleeting moment by impelling me to write to you. Indeed, it is solely owing to this despondent state of mind, that ought I have produced for those last four years proceeds. When this gloom frowns dreadful over the vista of my being, I but too much indulge the dreary prospect — exploring the wide domain of adversity terminated only by the impending darkness; hence it is,

> that whatever flows from my pen, or is laboured by my pencil, affects, in some degree, the tone of mind that possess [*sic*] me at the period of its production. [pp.1-2]

Watling's circumstances, his personality, and his aesthetic prejudices interact so that he perceives and expresses a "dreary prospect". His style is in striking contrast to the predominantly "emotionless" prose of White, Collins and, to a lesser extent, Tench. In Watling there is none of the annalists' objectivity, but the sense of alienation found in their works is especially strong in *Letters from an Exile* because the only emotions which the author is able to express in his situation are the outsider's feelings of rejection and despair. Instead of shaping the land to his creative will, Watling finds that he can only detail his sense of futility when confronting cruel experience which does not accommodate any of his aesthetic criteria. Like Tench he finds that the "face of the country is yet deceitful; having every appearance of fertility; and yet productive of no one article in itself fit for the support of mankind" (p.7). First-hand experience of the colony soon invalidates optimistic expectations:

> The flattering appearance of nature may be offerred as the best apology for those mistaken eulogiums lavished by a late eminent circumnavigator upon this place. Perhaps nothing can surpass the circumambient windings, and romantic banks of a narrow arm of the sea that leads from this to *Parramatta*, another settlement about fourteen miles off. The Poet may there descry numberless beauties; nor can there be fitter haunts for his imagination. The elysian scenery of a Telemachus; the secret recesses for a Thomson's musidora [*sic*]; arcadian shades, or classic bowers, present themselves at every winding to the ravished eye. Overhead the most grotesque foliage yields a shade, where cooling zephyrs breathe every perfume. Mangrove avenues, and picturesque rocks, entwined with non-descript flowers: In short, were the benefits in the least equal to the specious external, this country need hardly give place to any other on earth. [pp.7-8]

Watling's artistic predicament is epitomised in this passage. Initially he seems optimistic that the land possesses the qualities which suit both his aesthetic criteria and his floridly allusive diction. The perfumed zephyrs and flowers, the shades and bowers from pastoral traditions all *seem* to be in evidence everywhere. Then suspicions of trouble intrude with the offhand remark that the foliage is "grotesque", and finally Watling's melancholy must arise when the façade is stripped bare to show the deception and bathos beneath the "specious external".

Once the illusion is exposed, Watling cannot enthuse about the landscape, and he reassesses his original impression to concur with the previous writers who had perceived a waste land: "Bold rising hills, or azure distances would be kind of phaenomena. The principal traits of the country are extensive woods, spread over a little-varied plain" (p.9). It would be only by means of artifice that a writer or painter could render Australia attractive: "were I to select and combine, I might avoid that sameness, and find engaging employment" (p.9).

One of the few aspects of Australia which Watling does not find monotonous is the climate, which can often turn ominous, even somewhat apocalyptic:

> In the warmer season, the thunder very frequently rolls tremendous, accompanied by a scorching wind, so intolerable as almost to obstruct respiration; whilst the surrounding horizon looks one entire sheet of uninterupted [*sic*] flame. [p.9]

If the reference to such heat and the image of the fires painting the horizon connote a type of Hell, the comparison is appropriate. Once Watling had penetrated the inconsequential surface attraction of Australian nature, and once the suffering essential to the Australian society has broken his spirit, he finds only a disheartening emptiness in the country of his exile.

The descriptive work of the First Fleet annalists arose from a necessity to establish some certainties about a land which was suddenly located in the realm of fact after being for so long a site for varying degrees of fantasy. Once some objective observations had been corroborated, by experienced observers, more imaginative writers found they had raw material which they could shape to fit subjective themes. Once some "facts" had been posited they could then be interpreted in the way that Watling, for example, allowed his emotions to intervene between the Australian scene and the printed page.

Watling, of course, had first-hand knowledge of Australian hardship, but now that a canon of "facts" about the land had been "documented", an author did not need such experience in order to utilise life in the colony as a means of expressing a point of view. At the same time as Watling and the annalists were desecrating the image of Australia, Botany Bay was becoming an issue and an image for radical writers in England. These were years, particularly in 1793 and 1794, when William Pitt's nervous administration, ever-mindful of reformist iconoclasm brewing and exploding across the seas, in Ireland and France, was continually finding Jacobins under beds too close to the seat of English government. In Scotland there occurred the much publicised sedition trials of the five men who were to become known as the "Scottish martyrs". The most celebrated case involved Thomas Muir (a University of Glasgow M.A. and a University of Edinburgh advocate) whose lectures on Thomas Paine's *Declaration of Rights* and whose affiliations with the French and Irish rebels rankled the Establishment. After the controversial hearing at which he defended himself eloquently, Muir was sentenced on 31 August 1793 to banishment in New South Wales. Similarly convicted and banished about this time were William Skirving, Joseph Gerald, Maurice Margarot and Thomas Fyshe Palmer, who was an Old Etonian, Cantabrian and a one-time dinner acquaintance of Dr Johnson. (Boswell records a dinner date with Palmer and Johnson on 3 June 1781.)

The plight of the "martyrs" became something of a *cause célèbre* for radical writers, with William Godwin, for example, overtly sympathising with Muir and Palmer while criticising Pitt and his Scottish advocate, Dundas. As writers eulogised their exiled heroes, they depicted New South Wales as a gaol-land symbolically microcosmic of tyrannical England.

In a poem by George Dyer ("B.A. Late of Emmanuel College, Cambridge", and a close friend of Thomas Fyshe Palmer), the "martyrs'" indomitability, strengthened by their knowledge that they acted heroically and in good faith, is rendered even more exemplary in the context of the nature and society which the poet describes as their place of banishment:

'Midst howling winds, and foaming deeps,
No fear the guiltless suff'rer knows;
Peaceful amidst the storm he sleeps,
Fearless to unknown regions goes.

The guilt that makes ev'n tyrants groan,
Dares not invade the patriots [*sic*] breast;

The prisoner feels himself his own,
And triumph's [*sic*] most, when most oppress'd.

The bark that bears to barren lands
And barb'rous tribes a prize so dear,
Shall keep it safe from ruffian hands,
Or yield it to a nation's prayer.

Go, generous band, where honour calls,
Your chains are virtue's fairest prize,
Who nobly lives, and nobly falls
Stands but a step below the skies.

And thou, pure heart, shalt often send
The ardent prayer to heaven for me:
And grateful still I call thee friend,
And chearful would I follow thee.[24]

The heroism may be transcendent, but the land itself is barren and "barb'rous", and the society transported there is bound in tyrants' chains.

Similarly, in a poem by George Hamilton (Minister of Gladsmuir) entitled "The Telegraph: A Consolatory Epistle from Thomas Muir, Esq. of Botany Bay, to the Hon. Henry Erskine", the poet's Muir-persona addresses Erskine, the deregistered Edinburgh advocate and erstwhile supporter of the martyrs. Muir-Hamilton sympathises with Erskine and takes comfort in irony and fantasy by asserting that not even brutal Botany Bay could overcome their revolutionary fervour if Erskine were there with him on "this remote, this melancholy shore" where "desolation covers all the plain".[25] The persona does acknowledge the realities of the situation initially: "Here, it is true, incessant tempests lower,/But what are the tempests to the Tyrant's power./Here Heaven's own thunders scath the knotted oak,/But mild the thunder to the Despot's stroke" (p.5). The rhetoric causes the martyr to forget temporarily the society of "sullen Convicts [dragging] the clanking chain" (p.3), and in his rebellious mood he can ignore tempestuous nature. Even so, the poem does not deny the grim realities which prevail in the land of the martyr's exile.

The image of Australia as a land both of punitive nature and of the worst in British social injustice was not to be eradicated easily. In 1793 Thomas Watling had touched on this subject in mentioning that the military officers were always the first to flaunt Governor Phillip's moral strictures by taking convict mistresses, and that the male convicts were assigned to officers so that the prisoners became "the property of some haughty despot" (*Letters from an Exile*, p.20). The corruption of privilege was rife.

In 1797, four years after Muir's trial, Thomas Fyshe Palmer published the *Narrative of the Sufferings of T. F. Palmer and W. Skirving*, and in 1800 the trial and transportation of Joseph Holt, "General" of the 1798 Irish Rebels, stimulated much controversy.

Moreover, it was not only Jacobin hacks, in this disturbed political climate, whose poetic image of Australia was brought into agreement with that of White, Collins, Tench and Watling. In 1794, the year of Muir's and Palmer's transportation, Robert Southey — future poet-laureate and kindred Romantic spirit of S. T. Coleridge and William Wordsworth — was at Oxford, casting himself in the role of the ardent young radical, reading his Thomas Paine, and developing ideas of "dropping out" of moribund England and establishing an emigrants' "pantisocracy" (a community in which all are equal and all rule) based generally on the ideas of William Godwin. As long as the notion still seemed plausible, Southey, Coleridge and the other prospective pantisocrats dreamt of a new society, informed by literature and science, prospering on the banks of the Susquehanna River in North America.

Although he was always interested in colonies (in North America and Brazil) and possible emigration (to Portugal, North America, and Switzerland), Southey did not consider Australia as a plausible site for the pantisocracy. On the contrary, in this 1794 of the "Scottish martyrdom" and of the pantisocratic speculations, Southey published his *Botany-Bay Eclogues*[26] which, in accordance with the tradition of antipodean inversion, contradicted the expectations relating to bucolic poetry and presented a kind of Hades rather than an Arcady on earth.

The *Eclogues*, appearing under a William Lisle Bowles epigraph describing a region "Where a sight shall shuddering Sorrow find/Sad as the ruins of the human mind", trace the progress of a day in the penal colony, commencing with the poem "Elinor". This inverted pastoral depicts Botany Bay as a desolate and unresponsive place.

Elinor, transported for prostitution, leads a miserable existence at Botany Bay, turning each morning "Once more to daily toil, once more to wear/The livery of shame, once more to search/With miserable task this savage shore!" She muses nostalgically about her homeland, a fitting site for a true pastoral poem:

Still wilt thou haunt me, Memory! still present
The fields of England to my exiled eyes,
The joys which once were mine! Even now I see
The lowly lovely dwelling! even now
Behold the woodbine clasping its white walls,
Where fearlessly the red-breasts chirp around
To ask their morning meal.

But here at "the furthest limits of the world,/And blasted as [she is] with infamy", she can only survey "the drear scene,/ The marshy plain, the briar-entangled wood" and cower in anticipation of "all the perils of a world unknown".

Ironically, by describing New South Wales as a perilous "world unknown", Southey places his image of the colony in a well-known category, that of the harrowing land of emigration and exile described in Oliver Goldsmith's *The Deserted Village*. No poem dealing with the colonisation of faraway places could escape comparison with Goldsmith's piece, which was at once a paean to English rural virtues and a deliberate attempt to debunk dreams of paradise in North American colonies. Like Goldsmith in *The Deserted Village*, Southey in the *Botany-Bay Eclogues* emphasises the charms of English bucolic life by referring to comparative horrors in a faraway land. Botany Bay became defined in terms of the pastoral tradition of English poetry inasmuch as the colony stood as the antithesis of all pastoral felicity.

Now that some facts about New South Wales were documented, writers were beginning to incorporate the image supplied by the annalists into the corpus of imaginative English literature. As English writers continued the process of understanding and expressing Australian life they were combining knowledge gleaned from Australian experience with a system of images and attitudes which was inherent in their English culture. After the brief but necessary period of first-hand reporting on Australia, English writers began to respond to Australia vicariously and imaginatively. During the annalists' period, Australian experience was the dominant partner in a coalition with English culture as English authors created an image of Australia. Now the culture was coming to the fore, as objectivity gave way to imagination.

In many respects Southey applies the finishing touches to the daunting image of Australia, an image which had been latent in the "prediscovery" representation of the diminishing paradise, and which was clearly delineated in the writing of Watling and the First Fleet journalists. Also, there is in Southey's poetic image the beginning of the next dominant aspect of the English representation of Australia. For in the other three poems of the *Botany-Bay Eclogues* he draws attention to the decrepit state of English society and suggests ironically that in comparison to the evils of a social system which protects exploiting squires and press-ganging military recruitment officers ("Humphrey and William") and in which soldiers returning from valorously defending King and Country become forgotten men ("John, Samuel and Richard"), Australia is *potentially* an asylum from Old World troubles. Notwithstanding the horrors of Elinor's plight and the convicts' badinage about vice, garrison girls and venereal disease, Southey implies that Australia can come to be regarded (as indeed Quiros and Dampier before him had speculated) as a kind of Promised Land, a place where the persecuted may come to be "haven'd in peace in this corner at last" ("John, Samuel and Richard"). It is notable that the poems of Hamilton and Dyer cited earlier also contain such tentative implications.

The forbidding image of Australia was certainly a compelling and lasting one; but the Utopian yearnings of writers contemplating an enormous and still largely unknown land would not be dispelled. The earlier image of the diminishing paradise — the land which encourages optimism even in spite of continual disappointment — was still exerting an influence over writers, and it was almost inevitable that a more attractive Australia should also be popularised by English authors. This optimistic aspect of the image was bound to be superimposed on the foregoing impressions, as the picture of Australia became more detailed and complex. The new development is the subject of the next chapter.

CHAPTER THREE

Another Terrestrial Paradise (1800-1835)

And here shall Fancy in her favourite spot,
Arrange the wood, the waters, and the cot —
Add life and loveliness where nature fails . . .
Thus, in the flowing scene that round me lies,
Imagination paints her Paradise.
John Hamilton Reynolds, *The Eden of Imagination* (1814)

The Background

In 1813 Gregory Blaxland, William Lawson and William Charles Wentworth, members of a growing faction of free settlers in New South Wales, found a trafficable route across the Blue Mountains. For twenty-five years this small but precipitous range had proven as impenetrable a barrier against expansion on Sydney Town's western frontier as had the Pacific Ocean to the east. From the western slopes of the mountains the three adventurers surveyed extensive green plains which were waiting for agricultural and pastoral development. They hurried back to Government House with news that was to contribute to the development of an image of the colony as an unspoiled land: fertile, salubrious, and full of potential. They fostered new hope for paradise in the unknown regions of the south land.

The Blue Mountains crossing proved to be one in a complex of circumstances which caused an increasing proportion of the interested English writers to represent the colony more attractively than in previous decades when sinners and a sterile landscape had been dominant in the image of Australia. As industrialisation, the population boom, and the recession which resulted after the Napoleonic wars all contributed to the social malaise of England, the fortunes of Australia were perceived to be rising.

Under the energetic governorship of Lachlan Macquarie (in office 1810 to 1821) New South Wales was expanding, with a concerted building programme in Sydney being supplemented by increased exploration farther afield. West of the Blue Mountains grazing country was opened up. In 1816 the English government lifted restrictions on the emigration of free settlers to Australia, and during the 1820s the writings of Malthus impressed upon English people the possibility that England could be threatened by masses of its own unemployed and destitute malcontents.[1] Accordingly, immigration to Australia rose steadily during the 1820s until the great influx of settlers commenced in the mid-1830s. Moreover, Governor Macquarie's policy of granting unprejudiced pardon to ex-convicts (termed "emancipists") who wished to settle in the colony was the first step in a gradual process of removing some of the convict taint from the image of Australia. Macquarie's term of administration became a decade of development and prosperity, the pattern of which was to continue, with only the occasional faltering due to minor economic recession, until the 1840s.

As writers in England observed the social problems and the necessity of reform in the Old Country, the literary image of Australia became increasingly attractive. The Scottish martyrs and their supporters had indicated that, compared to corrupt England, Australia could be counted a haven. As Henry Erskine had implied, with an ardour more compelling than his poeticism, *any* new land was preferable to unjust England:

Then come, oh! sad alternative to chuse,
Come, banishment, I will no more refuse,

Go where I may, nor billows, rocks, nor wind,
Can add of horror to my tortur'd mind.

On whatsoever coast I may be thrown;
No lord can use me harder than my own;
Even they who tear the limbs and drink the gore,
Of helpless strangers, what can they do more.[2]

Moreover, it was not only radical representatives of the "politically-enslaved working classes of England"[3] who were aware of the shortcomings of life in England during these early decades of industrialised society. Anyone who required the essentials of life — land, lodgings and food — could be excused for dreaming of a happy land in the Antipodes. And there were many writers who were prepared to supply the public with the images that they wanted. In "a snug island" like one anonymous pamphleteer's version of Van Diemen's Land, for example, one might have "plenty of land, plenty of sheep, plenty of corn, plenty of all manner of vegetables. . .and plenty of as good fish and birds as we have here at home".[4]

Many authors could discern writing on the wall for England, and they implied that if the folly of Old England continued, the young colony would soon outgrow its allegiance to the crown. Drawing on the traditions of antipodean inversion, satirical writers could envisage a future in which an emergent Australia would overshadow a decadent England. In A. A. Watts's futuristic *Scenes of Life and Shades of Character* (1831) for example, the "Australasian Statesman in the year 2377" could reminisce about the "Decline and Fall of the English Empire":

> One time, at the opening of the nineteenth century, She [England] was able, single-handed to defy an united world! and to triumph finally in the cause of honour and freedom. . .
>
> But her time came at last! and as Tyre fell, or rather as Rome fell. . .so fell England: and the first symptom of her fall was, a hard-heartedness which took the place of the ancient English blunt good-nature. All the classes seemed infected by it. . .it was every man for himself.[5]

As the fictional statesman recalls, while such calamities were occurring in the northern hemisphere, "throughout the vast continent of Australasia" wealth "was flowing in; ease, comfort, and content, prevailed everywhere".[6] The sun might set on

England; but as it did, an age of prosperity might dawn on the southern region of the empire.

Emigrants' Literature

While it is not quite a premonition of Australian Utopia, Watts's article does suggest that, particularly in the years around 1831, emigration was an attractive theme in the popular British press. The social conditions were primed for writers to portray green lands on the far side of the walls of industrial England. And the farther away these luxuriant regions were, so the writers' imaginations could be granted more creative latitude. The distance between England and Australia was almost unimaginable, requiring as much as eight months' sailing; the colony could be regarded virtually as part of another world. Once imaginative writers felt free to use Australia as a fictional setting and once the fertile lands to the west of the Blue Mountains had been discovered, authors began to indulge their fancies in producing "other worldly" images which might satisfy readers' yearnings. Edward Gibbon Wakefield, whose *A Letter from Sydney* appeared in book form in 1829, was a major exponent of such "creative reportage".

The biographical details behind the composition of *A Letter from Sydney* seem to be drawn from the shoddiest penny-fiction, but the facts are that Wakefield developed theories of convict-free colonisation while he was serving a three-year prison sentence in Newgate after abducting and marrying a fifteen-year-old schoolgirl, Ellen Turner. When the elucidation of his emigration theories first appeared in serial form in the *Morning Chronicle* between August and October 1829, he was still in the gaol.

Wakefield's lineage gives some clue to the character of his political and economic theory. He was descended from royalty by virtue of his relationship to Robert Barclay who was an apologist of the Quakers and a descendant of King Edward I. The family had a history of radicalism. Wakefield's grandmother Priscilla wrote a feminist book, *Reflections on the Present Condition of the Female Sex, with Suggestions for its Improvement* (1798), and she also set up an independent savings bank in Tottenham; and his brother William eloped (successfully) with Emily Shelley-Sidney, cousin of Percy Bysshe Shelley.

The mixture of the aristocratic and the radical is manifest in Wakefield's political theory. Accused by Karl Marx decades later of being the model capitalist apologist, Wakefield developed in his "sufficient price" theory of colonisation a system of keeping the emigrant workers in their place: they were to be employed by moneyed landowners whose superiority was seemingly evident in the fact that they had sufficient income to purchase crown land at arbitrarily inflated prices. (In the last chapter of Book One of *Capital* Marx takes Wakefield to task in an analysis of the latter's *England and America,* 1833.) Espousing his theories with the zeal of a radical free-thinker Wakefield argued vehemently for the establishment abroad of what is in effect the most conservative of political systems: a type of free-enterprise serfdom in which, in theory at least, workers gradually improve their lot by dint of diligent toil for their masters.

Too often *A Letter from Sydney* has been examined solely as a treatise on the practical application of an economic theory, when in fact it is a subtle piece of creative literature in which the author's imagination supplies images which are necessarily fictional insofar as Wakefield had never set foot on Australian soil. Particularly important is the author's manipulation of the narrative persona. Presenting his "Letters" as factual journalism, Wakefield assumes the character of an established Sydney-sider who cries for his beloved country because heavenly Australian nature has for too long been sullied by a corrupt society and by authorities who have lacked the fortitude to maintain "that desirable proportion between the demand and supply of labour, without which, I say, no country can flourish".[7] Should that proportion be obtained, says Wakefield's Sydney-sider, then "I will tell you that Botany Bay is an earthly paradise" (p.113).

Wakefield's creativity extends not just to his characterisation of the authorial persona, but also to his deliberate manipulation of his readers. *A Letter* is written so that the present readers are "implicated" as "spies" receiving "privileged" information while perusing the confidential correspondence between the Sydney-sider and a long-standing intimate (fictional) friend in England. For example, when attempting to describe the native-born white

Australians, the Wakefield-character shares some private memories with the companion of his romantic youth:

> You remember that Genoese girl before whom you trembled, and I became faint, though she only handed us some grapes. . . Do you remember that bright laugh and how I patted her cheek, and told her that it was softer than her country's velvet? And how she blushed — do you remember that? — to the tips of her fingers and the roots of her hair? And how — do you remember how — peasant that she was, and but just fifteen, she tossed her head and stamped her little foot, with the air of a Queen? And afterwards. . . did we not feel jealous of each other for three days, though neither of us could hope to see the little angel again? Yes, you remember it all. Well just such another girl as that brings fruit to my door every morning. [p.147]

The very fact that the readers are perusing a tract that is ostensibly not intended for them serves to increase the rhetorical power of Wakefield's propagandist arguments insofar as the information supplied to the readers seems, on one level, all the more candid.

The Sydney-sider recalls the recent salad days of Australian farming immediately after the crossing of the Blue Mountains, and he proposes that such ideal conditions are possible all over the continent provided the right kinds of settlers are brought, in the right proportion, to the colony. (Which is to say, Australia requires large numbers of willing and experienced farm workers who are prepared to toil for landed masters. And lo, England abounds with unemployed agrarian workers!) Once the Blue Mountains are conquered and settlers have access to the "true" Australia of Wakefield's imagination, a type of paradise stretches away from Sydney:

> When their cows led them to those green plains, they could sew and reap without the labour of "clearing"; their cattle grew fat and multiplied rapidly: the asses' bridge was passed; and the advantage so quickly gained, was. . . imperishable. [p.126]

In his fervour to create an attractive milieu in which his social theories might be tested, Wakefield contributes to a developing image of cornucopian Australian nature:

> Timber, coal, iron, and other useful minerals abound; the harbours and rivers teem with fish; cattle of all sorts thrive and

> multiply with astonishing rapidity; every fruit that flourishes in Spain and Italy comes to the highest perfection; and Nature fully performs her part in bestowing upon man the necessaries, comforts, and luxuries of life. . .I can soberly declare that I believe this country to possess merits of a physical nature superior to those of most other spots on the globe. [p.102]

Indeed as F. G. Clarke has noted, quite apart from his contribution to economic theory, Wakefield's creation of a glowing image of Australian nature aligns him with the literary spirit of his age. For, "Wakefield has often been described as a utilitarian, but inasmuch as he dreamed of establishing an agricultural arcadia in Australia, he was in the mainstream of the romantic movement".[8]

A Letter from Sydney is the exemplar of propagandist emigrant literature which extols Australia as a land of promise. It is a genre with pretences to journalistic realism, but beneath that guise writers create a world to comply with their desires or prejudices. Such literature was particularly prevalent in the 1830s after the founding of the South Australian Land Company under the auspices of the National Colonization Society, of which Wakefield was originally a member. Axe-grinding authors who had land or friends involved in the project, or who wrote specifically for the growing market of people considering emigration, began to describe the convict-free society of South Australia as an egalitarian, working-people's community, perfectly harmonised with a beneficent Australian nature. According to T. Horton James in 1838, it "was pleasing to see in Adelaide the importance and respectability of the labouring classes"; the esteem granted to "shepherds, stockkeepers and such like" was so considerable as to "lessen the distinction between master and man". James remarks that as he went "strolling up to the tents, and near the huts of the labouring people, they all seemed healthy and happy".[9]

Was this perhaps the best of all possible worlds? Certainly, by the 1830s readers could indulge their fantasies by accepting what they were being told of life in the Antipodes. The image of the happy workers' democracy was not confined to South Australia. As Thomas Bartlett assesses the well-established genre in 1843, emigrants' literature about Australia appealed to readers' yearnings so that "unshackled by dull reality, [readers'] ideas wander in the regions of romance, from whence it is natural to suppose, that none but pleasing and delightful images will be drawn".[10] With the aid of readers' gullibility writers exploiting the potential emigrant market wrote of an "arcadian life in a country in which there is no cold winter's blast, no snow and where ice is a matter of history" (p.3). In this version of Australia, settlers could "luxuriate in the finest climate in the world, and at the same time. . .amass a large fortune by the exercise only of common prudence" (p.3). Who indeed would decline "to enjoy the pleasures of continued summer. . .and to revel in the possession of almost perfect health" (p.3)?

Imagination Paints Her Paradise

The emigrants' literature arose at a time when writers dealing with Australia felt less constrained to present strictly veracious images. After the initial period of apprehension, when the First Fleet annalists documented the early years, the prospect of fertile regions inland from the Blue Mountains stimulated writers to represent Australia in glowing terms despite the fact that the majority of them had never visited the land. Their fantasies about a country that they could create in their writing influenced the image of Australia more than the land itself did. In the process of achieving an equilibrium between English culture and the environment in Australia (the process set in train by the First Fleet annalists), the emphasis swung temporarily over to the English culture as writers projected traditional optimistic expectations onto the region.

Emigration propaganda alone could not have brought about the widespread change of attitude toward Australia which occurred in contradiction of the daunting image which had prevailed at the turn of the century. More universal influences were at work on the image. First there was the question of wish-fulfilment, as writers created in their imagination the characteristics of an exemplary society and environment, and then ascribed their private Utopian yearnings to the actual geographical entity of Australia. As Thomas Hervey acknowledged in 1824, whenever discussion turned to the Antipodes:

> Fancy built new regions in the main
> . . .And, where the vast antarctic waters roll,

She reared a continent against the Pole
. . . Philosophy, in thought, would oft repair
To theorize, and gather systems there;
And poets, in Utopian mood, would stray,
Within its shades to dream an hour away.[11]

Moreover, poets' Utopian moods were already well developed by longstanding expectations of wonders to be found in *Terra Australis*.

Inevitably, when a new world is opened up, the dreamer in a writer stirs to supply felicitous images of unlimited potential in an unexploited realm. This happened with English writers' initial responses to America. The New World became the New Canaan, and Michael Drayton was not alone in his evocation of Virginia as "Earth's onely Paradise".[12] For example, in 1613 Alexander Whittaker assured his readers about Virginia:

> Wherefore, since God hath filled the elements of earth, air, and waters with His creatures, good for our food and nourishment, let not the fear of starving hereafter, or of any great want, dishearten your valiant minds from coming to a place of so great plenty[13];

and Robert Thorne was most optimistic about the prospects of the "Indees occidenalls" in a "Declaration" anthologised by Richard Hakluyt: "without doubt [merchants] shall find there ye richest lads [*sic*] and Islands of the worlde of Golde, precious stones, balmes, spices, and other thinges that wee here esteeme most".[14]

However, such representations of little-known regions are not simply a question of wish-fulfilment. As Harry Levin indicates with specific reference to the Renaissance and the Americas, but with general relevance to all travel-writing:

> [authors] could draw on a rich backlog of fabulous lore about aborigines, namely the myth of the golden age. Hence it is not surprising that whenever the voyagers undertook to describe the inhabitants [and the general characteristics] of the new lands they had been exploring, the Ovidean *topos* was likely to come into play, almost as if it had been touched off by a reflex action. Life at its barest and least sophisticated was somehow decked out with a set of trappings inherited from the learned conventions of literature.[15]

And in a Christian culture such as nineteenth century England there is also the Biblical variant of the golden age myth, namely Genesis, which can be stimulated by the same type of reflex action. The stock paradisaic images of a happy rural society which is needless of laws, blessed with perennial harvest and constant good health in a perfect climate, could all be expressed in Edenic terms.

Now that the content of Australian images was conforming to traditional English ideas of felicitous lands, the diction and motifs employed to express that content were not being challenged to cater for new experience. English literary language could already cope well enough with the task of portraying Australia as some kind of paradise.

In fact, one need not refer to newly discovered *lands* to demonstrate this mode in which traditional language can shape new experiences into old moulds before the experiences can cause a reworking of the language. Paul Fussell has examined World War One from this perspective:

> The point is this: finding the war "indescribable" in any but the available language of traditional literature, those who recalled it had to do so in known literary terms. Joyce, Eliot, Lawrence, Pound, Yeats were not present at the front to induct them into new idioms which might have done the job better.[16]

In the case of Australia, writers who wished to present an image of the country but who had no direct experience of it could draw on what Bernard Smith has called "a stock of attitudes and preconceptions"[17] about happy lands far away in time and space.

Sadly there was no Shakespeare or Wordsworth who responded in an innovative fashion to the idea of Australia up to the mid-1830s. Wordsworth in England took such traditional themes as the splendour of nature or the virtues of rustic individuals and society, and fashioned a new poetic language in order to create a new poetic experience. Those who were concerned with portraying Australia, however, were generally either incapable or not desirous of transcending clichés. Their allusive language served to render the unique subject of Australia in Old World language and traditional images of terrestrial felicity. The influences which Bernard Smith discerns in Thomas Watling's writing may also apply to other authors:

> When Watling talks of Elysian scenery, Arcadian shades, and classic bowers, we observe the powerful images which he derived from his education, acting as a filter through which he saw and commented on the local scene. He has joined the mythical with the actual.[18]

Watling sought to describe Australia in unusual fashion: he implicitly criticised it for being unlike the preconceptions of "the elysian scenery of a Telemachus; the secret recesses for a Thomson's musidora; arcadian shades or classic bowers" (Watling, *Letters from an Exile*, p.8) which he counted worthy of artistic treatment. He thereby utilised clichés of earthly paradise in a negative fashion by indicating their untenability when tested against lived Australian experience. Much more representative (outstanding perhaps only in its singular lack of imagination!) is J. H. Tuckey's attempt to describe pristine Australian nature:

> Nothing could offer a more perfect picture of reposing solitude, than the wilds of Port Philip [*sic*] on our first arrival. Here Contemplation, with her musing sister Melancholy, might find an undisturbed retreat. Often at the calm hour of evening I have wandered through the woods,
>
> Where the rude ax with heaved stroke
> Was never heard the nymphs to daunt,
> Or fright them from their hallow'd haunts.
>
> The last hymn of the feathered choiristers [*sic*] to the setting sun, and the soft murmurs of the breeze, faintly broke the death-like silence that reigned around; while the lightly trodden path of the solitary savage, or the dead ashes of his fire, alone pointed out the existence of human beings.[19]

While the nymphs commune with the spirits of Contemplation and Melancholy, the birds sing their hymns in a strange world, but it is not new.

As the paradisaic image of Australia developed, the grim garrison depicted by White, Collins, Tench and Watling faded from view. In its place arose a fantastic "Land of the free!" whose "kingdom is to come —/Of states, with laws from Gothic bondage burst,/And creeds by chartered priesthoods unaccurst", as Thomas Campbell envisaged it in 1828. [20] The imagination supplies the images from traditions of the golden age when there "was no fear of punishment. There was no threatening law/In brazen tables nailed up to keep the folk in awe".[21] As James Montgomery wrote of an island paradise set just off the coast of latter-day South Australia:

Here was the infancy of life, the age
Of gold in that green isle, itself new-born,
And all upon it in the prime of being,
Love, hope and promise; 'twas in miniature
A world unsoil'd by sin; a Paradise
Where death had not yet entered; Bliss had newly
Alighted . . .
Plants of superior growth now sprang apiece . . .[22]

Similarly T. K. Hervey could add a sense of exoticism to his vision by describing the discovery of Australia in terms of one of the most celebrated (even then) of classical myths:

Thou giant secret of the liquid waste,
Long ages in untrodden paths concealed,
Or, but in glimpses faint and few revealed,
Like some chimera of the ocean-caves,
Some dark and sphinx-like riddle of the waves,
Till he — the northern Oedipus [i.e. Captain Cook] unfurled
His venturous sail, and solved it to the world![23]

Alternatively, a poet might rely on the English pastoral tradition. Australia could become William Wickenden's expansive English country garden:

Awake, my muse, recal [*sic*] the wandering strain,
Behold, Britannia's banners grace the plain,
Her fields of corn o'er every valley spread,
Her oaks encircling every mountain's head,
Where in light chaplets smiles the blushing vine,
And o'er each porch its purple clusters twine,
Where sloping woodlands, smiling lawns between,
Blend with wide seas of everlasting green,
Where Spring, exulting, decks the passing hours,
And from her urn throws never fading flowers.[24]

Any new world worth extolling must possess an ideal climate, and of course "the extraordinary healthiness of the climate of

New South Wales"[25] circa 1830 becomes so well-attested that its "salubrity . . . is proverbial".[26] All creatures great and small thrive in the atmosphere. As P. M. Cunningham describes the country which he visited in the 1820s, human beings seem truly blessed:

> No better proof can indeed be given of the *healthfulness* of Bathurst, than that the only death owing to natural causes from the period of its first settlement took place in 1826, after a space of twelve years.[27]

And so do livestock:

> The diseases of sheep and cattle in this colony are indeed scarcely worth commenting on; so rarely do fatal effects result, most of the sheep dying of sheer old age. How different this is to what we observe in European countries.[28]

Here is universal longevity worthy of the golden age when the "fertile earth as yet was free, untouched of spade or plough,/ And yet it yielded of itself of everything enough".[29] Fertility prevails throughout the land: "the effects of the climate of Australasia, it is well known, are to increase, in a high degree, the productive powers of animals of all descriptions: man is by no means an exception."[30] The variety of produce is almost cornucopian in a land where even "the swine are fed on peaches and apricots"[31]:

> Their gardens [in Van Diemen's Land] exhibited raspberries, strawberries, melons, pears, plums, nectarines, and apricots; and their young orchards, thriving rows of cherries, citrons, guavas, mulberries, figs, pomegranates, quinces, and medlars, with lemons and oranges in sheltered situations, and even the olive, which had been lately introduced into the island . . . the huge hedge rows were filled with Spanish chestnuts, walnuts and almonds.[32]

Is this the same land as the barren realm of suffering and death John White describes in his *Journal*? Clearly it is not. One is the representation of a scientist's first-hand experience of gruesome actualities in Australia; and the other is a region where authors' imaginations have been allowed greater latitude, a region comprehensible in pre-defined terms drawn from literary traditions about exotic territories. As soon as the English literary mind confronted the idea of a felicitous new land of Australia, the literary language inevitably came into play.

To put it most crudely, the authors who depicted Australia during the first three decades of the nineteenth century were often simply bad writers. They were not innovative enough to break with established themes and forms dealing with exoticism as they attempted to evoke what was actually a new experience in a new land.

Because Australia was so distant and so large, and because the alluring interior was still mostly unknown to English people, these writers could fossick in their imaginations and find, especially in the envisaged interior, an Aladdin's cave of splendour. As Jonathan Swift had realised more than a century before, a land far away in space (and therefore in time) can seem to be so distant from actuality that it can be located in the regions of fantasy. In a sense the glowing images of Australian salubrity gained credence simply because of the effects, on imaginations, of the distance between Australia and England. At such "unreal" remoteness, an "unreal" world could justifiably be envisaged.

This aspect of the fantasy and mystery which may be associated with Australia — in the manner of Swift in *Gulliver's Travels* — is most apparent in a Utopian fantasy of 1837 entitled *An Account of an Expedition to the Interior of New Holland*. It was written by Lady Mary Fox (born 1798) who was the eldest daughter of the Duke of Clarence (later William IV).

With reformist vision and democratic spirit, Lady Mary utilises the mystery of distant Australia in conjunction with specific knowledge culled from journals in order to present a tale about a rational and equitable society exemplary to contemporary England. By choosing the location of far away Australia, the land which so many contemporaries were depicting so euphuistically, and by referring to selected mundanities of Australian life such as the seasons and the local weather conditions, she contrives to imbue her fantastic tale with a degree of authenticity.

The plot follows the adventures of Mr Hopkins Sibthorpe, an Englishman who leaves Bathurst (*actual* Australia) with a selected party in August 1835 (*actual* time) to explore the interior of the country to the west. With deliberate attention to local colour Lady Mary (who poses in the narrative as editor of Sibthorpe's journals) remarks that the party leave in August because it is then winter in Australia and there is less problem at that time of year with heat and possible dehydration. The party intend to travel by canoes across marshes and lakes west of Bathurst until they reach fertile territory on the shores of a large body of water outside the ambit of present knowledge of Australia.

So the fantasy begins. Like William Dampier, Pedro Fernandez de Quiros, John Callander and nineteenth century explorers who searched for the inland sea, Fox represents Australia as a realm in which an idealised territory can be imagined on the other side of the horizon of known Australia. In 1766 for example, Callander had refused to dismiss the possibility of finding "some civilized nation in the interiour [*sic*] parts of this country [*Terra Australis*], who are as utter strangers to us, or our arts, as we can be to theirs", and he had then evoked visions of an Australian El Dorado by referring to a comparable history with the great Inca civilisations of South America (Callander, *Terra Australis Cognita*, vol.I, p.14. The parallel passage in de Brosses is Tome I, pp.20-21).

The idea of a paradise concealed from immediate view in Australia was a seemingly universal one and not simply confined to writers familiar with the traditions of travel literature. According to D. D. Mann in his *Present Picture of New South Wales* (1811), an "absurd notion had uniformally [*sic*] existed amongst the convicts that it was possible, by penetrating into the interior, to discover a country, where they might exist without labour and enjoy secrets hitherto unknown".[33]

To similar effect Lady Mary Fox sends Sibthorpe and his party into the interior. The explorers travel for days on a lake which becomes a river, all the time putting distance between themselves and known Australia until they sail into a series of lakes, the largest of which is surrounded by "a most extensive and delightfully fertile region, watered with numerous streams from [the] mountains".[34] The natives there are "of a less savage aspect than those in the vicinity of our settlements" (p.6). Also there are signs of civilisation, such as animals which they identify as boars, which were "well known not to be indigenous in New Holland" (p.7). They are destined to encounter a splendid "civilized nation of European origin, which had in so remarkable a manner, been kept separate hitherto from the rest of the civilized world" (p.1).

The history of the nation dates back to the Reformation when a group of English and German idealists "meditated a removal to some distant region, in which they should escape finally from strife and oppression" (p.12). Rather than opt for America they headed south, "induced by some glowing descriptions they had heard, but which proved [until then] to consist chiefly of fable or exaggeration, to seek for the long-famed southern continent, the 'Terra Australis Incognita'" (p.12). After a short period on the coast these travellers in the imagination headed inland and found at the heart of New Holland the source of the legends. They established a settlement which "from its singular beauty of situation. . .[was] called Eutopia (fine place), probably with something of a covert allusion also to the well-known fabulous Utopia (no place)" (p.26).

Once Hopkins Sibthorpe arrives there, most of Lady Fox's manipulation of the image of Australia is complete. Now the attention focuses on England, as Fox contrasts the social organisation of the Old Country with that of the south land. The extraordinary colony is founded on rationalist ideals. All behaviour involving emotional reaction, passion, and even rhetoric, is condemned as "savage". All topics (such as the "Gothic barbarism", p.48, of the English custom of duelling and the concept of honour) are analysed discursively in lengthy Socratic forums at dinner parties. Government is democratic, and mostly designed along republican lines, with inherited privilege outlawed and with administrative positions being held according to merit. Prisons (though hardly required) are run on humanitarian principles, with rehabilitation rather than punishment being the professed aim. All religious affairs are conducted in a spirit of ecumenicalism, with seventeen different religious communities co-existing without rancour.

By choosing Australia as the site for her Utopian (or Eutopian) vision, the author is responding *and* contributing to a well-established literary image. As the culmination of a tradition which dates back past Jonathan Swift and Pedro Fernandez de Quiros to antiquity, Australia in the 1830s is portrayed as a land whose limitations are as yet unimaginable. However, the crucial difference between the image in Swift's time and in the 1830s is that in the latter period Australia is actually being colonised and a *real* society is being established there. In Swift's time Australia was a fantasy land whose evocation could be used to comment on the "real world". However, in the 1830s Australia is a "real world" which is still saturated with fantasies ascribed to it from without as well as within as the interior is regarded so hopefully by prospective colonists.

By a most conservative assessment, the image of Australia which is presented in Lady Mary Fox's *Account* entails a land whose future is still malleable and whose pristine condition justifies idealists' hopes in the quality of life which could be developed deliberately in this latest new world. The fact that the gaol community at Sydney is a butt for the author's cynicism does not detract from the optimism, for the penal colony need not be regarded as essential Australia. Rather, it can epitomise all that is reprehensible in English society. In a reaction reminiscent of Francis Bacon's comments about the Americas (in which he declared it "shameful" and "unblessed" to take the "Scumme of People, and Wicked Condemned Men, to be the People with whom you plant"[35]), the Eutopians are aghast at Sibthorpe's information about the Botany Bay prison:

> To people a new settlement with convicted criminals, to form a nation of the scum and refuse of mankind, appeared to them so preposterous, that for some time they could not help supposing they must have misunderstood their informants. "To bring together a number of villains", they said, "to a country where good character is not the rule, but the exception, allowing them free intercourse with each other must be the most effective mode of hardening and confirming them in wickedness". . . [p.30]

Provided the taint of convictism can be overcome — either by settlers who travel westward to the imagined fertile regions, or by an increase in the numbers of free colonists in the established settlements — Australia could still be envisaged as a blessed land.

Lady Mary Fox's *Account* can be seen to have developed out of images from the past. By reinterpreting the long-established tradition of the south land as a diminishing paradise she was able to portray an attractive land with many attributes verifiable in the present, and with future prospects which seemed limitless.

Where the author is perhaps atypical in her rendition of the happy land with the still happier future is in her portrayal of the rationale behind the ideal type of society which must exist at the heart of imagined Australia. Her Southlanders live in a sophisticated community where reason and discourse are the guiding influences and where work and entertainment are conducted in well-planned, functional cities. By way of contrast the society imagined in the majority of optimistic contemporary responses to Australia is markedly simple, intuitively ordered, and rural; it is in fact distinctly pastoral.

In England the 1830s saw further industrialisation and subsequent expansion and overcrowding of unhealthy cities. The resultant nostalgia for rural tranquillity is manifest in Romanticism, of course, but the traditions of English pastorals, with their familiar images of unthreatening and well-ordered landscapes and communities, also provided lesser poets with expressions of escapist themes. Inevitably the idealisation of rural life influenced attitudes to Australia. For example, vilification of the city is basic to Edward Gibbon Wakefield's visions of a prosperous agricultural Australia developing away from convict Sydney. In the first half of the nineteenth century, there developed the "Sydney versus the bush" contrast which has become a tradition in Australian literature and which is most obvious in the work of A. B. "Banjo" Paterson, Henry Lawson, and more recently, Patrick White. G. H. Haydon's avowed preference for bush life in 1846 is representative of the English attitude which became established particularly during the 1830s and 1840s:

> Illness is almost unknown in the bush; a life there is far preferable to living in the towns . . . The bush, notwithstanding the rough life led in it, is the stronghold of hospitality and good feeling.[36]

A more explicit polarisation of attitudes is found in Alexander Harris's *Settlers and Convicts*. Harris simply aligns the city and the bush with evil and good respectively. The Rocks area of Sydney is described as a squalid zone of bordellos and sly-grog houses frequented by "runaway convicts, who were in strict 'hiding' in the day-time, and only 'showed out' by stealth at night, creeping through the darkness up and down those intricate streets to the place of assignation for some desperate deed".[37] By way of happy contrast, an evening spent in the bush is idyllic, with a catalogue of simple delights rewarding the honest worker:

> The success of the day, the prospect of a good cutting or an advantageously shaped log on the morrow, the pleasant perfume of the pipe, the cheering pot of tea again and again repeated, with each new yarn, or joke, or laugh, the busy and pompous excursions and barkings of the dog, the pattering shower, the clouds of fireflies that dance along in their countless angular courses where the cold stream tumbles among the great stones in the bed of the creek, such are the objects which occupy [the sawyer's] thoughts; and it were well that all things that can occupy our attention and our thoughts had as little in them to excite unwise desires or fears. [p.85]

Settlers and Convicts is representative of much of the literature concerning Australia at this time. With little being known about the colonies, there was both a demand for information about them and a tendency to utilise them as a comparatively exotic locale for fiction. In works such as *Settlers and Convicts* a writer could detail the conditions of life in Australia by following the fortunes of a central character, normally the authorial persona, who travels and works throughout the land, experiencing the colony at first-hand.

Harris did live for some time as a free settler in Australia before returning to England and later living in Canada, where he continued to write, until his death in 1874. In *Settlers and Convicts* he presents a compilation of several literary forms loosely bound together by a picaresque narrative (which is approximately autobiographical) concerning the "emigrant mechanic" who tells the tale. Throughout the work the author punctuates the narrative with much standard travel literature information. There are tables of retail prices of essential commodities; lists of articles necessary for establishing a comfortable farmhouse; descriptions of the climate and terrain of the major areas of settlement; and much general advice to prospective emigrants.

Harris is similar to the First Fleet annalists insofar as all these authors had direct experience of Australia and were writing about their lives in the country. Also they all produced works characterised by a certain diversity of tone as the multiple purposes of the works — empirical compilation, objective reportage, interpretative discourse, narration of plot — did not always harmonise. Certainly there is still a sense of the annalists' objective recording in *Settlers and Convicts* as Harris supplements his semi-autobiographical tale with an attempt to present a commentary on the social gamut of the colony, from the urban convicts to the landed "gentry" in the grazing country. However, the differences between Harris's and the annalists' work are pronounced, deriving from and exposing the changes which had occurred in the condition of the colony and in the situation of the writer concerned with Australia. The annalists were unable to consider the colony as a setting for fiction: their training and their status as recorders of the external and historical details of a society which was struggling to survive left the authors few opportunities to consider the country in terms of the metaphoric or symbolic overtones applicable to fiction. Harris, on the other hand, was less concerned with the details of survival or the beginnings of history and tradition. He was free to regard Australia as a literary setting rather than as a demanding experiment in life and death whose data had to be recorded.

In fact, as Harris's knowledge of Australia broadened he became even less concerned with precise recording than with expounding imaginative themes which could be elucidated in the Australian setting. As W. S. Ramson has observed, Harris moved from being something of a "social commentator" in *Settlers and Convicts* towards being the "selective", creative author of *The Emigrant Family* (published two years later in 1849) who "makes an impressionistic reordering of even the geography of the colony to accommodate his vision, reshaping the colony into a single stage on which the drama of his and everyman's life is displayed".[38] Although there is still much of the practical emigrants' handbook about *The Emigrant Family*, Harris's development is evident and his work can stand as the epitome of the change in the writer's status generally in Australia during the colony's first sixty years, as authors allowed their imaginations, and not solely the objective facts about the land, to shape any literature concerned with Australia.

In *Settlers and Convicts* the emigrant mechanic's adventures progress from unemployment in the city to satisfying work as a woodman in the bush, where, apart from sharing the camaraderie of a pastoral type of society, he survives adventures such as a flood, an attack by bushrangers, and unjustified arrest by spitefully overbearing constables. Eventually he saves a modest amount of money and embarks for Old England.

Harris does portray Australia as a land of opportunity, but practical experience had acquainted him with some of the country's shortcomings, and he does not present a completely favourable picture of the country even though his writing is aimed at the emigrant market. Harris is his own man, not prepared to suppress unpleasant information in order to please his publishers and his public. His hatred of the authoritarianism which arises from the penal society of the city moves him to depict the brutal side of life in the colony. Harris's renditions of the flogging of convicts, for example, are not for the squeamish:

> I saw a man walk across the yard with the blood that had run from his lacerated flesh squashing out of his shoes at every step he took. A dog was licking the blood off the triangles, and the ants were carrying away great pieces of human flesh that the lash had scattered about the ground. [*Settlers and Convicts*, pp.25-26]

The horror affects all elements of the society. One character recalls seeing "young children practising flogging on a tree, as children in England play at horses" (*Settlers and Convicts*, p.24).

With such visions of the gaol-society occurring throughout Harris's writing, his image of an alternative society away from the decadence of the city becomes all the more attractive. The future of the colony lies in a rejection of the old social hierarchy based on class distinctions and the dominance of certain sectors of the community over others. As Harris asserts in *The Emigrant Family*, the true Australians exist in classless, cooperative communities in which "fellowship of country has already begun to distinguish them and bind them together in a very remarkable manner. Whenever they come into contact with each other, even when considerable difference of rank exists, this sympathy operates strongly".[39] Away from moribund England and the heavily populated cities, writers felt they could locate regions "where the jarring din of politics gives place to the pleasing and profitable hum of industry; and where strife and enmity are suppressed by the pacific principles of Christianity".[40]

Although all is not exemplary in Harris's Australia, the regions in the bush are envisaged most optimistically. In this respect, Harris's image of an alternative to Sydney society recalls Lady Mary Fox's vision of the prosperous and happy society of Southlanders who are aghast at the reports of the convict system and who set up an ecumenical meritocracy which requires "no subjection of one race of men to another on the ground of colour or caste" and which makes "all subjects of the state necessarily admissable to the rights of citizenship" (Fox, p.22). Once the free society begins to outgrow its convict beginnings, Australia can be represented as a land in which people are free to develop according to their own worth. The citizens of the bush can exist in a type of Australian golden age whose rationale, as Edward Bulwer Lytton judged it, is based not so much on "intellect as a peculiar turn of intellect, and a fortunate combination of physical qualities, easy temper, and quick mother-wit".[41]

Such an attitude did not necessarily deny the flaws and disgraces of Australia, as Harris's works exemplified. The admission of shortcomings such as the barbarity of the convict system and the apparent growth of vice and crime in the cities marked the development of a certain balance between fancy and experience in the creation of an image of Australia. Writers had begun to use the colony as a stage for fictional dramas, but they were also aware that the country was simply another part of the actual, imperfect world, and they were aware that this fact had to be acknowledged.

William Thomas Moncrieff's play *Van Diemen's Land!* is a case in point. Moncrieff (1794-1857) was the son of a London tradesman. He began to climb the social ladder early when at the age of ten he established himself as a song-writing prodigy at the same time as he was employed as a solicitor's clerk. In 1810 he began writing plays, and he subsequently became a prolific author who composed "considerably above two hundred [pieces]. . .that have, at various times, appeared successfully on the Stage."[42] As he was for some time manager of the Regent's Theatre (later the Queen's Theatre), he had an entrepreneur's sense of what would be popular, and he was plainly just as concerned with the quantity in the cash-box as he was with the quality on the stage. As the Preface of the 1851 *Selection* of his plays informs us, Moncrieff was "[engaged], from the very commencement of his career, in management", and therefore "the dramatist [in him] was ever held by him secondary to the manager. The pieces were furnished to meet the temporary wants and exigencies of the Theatre at which the Author happened at the time to be engaged".[43]

Van Diemen's Land! was written and performed in 1830 while Moncrieff was employed by R. W. Elliston, manager of the Surrey Theatre. According to Moncrieff, this play which achieved "extraordinary popularity" was written at the suggestion of Elliston who had two sons in Van Diemen's Land managing a "highly flourishing store and hotel".[44] (It is not unfair to say that Elliston also had an eye for an exotic and popular dramatic subject.) The resultant play is a theatrical hybrid of drama, opera, masque and ballet. (Indeed, it is not too fanciful to regard *Van Diemen's Land!* as a direct, though degenerate, descendant of John Gay's *The Beggar's Opera* — the definitive mock-operatic "anti-pastoral" about low-life and roguery.) A chorus introduces most of the scenes with ditties sung to the tunes of contemporary popular songs, which frequently prompt the characters into spirited song and dance.

As a *coup de grâce* Moncrieff includes two panoramas of picturesque scenes which complement the action. In Moncrieff's opinion, with respect to *Van Diemen's Land!*, the "Panorama [designed by a Mr Marshall], in the play, was a masterpiece of art, painted with such rare fidelity" (vol.4, p.vi). The device appears twice in Act I and serves to introduce the audience, as well as the characters who tour the island, to Moncrieff's vision of Van Diemen's Land. Given the opportunity to express himself both pictorially and verbally, Moncrieff emphasises the "highly picturesque views" which distinguish the imagined landscape. Scenes featured in the panoramic exhibit include the "romantic country" between Hobart Town and Squashmoor Village; the audience is treated to representations of the River Derwent, Herdsman's Cove, Blue Hills, and a "Forest of Gum Trees" (p.20).

The changing pictures form an ideal backdrop to the plot, which is three-fold. Plot (a) is concerned with an ingenuous group of free settlers who have just arrived in the colony. One of the group, Frederic, is pining for his lost love, Eliza, who has been wrongfully convicted and transported. Of course, the lovers meet here in this penal settlement, and Eliza is eventually vindicated when the real culprit of the thefts confesses on his death-bed. Plot (b) involves bushrangers who capture Frederic and Eliza and who plan to rob and murder the new settlers. Plot (c) entails much local colour, with singing and dancing Aborigines who are gradually converted from their attitude of "an eye for an eye", to friendly cooperation and inter-marriage with the settlers. The Aborigines are also instrumental in the eradication of the bushranger menace.

Plot (c) is examined in chapter five of this book. Plots (a) and (b) ought to be treated now because of their references to the idea of a paradisaic present and future in Australia.

Moncrieff is definitely fascinated by the prospect of life in a fertile and temperate new world. As indicated by the panorama, the landscape which he envisages is distinguished by its grandeur and luxuriance. Such uncorrupted nature seems a setting in which his liberal vision of an unprejudiced society might become reality. Certainly Moncrieff is not prepared to condemn the convict inhabitants of the island, particularly considering how many of them originally came from the corrupting city environment of London. A convict chorus sings the axiom: "Let moralists gravely declaim against vice,/But the man was ne'er born that hadn't his price —/Opportunity makes us all rogues in a trice" (p.21). The implication is that a respectable life in England is extremely difficult unless one is newly rich or a lordly profiteer from "aristocratic avarice and over-weening power" (pp.16–17). Indeed, even the eminently honest character John Hardy, leader of the new settlers and father of the lovelorn Frederic, has been forced by unemployment and imminent poverty to leave England after he has lost his long-standing job as a cutler at the Exeter Change. By contrast with England, Van Diemen's Land seems, as Hardy himself exclaims on arrival, "a noble island" where one can "breathe the air of freedom. . .how different from smoky, thankless London" (p.10). Hardy reinforces the play's anti-city bias when he chooses his convict servant (albeit in misjudgement of the felon's character) because he is a "country-looking fellow" whose "rustic habit should not cloak much guilt" (p.16). Yet again the opposition between the evil of the city and pastoral innocence is basic to an English writer's image of Australia.

In a rural setting like Van Diemen's Land any individual's personality ought to improve. The characterisation of Mr Blithe, a long-term settler in the colony, bears testimony to the contention. Moncrieff portrays Blithe as a model of the new man, an Australian advocate for the possibilities of life in the classless society. "Only exert yourselves", he advises his assigned convicts, "you're sure to get on". And although there is comic irony in his next observation that a murderer named Tom

Gore became the first doctor in the colony, Blithe's egalitarian sympathies are so sincere as to seem extreme: "I don't care what a man is, so long as he isn't a gentleman. A cobbler's worth twenty gentlemen" (p.22). Moreover, his is a sincerity which the rank and file (so called in Old World thinking) can respond to. Convict Hardy Vaux recognises Blithe's good qualities: "We might have fallen into worse hands than Master Blithe's, gentlemen; he knows the world — has seen life — understands things — perhaps has been transported himself in his time" (p.22). By virtue of his wisdom of experience, rather than through pre-defined class distinctions, Blithe warrants the convict labourer's respect.

At the same time as he succumbs to the stock attitudes about a felicitous Australia, however, Moncrieff is aware that all is not gold in *actual* Australia. Even though he was patently concerned to make money from all of his shows, either as author or manager, in this case he felt obliged by the demands of plausibility not to portray the colony as a totally enchanting fantasy-land. He knows too much to allow standard visions of ideal Australia to pass unqualified. There are indications throughout the play which suggest that Moncrieff's Van Diemen's Land was not entirely a region in his imagination. For example, Hardy Vaux was in fact an historical figure who was transported three times to Botany Bay for assorted charges of petty larceny. An affable and inveterate rogue, Vaux attained some celebrity when he published his *Memoirs* (1819) which were edited, with a morally instructive introduction, by Supreme Court Judge Barron Field. Moncrieff's characterisations of historical entities such as Vaux, Mike Howe, the Tasmanian bushranger, and Bennelong, the Botany Bay Aborigine who visited England with Governor Phillip, all serve to demonstrate that he was aware of some of the contemporary literature about the colony. Also, his awareness that convicts in Van Diemen's Land served standard sentences of either seven or fourteen years indicates that he carried out a degree of preliminary research, and was concerned to some extent with historical authenticity.

He undercuts many of the fallacies about Australia in his characterisation of James Gooseberry, a buffoon who arrives in the colony with outlandish expectations of rapid wealth and respectability. As he stretches his legs on the Hobart docks after the voyage from England, Gooseberry ruminates:

> I'm quite longing to become a landed proprietor: five hundred acres!. . .it would make me lord of the manor in England. I trust there'll be a preserve or two on the grounds, that I may have a pop at the partridges, for I'm rather fond of game. [p.11]

In projecting English criteria onto his expected Australia, Gooseberry has taken the emigrant literature to heart. Deliberately indicating the falsity of propagandist writing, Moncrieff introduces a character named Bolter, who is a free settler who (in his own words) "thrives" on the gullibility of the "rogues and fools, convicts and settlers" who arrive in the colony (p.9). Bolter's welcome to Hardy's and Gooseberry's party could be drawn from any piece of emigrants' literature: "Welcome to Van Diemen's Land, gentlemen — the finest country in the world for health, wealth, and no rent and taxes" (p.10). Coming as it does from this prototype of the Australian con-man, the declaration must be taken with several grains of salt. Moncrieff is not about to endorse an unreservedly favourable image of the colony.

Furthermore, in the bushranger sequences of the play, Moncrieff comprehensively undercuts the romanticised portrayal of a Robin Hood figure who flees into the bush to escape the oppression of an evil society. Michael Howe, the bushranger-character based on one of Van Diemen's Land's most notorious historical figures, is a tormented and unhappy desperado who is willing to abduct innocent women and murder inexperienced settlers in order to survive. Here is no innocence and pastoral self-sufficiency. Contrary to the clichés, Moncrieff does not represent the bush specifically, and Australia generally, as an ideal realm. He is willing to face some of the more disquieting facts about actual Australia.

In effect, although Moncrieff is attracted by the optimistic image of Australia and although he can discern many advantages to life there (in the present as well as in the future), he is not prepared to ignore the deficiencies of the country. He is aware of flaws in the arcadian image, but ultimately he does not develop any new and more pertinent image; he simply rejects, tacitly, the representations of Australian felicity.

His attitude is similar to that of Barron Field, who affirmed that stock English images are not entirely relevant to Australian experience. Field (1786-1846) was a Supreme Court Judge in

New South Wales between 1816 and 1824. When in London he frequented the literary circles, and he was friendly with Charles Lamb and Leigh Hunt and was acquainted with William Blake, William Wordsworth and S. T. Coleridge. His term in the colony was not entirely happy. He quarrelled with Governor Macquarie and felt himself an alien in an unappreciative community, as is evidenced in his poetry and journalism. A staunch proponent of traditionally English aesthetic values, Field admits that such criteria do not apply to Australian experience. He discerns a land "where Nature is prosaic,/Unpicturesque, unmusical, and where/Nature reflecting Art is not yet born".[45] Unlike others who found Australian nature unfamiliar, Field refuses to disguise the reality by describing it in irrelevant English terms:

> New South Wales is a perpetual flower-garden, but there is not a single scene in it of which a painter could make a landscape, without disguising the true character of the trees.[46]

Nor does he seek new criteria by which to assess and express peculiarly Australian nature and society. He simply rejects the land out of hand:

> No tree, to my taste, can be beautiful that is not deciduous. What can a painter do with one cold olive green?. . .forever fair is never fair; and without January, in my mind, there can be no May. All the dearest allegories of life are bound up in the infant and slender green of spring, the dark redundance of summer, and the sere and yellow leaf of autumn. These are as essential to the poet as emblems, as they are to the painter as picturesque objects. . .I can therefore hold no fellowship with Australian foliage, but will cleave to the British oak through all the bareness of winter.[47]

Field is reluctant to modify his aesthetic values in order to find merit in an Australian setting, as the above quotation demonstrates, with its discourse shaped by northern hemisphere seasonal patterns. Holding no fellowship, therefore, he is pleased to opt out of what he construes to be an uninspiring land: "a ship is poetry to me, /Since piously, I trust, in no long space,/ Her wings will bear me from this prose-dull land."[48]

Like Harris and Moncrieff, Field is concerned to indicate that unreservedly favourable images of an Australian paradise cannot prevail. Expectations of a cornucopian nature and a perfect society in Australia simply do not withstand the tests of experience. By rejecting the unreservedly optimistic fantasies of fiction writers who invested Australia with traditional English images of an exotic paradise, authors like Moncrieff and Field anticipated writers who would frame images deriving from their own practical activities in the actual region of Australia. A more informed view of the country, a view arising from lived experience in conjunction with imaginative attempts to interpret the land through the writer's self, would have to supersede the somewhat inadequate images of the First Fleet annalists' objectively rendered Australian deprivation and the excessively derivative visions of luxuriance conjured by relatively "inexperienced" writers in the 1820s and 1830s. A balance between recording and interpretation still had to be attained. The writers who progressed toward this middle ground were the explorers of the 1830s and 1840s who presented their renditions of the land by drawing on their own practical activities in the interior, where they sought solutions to Australian mysteries at the same time as they established their own senses of identity in the last pristine regions of the great south land. They helped write the next chapter in Australian cultural history.

CHAPTER FOUR

Experience in Purgatory (1835-1850)

On these wild shores the hand of Grace
Shall probe my secret soul; shall cleanse its wounds,
And fit the faithful penitent for Heaven.
Robert Southey, "Elinor", in *Botany Bay Eclogues* (1794)

So there is a sense, then, in which the idea of Australia is a central, almost mystic, symbol in our literature. It is a vision of a certain kind of innocence, not childlike but regenerative; a purification which is the result of hardship and endurance, of sacrifice of personal ease, sacrifice perhaps of life itself.
Judith Wright, *Preoccupations in Australian Poetry* (1965)

Between Heaven and Hell

By 1835 the English image of Australia lacked definition. A complex representation had developed in the English mind, as if etched on a *tabula rasa*. Prior to 1770 the only markings evident on the tablet signified a land of mystery, bright and alluring, yet shaded marginally by the scepticism arising from the initial inconclusive encounters with the southern continent. After 1800 images of a hellish realm of suffering were apparent, over which were later inscribed representations of fecundity and pastoral repose. Out of the entanglements of these delineations a sharply focused image was yet to arise. The fundamental forms were already inscribed on the tablet of the English consciousness; the excesses and irrelevancies had to be eliminated and the pertinent aspects needed to be highlighted. Indeed, by the end of the 1830s, after almost half a century of colonisation, an enduring image of Australia would begin to form out of the trials and errors involved in testing images of the country against the increasingly well-documented experience of Australian life.

Earlier authors had pointed a way forward. Robert Southey in his *Botany Bay Eclogues* of 1794, and the apologists for the Scottish "martyrs" had all described a region of desolation and suffering which was paradoxically also attractive because it offered hope for people who despaired of justice or redemption in moribund England. By the mid-1830s, after the version of a bountiful Australia had been popularised, many more writers found that they needed to develop a new understanding of this colony which had been described as both the devil's and God's own country. An interpretation was required which encompassed both the bitter experience of a convict society struggling in an alienating landscape, and the optimism essential to the development of a new country.

As the history of the colony unfolded, greater numbers of English people were emigrating, and the first generations of free Australians were growing up. Observers were compelled therefore to acknowledge the south land as a "real" and contemporary world, rather than a nebulous nether region to which fancy could fly without constraint. As the previous example of America had demonstrated, there comes a time when new-world dreamers must acknowledge that they are dealing with actualities. Because it was a real world rather than a literary paradise, Australia was subject to variations of fortune: the climate could be unco-operative, and recession could afflict the economy, as became obvious during the 1827 and 1843 droughts. The revelation could be disheartening as writers discerned the natural realm not conforming to literary notions:

> And now [1843] that the fruits of the earth have ceased to grow,

> the heavens to drop rain, and the rivers to run, I suspect that this, like many other Australian El Dorados, will end in nothing.[1]

The image of Australia had reached a stage in its development where writers with direct experience of the land were required to "legitimise" the image.

Generally a note of caution rather than despair was introduced. Writers began to reassess their vision of Australia; they were bringing the paradise back down to earth. In the first stage of this process some fundamental truths about the country had to be confronted. There was no denying that an authoritative group of writers — White, Collins, Tench, Watling, for example — had presented a convincing picture of alienation in a strange and distant country. The Australian environment was seemingly designed to accommodate a society of desperate and guilt-ridden sinners. As Barron Field observed as late as 1825, the habitat could seem (to English sensibility) an "afterbirth" of Creation. It was a land "Not conceiv'd in the Beginning/ (For God bless'd His work at first,/ And saw that it was good),/ But emerg'd at the first sinning,/ When the ground was therefore curst".[2] As time passed, nature occasionally vindicated Field's opinion, most implacably in the droughts of 1827 and 1843.

How then to reconcile the differing interpretations of the new land? At one extreme there was a region of suffering and deprivation; at the other a land of freedom and plenty. Could it be that both of these attitudes, which seem mutually exclusive, ought to be taken as correct?

One answer, from a modern standpoint, can be heard echoing from the work of Jonathan Swift, a writer who was remarkably influential in the formation of the English image of Australia.

In two separate sections of Swift's *A Tale of a Tub* the narrator refers to a *Terra Australis* recently rendered "cognita". In the nature of the tale, each of these references is significant on both the literal and the allegorical levels; and, perhaps in the nature of Swift, the author is remarkably prophetic in each instance, on both levels.

In "Sect. IV" of *A Tale of a Tub* the increasingly autocratic Lord Peter purchases "a large Continent lately said to have been discovered in *Terra Australis incognita*":

> This Tract of Land he bought at a very great Penny-worth from the Discoverers themselves, (though some pretended to doubt whether they had ever been there), and then retailed it into several Cantons to certain Dealers, who carried over Colonies, but were all shipwreck'd in the Voyage. Upon which, *Lord Peter* sold the said Continent to other Customers *again*, and *again*, and *again*, and *again*, with the same Success.[3]

A note at the bottom of the same page (of the 1720 edition) informs the reader that this "Continent is taken by some to mean Purgatory, & by others Heaven". Later in the same edition, the authorial persona proposes a "Project, For the universal benefit of Mankind", which would entail the publication, in ninety-six folio volumes, of "an exact Description of *Terra Australis incognita*", which has been "collected with great care and pains from 999 learned & pious Authors of undoubted veracity". Expressing his opinions in the terms of a well-established tradition of emigration-propaganda which was liable to parody, the author proclaims that:

> This Work will be of great use for all men, & necessary for all familys, because it contains exact accounts of all the Provinces, Colonies and Mansions of that spacious Country, where, by a general Doom all transgressors of the law are to be transported: & every one having this work may choose out the fittest & best place for himself, there being enough for all, so as every one shall be fully satisfied.[4]

On the literal level these two passages describe an Australian continent which is expansive and full of potential, but which at the same time is difficult to locate in actuality. This attitude to *Terra Australis* is consistent with Swift's representation of New Holland in *Gulliver's Travels*. In both works the south land may be regarded as a diminishing paradise where searchers attempt to locate the source of a dream in the concrete world of geography. Swift makes this point explicit in *A Tale of a Tub* when the narrator promises to supply, in addition to the ninety-six folio volumes, a "Map of the Capital City" of the *Terra Australis*, contributed by "a known Author who took an exact survey of it in a dream".[5]

Uncannily prophetic on the literal level is Swift's assertion that the land will become the home for transgressors of the law. It seems that even in 1704 the south land was a logical export site for England's problems. Most importantly this question of wrongdoers provides a link between the literal and the allegorical levels. Given the acceptable premise that *A Tale of a Tub* is an allegory on the Reformation, it can be argued that the mysterious southern land of frustration and hope stands for Purgatory. The clues are supplied by the references to Lord Peter's profitable sales both of prime Australian real estate, and of insurances for people bound for the distant shores of this land below England. Lord Peter is seen as no more respectable than any upstart racketeer. It is not difficult to draw parallels between these transactions and the Catholic church's sales of indulgences to transgressors embarking on the longest and last journey, to the afterlife.

At the same time as Swift was being vehemently critical of the concept of Purgatory as it was exploited by institutional religions, he was also being unwittingly prophetic about the development of Australia as a literary image. In the nineteenth century many English writers attempted to attain a balance between the bleak and the florid responses to Australia which arose during the first fifty years of settlement. They portrayed the colony, implicitly rather than explicitly, as a type of Purgatory, a realm of suffering and concomitant reward. Although "Purgatory" is a term rarely, if ever, invoked by writers describing Australia in the years 1835 to 1850, the label is a legitimate critical aid which may be employed by the modern reader to encompass accurately the characteristics of the new image of Australia which arose from the muddle of observations and aspirations which had accrued over the decades. A comparison of Australia to Purgatory is pertinent insofar as the colony was construed as a society of guilty sinners suffering in a bizarre environment. As it was represented, Australia could be a site for absolution. Moral rectitude and a sense of acceptance into a legitimate community could be achieved by purging convict guilt in a process of penitent suffering. At the end of the trial the rewards of one of the earthly kingdoms of God might be available.

In the early years of colonisation the isolation of the continent and the virtual absence of damning social conventions render the colony ideal for personal regeneration. This is in marked contrast to England, where, in P. M. Cunningham's estimation, "once [an individual's] fair name is blasted, he becomes . . . an outcast from honest society, is looked upon with a suspicious eye, and his misdeeds [are] thrown in his teeth on occasion of every petty dispute".[6] Moreover, it is not only the sinner for whom Australia may represent an escape from the past. Innocent victims of recession, industrialisation, or aristocratic corruption may begin life anew by emigrating. As W. H. Leigh explains, once the emigrants depart from England "the land where their forefathers are sleeping is left forever" and a new time-sphere is entered:

> The past must be viewed, with all its pleasures, its vicissitudes, or its pains, as a blank which is never to be noted; and the future must be gilded with the ray of all-radiant hope, to light him cheerfully to a more peaceful, a happier goal.[7]

This anticipation of a new order in the antipodes dates back to the days of Quiros. As the quest for the diminishing paradise continued even after the east coast of New Holland was located and colonised, the prospect of future Australian felicity could console those dreamers who were confronted with more daunting experience in the present. As the penal colony struggled for survival, and the known areas of the country yielded no golden fleece, writers and settlers contemplated the western horizons and imagined a promised land. Therefore, as the pattern of the diminishing paradise continued, hopes were spiralling in on the interior — the heart of the land — as the centre of Australian dreams. The discovery of fertile land behind the barrier of the Blue Mountains seemed to validate the fantasy, and the interior glowed alluringly in the imagination. It may be recalled that Lady Mary Fox's ideal republic is located in a fertile heartland, and her creation can now be recognised as part of a literary tradition. The fact that known regions of bleakness encircle the interior and must therefore be traversed before a paradise is achieved only serves to validate the quest. As T. J. Maslen asserts in 1830 when he imagines the interior, "if there are desert tracts of large extent, there are also doubtless many highly fertile, beautiful, and, perhaps, curious portions of country, possessing novelties which the imaginations of the geographer and the traveller would never have anticipated".[8] At the heart of the imagined land there is the source of the dreams: "what the *interior* consists of, it is almost premature even to conjecture".[9]

The preoccupation with the interior is a part of the attempt to resolve the conflicts between settlers' knowledge of suffering in Australia and the traditional aspirations for a southern paradise. Therefore the writings of the explorers who sought to map out the Australian interior are crucial to the elucidation of an image of the Australian Purgatory, for these writers tested their aspirations by exposing themselves to the elements in an attempt to solve the final mysteries of the continent. There were to be no more uninvestigated horizons behind which the diminishing paradise might be concealed. The writings of Charles Sturt, Thomas Mitchell and Edward Eyre are major works in the canon of English literature about Australia because each writer investigates the myths of the inland sea and the great central river system. Their interpretations of their experiences were to have a pronounced influence on the way Australia was to be regarded in years to come, and their texts will therefore be examined at length later in this book.

The notion of an Australian Purgatory wherein disappointment and adversity may be seen as necessary preludes to the attainment of some blessed realm is certainly plausible in terms of the concept of the diminishing paradise. Equally influential in this respect is the idea of antipodean inversion. Admittedly, assertions that in the south land night is day, and winter is summer, that birds do not fly, and that paradoxes are the norm, are all clichés first proclaimed in ancient times. However, clichés only become so through repeated assertion, and in the nineteenth century there is scarcely a writer concerned with Australia who does not marvel that:

> Every thing in Australia seemed formed on a plan the reverse of every thing in other parts of the world; that the swans were black, the rivers flowed from the sea-shore into the interior; that the mountains were the most fertile, while the plains were the most sterile parts of the soil; that even the animals were as singular as the country.[10]

And while most writers were not as hostile as Barron Field, who adjudged Australian nature to be accursed, few denied that in the Antipodes . . . quite athwart goes all decorum:

> Whether Botany Bay was made in a merry mood of Nature, or whether it was her first essay in making continents, we shall

> never know; but we may be quite sure, that every thing found there will be diametrically opposite to the ordinary productions and inventions of the Old World.[11]

In such a contrary world, evil can become good, and suffering can lead to happiness. Even Charles Darwin, who admits no regret at leaving Australia when the *Beagle* sets sail after a brief sojourn there, acknowledges that the moral inversion apparent in the colony is remarkable:

> As a means of making men outwardly honest, of converting vagabonds, most useless in one hemisphere, into active citizens of another, and thus giving birth to a new and splendid country — a grand centre of civilization — it has succeeded to a degree perhaps unparalleled in history.[12]

As Commander John Lort Stokes (who was captain on the *Beagle* in later years) observes, even Australian nature can exercise astonishing regenerative powers, with rainfall causing a landscape to change overnight from "a thirsty looking plain to a rich green spot".[13] So, according to *Blackwood's Edinburgh Magazine*, against such a background, a parallel "experiment in the faculty of renovation in the human character [might find] its field in the solitude of this vast continent".[14] Or as H. Rogers explained at greater length:

> Nay, if we look at New Holland, we see that even the very vices of England are pressed into the service of civilization! As though every particle of our soil were too precious to be lost, the very scum and refuse of our population is, like other refuse, swept off to fertilize a barren waste. The very convicts of England (strange destiny!) will, perhaps, be the patriarchs of a great and powerful nation.[15]

The sinners may become saints, and the sins of the parents need not be visited upon the children. When writers observe the first generations of native-born white Australians they assert with almost total accord that there is a new and exemplary Anglo-Saxon race arising in the Antipodes. The new Australians, dubbed "currency lads and lasses" (as opposed to sterling), are presented as physically splendid. Those who do not fit P. M. Cunningham's stereotype are embraced in Edward Gibbon Wakefield's enthusiastic descriptions. Cunningham observes a new-world type: the currency children "grow up tall and slender, like the Americans, and are generally remarkable for that Gothic peculiarity of fair hair and blue eyes".[16] Wakefield draws his model from the more exotic realms of the Old World:

> The same human form which more than two thousand years ago was embodied by Phidias and Praxiteles, is still considered the model of perfection by all refined Europeans. Where does that form most commonly breathe? In Greece, and even in the very Cyprus, where Adonis was conceived, and where the Goddess of Beauty had two temples. You may laugh or sneer; but the latitude of Sydney corresponds exactly with that of Paphos; and it is no less true that the native Australians [i.e. the currency lads and lasses in this context] bear a stronger resemblance to the modern Greeks than to any other people.[17]

More significantly, currency folk are perceived as *morally* exemplary. Cunningham asks rhetorically: "what more can be said in their favour, than that they are little tainted with the vices so prominent among their parents!"[18] Indeed, Commissioner Bigge adds a sense of historical veracity to the representations found in the travel literature when he asserts in his official parliamentary report on the colony that:

> The class of inhabitants that have been born in the Colony affords a remarkable exception to the moral and physical character of their parents . . . they inherit neither the vices nor the feelings of their parents.[19]

From transported English outcasts a new and vibrant civilisation is seen to develop in a wild and uncorrupted environment. From this point of view it is appropriate that several authors compare the nascent Australian communities to ancient Rome in its earliest days. James Tuckey, for example, in his *Account of a Voyage to Establish a Colony at Port Philip* maintains that all he beheld in Port Phillip prompted him to dream of "a second Rome, rising from a coalition of banditti". As the idea takes hold he envisages the colony "giving laws to the world, and superlative in arms and arts, looking down with proud superiority upon the barbarous nations of the northern hemisphere".[20] In fact this notion of the new southern Rome dates back at least to Charles de Brosses and John Callander. Callander did not hesitate to translate de Brosses's optimistic speculation about the possibility of colonising the south land with convicts:

> Besides, were a number of such people obliged to live together, they would soon find the necessity of forming a regular society; for anarchy quickly destroys itself. After all, if we look to the origin of many colonies, we shall find them frequently to have taken their rise from idle, or unfortunate wanderers, and often composed of the worst kinds of people. The infancy of states, like that of man, is often void of law or reason. *Sisiphus* the robber built *Corinth; Romulus* founded *Rome* at the head of a troop of banditti . . .[21]

By the time speculation had become actuality, the language and the images for describing a penal colony were well established. For example, an anonymous journalist for the *London Magazine* sees the officers of the First Fleet as "the Romuluses of the colony".[22] And even Barron Field concedes that although "the flow'ry name/Which science left" to Botany Bay "has become a scorn/And hissing to the nations", there is potential for this "discordant state" to develop just as "fairest Rome became".[23] And Charles Darwin, in a letter to his sister during his visit to Sydney, is reminded of bygone days of grand empires when he asserts that ancient Rome "would not have been ashamed of such an offspring".[24] From the beginnings of guilt, exile and hardship in a primitive land, legendary splendour might ensue.

The image of Australia as a new Rome is an apposite variant on the representation of the Australian Purgatory. There could be no denying the colony's sinful beginnings and cruel environment. But what manner of Purgatory was this? And what were its rewards?

Between Fact and Fiction, Between History and Myth

By the 1830s the habitable regions in the hinterland around Sydney, in the environs of Hobart and Port Phillip, and on the plains to the west of the Blue Mountains had all been adequately surveyed and therefore divested of mystery. They appealed less to writers' and readers' imaginations than the unknown expanses in the interior of the continent. Accordingly, as part of a "symbiotic" relationship between myth and history, dreams of inland fecundity drew explorers away from the civilised areas on journeys toward uncharted pristine regions. Because the heart of Australia was the subject of so much literary speculation, the unknown interior had become virtually a symbol of the essence of Australian experience. Interest was high and the explorers often published the narratives and impressions which arose out of their expeditions.

The two decades after 1830 developed as a "golden age" of travel literature concerning Australia. The content and the form of the published journals dealt with concerns crucial to the English image of Australia: the quest for a type of promised land in the interior; the efficacy of suffering and perseverance in the land of antipodean inversion; the attempts to understand and express Australian experience in the English language. The journals were presented in England as popular travel literature, and they were widely read and reviewed. For example, Thomas Mitchell's *Three Expeditions* had gone into its second edition a year after publication, and Charles Sturt's *Two Expeditions* and Edward Eyre's *Journals* received review coverage in major periodicals such as *The Athenaeum* and the *North British Review*. The explorers' writings were the most cohesive and popularly circulated accounts of Australia during the colony's decades of early maturation. As experientially validated compendia of aesthetics, geography, history and myth they comprise a body of literature which was to alter English impressions of Australia and which was in turn to underlie the development of the Australian ethos until the present day.

The authors of the journals are operating in a literary territory somewhere between documentary and fiction. They are presenting quests after undefined but alluring goals, quests enacted in actual historical time, across a real geographical landscape. Yet simultaneously, because they are English people investigating and describing this unspoiled land which is so very far in time and space from the quotidian realities of comprehensible Old England, and because Australia had been for centuries synonymous with elusiveness and mystery, the explorer-writers traverse a literary symbol as much as a concrete geographical entity. Their motives originate in a response to the myth of the diminishing paradise at the same time as they are associated with mundane questions of daily employment and colonial expansion. Their responses to and representations of what they encounter on treks toward the centre of Australia are inevitably steeped in connotations pertaining to the legendary continent — land of despair, land of hope. The journals become as much a part of composed national myth as of national history. These writers probe the heart of the south land, literally and metaphorically.

The explorers were dealing with a region which had fostered longstanding literary connotations. Also they were writing at a time when an Australian ethos was largely unformed and liable to be influenced by any new information which writers might supply about important areas of the continent. For these reasons the explorers' journals need to be treated as "proto-myths", as works which contributed to the elucidation of the image of Australia.

The published journals may not have been created as fiction or as orthodox "creative literature". However, given the undoubted quality of much of the writing, the breadth of the readership, and their time of composition, these works ought to be analysed as effective imaginative literature which appealed to readers' opinions and fancies and which contained literary characters, plots, themes and even symbols produced by minds that were attempting to interpret new experience and render it comprehensible. The journals do not present merely objective recording of data. The explorers regarded themselves as men with a mission to discover and publicise the most important secrets of the south land. Sturt, for example, wrote to his friend George Macleay that "there is a destiny for us all, and unconsciously we are the instruments in our own hands of its fulfilment" and that he "had for years a presentiment that that task [of 'penetrating to the Centre'] was preserved for [him]".[25] To similar effect Sir Thomas Mitchell claimed that the unknown tracts of Australia were not merely of geographical importance:

> Curiosity alone may attract us into the mysterious recesses of regions still unknown; but still a deeper interest attaches to those regions, now that the rapid increase of the most industrious and, may we add most deserving people on earth, suggests that the land there has been reserved by the Almighty for their use.[26]

It was no workaday project that these travellers were undertaking. In many respects they were mapping out the terrain of their own desires and ambitions. A completely objective rendering of their experiences in the interior was therefore not to be expected. Moreover, against the background of what had gone before in literature about Australia — the descriptive objectivity of the annalists, and the more interpretive, personal work of Watling and Tench — it is not surprising to find that the explorers' imaginations are given some latitude in the expression of the Australian experience and environment. As Val Vallis has explained in reference to the development of a regional artistic vision, description must inevitably give place to expressive projection of personality: "Sheer description is the lowest level of poetic craft. The next move, to embody attitude in the description, is the first drift from reportage towards the mysterious regions of the Symbol".[27] Or, to return to Hegel as he was invoked in the Introduction to this book:

> Man realizes himself through practical activity, since he has the impulse to express himself, and so again recognize himself, in things that are at first simply presented to him as externally existent. He attains this end by altering external things and impressing on them the stamp of his own inner nature, so that he rediscovers his own character in them. Man does this in order that he may profit by his freedom to break down the stubborn indifference of the external world to himself, and may enjoy in the countenance of nature only an outward embodiment of himself.

The explorers' literature arises from the expression of action in the Australian environment. The writing itself, the product of the experience of authors who have "imbibed" the land, takes the image of the country past description towards realms of symbol wherein the individual in Australia can begin to make sense of his or her own existence there.

The individual writer begins to take more control over the way the land is envisaged. The human self becomes more assertive as human beings and the externally existent continent meet half-way, so to speak, in the process of creating literature about Australia. The "purgatorial" image of the land, which will be found in the explorers' literature is a "mature" image because it is produced by authors who are experienced and who have tested their preconceptions, old images and suspicions, and have returned from the mysterious centre with new knowledge derived directly from the interaction between their selves and the country.

Sturt, Mitchell and Eyre shaped an image of the land even as the land shaped them. They created myths while chronicling history. It was work such as theirs which prompted Mark Twain to assert decades later:

> Australian history is almost always picturesque . . . It does not read like history, but like the most beautiful lies. And all of a fresh new sort, no moldy [*sic*] old stale ones. It is full of surprises, and adventures, and incongruities, and contradictions, and incredibilities; but they are all true, they all happened.[28]

Part One
Exploring Purgatory

Any analysis of the nineteenth century accounts of travels to and within Australia must refer at some stage to Barron Field's "Journal of an Excursion across the Blue Mountains of New South Wales", which is included in a compendium entitled *Geographical Memoirs on New South Wales,* of which Field is the editor. In this lengthy article Field sets up a narrative pattern which is to recur in the works of all the writers who detail journeys toward the centre of the land. The travellers set out with expectations of attaining a felicitous land, but they encounter natural obstacles which they can hope to surmount only through dogged application, and even suffering. For the party in Field's narrative, there are the Blue Mountains with the craggy outcrops of the "Three Sisters" standing sentinel over the lands which the travellers seek. The crossing of the mountains is presented as a series of tribulations, the commencement of which occurs "at Emu Ford over the river Nepean . . . Crossing this stream is always a work of such time and trouble, and sometimes of such difficulty and danger that it is half a day before [the traveller] rides or rows through it".[29]

Trial follows trial. There is Lapstone Hill to be conquered. But for those who persevere, the rewards are described in terms of the legends of opulence. A vantage point in the western foothills "affords the first view of the promised land of Australia, after the wilderness of the Blue Mountains" (p.430). Here is a region which, unlike other tracts in a less dramatic landscape, truly merits comparison with Canaan:

> In Van Diemen's Land they have a river Jordan, and plains of Jericho; but the river is so called (I suppose) because it may be occasionally passed over on dry ground; and the plains are not equal to Bathurst Plains. After three days' starving among the mountains, your cattle now get plenty of green grass. Encamp then at the first bite; for there is water enough, and the station under Mount York is very picturesque into the bargain, *que ne gâte rien*. [p.430]

Moreover, closer inspection of the vista validates the enthusiasm. The narrator travels west across the Macquarie and Bathurst plains: "I could hardly believe I was travelling in New Holland this day; so different — so English — is the character of the scenery — downs, meadows and streams in the flat — no side scenes of eucalyptus" (p.443). When it is recalled that Field elsewhere condemns Australian nature for not meeting English criteria of pastoral luxuriance, it is apparent that the Bathurst plains are being accorded the highest of praise. Indeed, to Field's way of thinking, this area is so atypical of the rest of Australia that he is moved to reiterate his reference to Canaan, a haven for exiles who have struggled through alienating deserts: "This is truly a land flowing with milk and honey" (p.445).

In "Journal of an Excursion" travellers encounter a trackless landscape which tests their fortitude but which, if conquered, also leads to a land of contrary splendour. The plot structure ratifies, albeit implicitly, the daunting aspects of Australian experience as valuable insofar as the rewards for perseverance are shown to be ample. This pattern in Field's narrative derives both from his lived experience in Australia and from his own aesthetic and social biases. The image of the land which emerges from Field's writing is a product both of the nature of the Australian continent and of his own cultural background. Australia *is* a land of vast barrenness alleviated by fertile havens, and a direct recording of travel through these geographical features must give rise to narration which outlines a pattern of tribulation and reward. However, through the writer's invocation of cultural values and literary language, an image charged with connotations can develop. In Field's description of the attainment of a "promised land" west of the Blue Mountains, both the immanent nature of the land, directly recorded, and the culturally determined personality of the writer have combined in the production of an image of the country.

Charles Sturt: A Country of the Mind

The purgatorial narrative pattern and image of the land recur throughout the canon of travel-writing during the age of exploration which occurred after the crossing of the Blue Mountains. The most comprehensive accounts of purgatorial experience in Australia occur in the published journals of Charles Sturt and Thomas Mitchell.

Sturt was born in India in 1795, the son of a magistrate with the East India Company in Bengal. After an education in England, which included two years at Harrow, Sturt joined the army with career ambitions, and in 1841 fought in the Spanish campaigns and in Canada. He later spent three years in France as a member of the English occupation army. The turning point of his life came in 1826 when he embarked for Australia as captain of a regiment in charge of convicts. He arrived at Port Jackson eager to participate in the investigation of the country where "the stillness of that once desert shore is now broken by the sound of the bugle and the busy hum of commerce".[30] He secured a post as military secretary to Governor Ralph Darling, and through this influential connection Sturt negotiated the financial backing required to realise his ambitions of continental exploration. Between 1828 and 1831 he completed two expeditions which, after he published his journals in 1833, were to become legendary.

His account, *Two Expeditions into the Interior of Southern Australia*, details journeys into the "unexplored country to the westward of the Blue Mountains" (vol.I, p.x). By Sturt's own assertion, the book is worthy of consideration because it presents a vision of Australia which derives from his extensive practical activity in the environment. He purports to be able to provide an authentic, mature account of the country, in contradiction to "so many individuals" of his acquaintance "whose ideas are totally at variance with its actual state" (vol.I, p.x). Sturt's writing is invested with the authority of experience.

As the history of this experience is set out, Sturt and his party trudge across desert wastes, transporting adapted whale boats to parching rivers which trickle westward into the continent's mysteries. The first expedition traces the route of the Macquarie River; and the second describes a truly epic trek along the course of the Morumbidgee (Sturt's spelling) and Murray rivers. The expeditions, although organised and enacted as separate ventures, are described within one published work. One effect of this arbitrary choice by Sturt and his publishers is that the reader is encouraged to consider the two expeditions as components of a single cohesive narrative. The reports of first-hand experiences have been imaginatively organised to a certain extent so that the reader is encouraged to interpret the accounts in a particular fashion.

The "Preliminary Chapter" is informative both about Sturt's attitudes to Australia and about his creative organisation of events into a cohesive narrative. As Michael Langley has observed, Sturt's writing contains important "moments of meditation".[31] During these contemplative stages of the narrative the author detaches himself from time, space and the events in progress, and interprets the presented "facts" so that there can be no doubt in the reader's mind as to the meaning of all that is occurring. The "Preliminary Chapter" is such an instance. It anticipates the narrative and directs the reader's expectations so that he or she will extract a specific meaning from the text. Ostensibly the chapter is a "state of the nation" review of the colony's fortunes in 1833. But within the discussion Sturt establishes his major themes, which he has learned from his encounters with untamed Australian nature and which he hopes his readers will deduce vicariously. In fact Sydney Town, as he describes it, symbolises the preoccupations in his writing. It is a prosperous community which achieved its status through a peculiar process:

> The labour and patience required, and the difficulties which the first settlers encountered in effecting these improvements, must have been incalculable. But their success has been complete: it is the very triumph of human skill and industry over Nature itself. [vol.I, p.xv]

Labour, patience, the triumph of humanity over nature: these are to be the recurrent concerns of *Two Expeditions into the Interior*.

In the "Preliminary Chapter" Sturt also contrives to make it appear obvious that, in a society still in its infancy and still curious about its own potential, an account such as his is necessarily of national importance insofar as he claims to be testing mere conjectures against his own authoritative knowledge of the colony. At this stage when opinions about Australia are still forming, his views contribute considerably to the development of a national image. In effect the reader is witnessing the composition of early white Australian mythology.

So, with the reader's preconceptions adequately formulated, Sturt embarks on the journey. As it is primarily the narrative structure — the manner in which Sturt arranges the events and perceptions from his lived experience — which informs the reading of Sturt's image of Australia, it is vital that the "plot" of the expeditions be presented in some detail. As the daily fortunes of the travellers are methodised into a pattern, their experiences become meaningful.

The account begins in earnest with the outset of the first expedition in 1828. The drought which commenced the year before is still unbroken. Sturt sets the scene, observing that during the last year "the surface of the earth became so parched up that minor vegetation ceased upon it. . . It almost appeared as if the Australian sky were never again to be traversed by a cloud" (vol.I, pp.1-2). The party travel uneventfully across known Australia *en route* to lands of mystery. They cross the Blue Mountains, and pause in Bathurst, which prompts the author into a meditative moment. Now that he has arrived in this flourishing township he asserts that he has never been "more impressed with the importance of the service upon which I was employed, or more anxious as to the issue, than while contemplating the rapid advance of agriculture upon its plains" (vol.I, p.5). The way into a region such as the Bathurst plains is not necessarily easy, but the rewards are undeniable once Sturt has overcome the "formidable bar to. . . prosperity which [he] had left behind [him], in the dark and gloomy ranges which [he] had crossed" (vol.I, p.5). Perseverance in the face of adversity bears dividends in Sturt's version of the western country.

The travellers continue westward, following the Macquarie River, and penetrating a bizarre region increasingly afflicted by drought. As the sun sets one evening they arrive at a depleted natural reservoir. A scene then ensues which would seem fantastic in any other setting:

> As soon as the sun dipped under the horizon, hundreds of birds came crowding to the border of the lake, to quench the thirst they had been unable to allay in the forest. Some were gasping,

> others almost too weak to avoid us, and all were indifferent to the reports of our guns. [vol.I, p.16]

As they are described, the events and apparitions in the landscape are becoming less recognisable as part of normal worldly experience.

The travellers approach territory which is completely unsurveyed. They reach the site of John Oxley's camp of ten years before, and find it undisturbed; the camp-fire ashes and the tent-trenches have remained just as they were left one morning a decade earlier. A modern reader is tempted to compare Oxley's tent-trenches to Neil Armstrong's ever-lasting footprint on the lunar landscape. That is excessively fanciful, certainly, but without doubt Sturt himself is disturbed enough by the otherworldly "ghost-camp" to wonder whether his fortitude and good fortune can hold out so that he might "penetrate beyond the point which had conquered [Oxley's] perseverance" (vol.I, p.26).

Indeed, Sturt's tribulations have hardly begun. The party strike out into the unknown. They struggle across the marshlands into which the Macquarie trickles. On the other side of the swamps there is a plain engulfed by bushfire. They wander across the charred waste, and the landscape becomes even more infernal as they encounter no water and the sun bakes a desolate expanse.

At this crisis in the narrative, portentous events occur:

> Hope never forsakes the human breast; and thence it was that, after we had secured the horses, we began to wander round our lonely bivouac. It was almost dark, when one of my men came to inform me that he had found a small puddle of water, to which he had been led by a pigeon.
>
> It was, indeed, small enough, probably the remains of a passing shower; it was, however, sufficient for our necessities, and I thanked Providence for its bounty to us. [vol.I, pp.45-46]

A party wandering in a desert; direction and sustenance provided by Providence: here are elements of an exodus myth. On more than one occasion Sturt proclaims that his travellers have been treated by fate in the manner of a chosen people. He meditates at the conclusion of the first expedition: "Something more powerful, than human foresight or human prudence, appeared to avert the calamities and dangers with which I and my companions were so frequently threatened" (vol.II, p.6). Sturt is not presenting unadorned factual reportage of experience in the style of John White and David Collins; rather, by manipulating religious and mythic allusions so adroitly he is investing his tale with an added potency, with a certain oracular credibility.

Revived by the variant manna from Heaven, Sturt presses on into more torment, into an area which is almost sublime in its desolation:

> There was scarcely a living creature, even of the feathered race, to be seen to break the stillness of the forest. The native dogs alone wandered about, though they had scarcely strength to avoid us; and their melancholy howl, breaking in upon the ear at the dead of night, only served to impress more fully on the mind the absolute loneliness of the desert. [vol.I, p.73]

Even the Aborigines are starving. "How then", muses the author, "could an European expect to find food in deserts through which the savage wandered in vain?" (vol.I, p.74).

In answer to his own question he decides to return to civilisation, and the party retrace their course, receiving "aid from Providence" and "the bounty of heaven" whenever they are beset by the "most trying circumstances" (vol.I, p.97). They travel through countryside which, in Sturt's description, appears almost unnatural. There is Oxley's Tableland, for example, which "consists of two hills that appear to have been rent asunder by some convulsion of nature" (vol.I, p.81). And there is the vast marshland which is evaporating into desert in the unremitting drought: "It was . . . so shallow as to expose the backs of the fish in it, and a number of crows had congregated and were pecking at them" (vol.I, p.110). At this stage the party reach the Darling River, where "the stillness of death reigns" in the environs (vol.I, p.108).

However, after traversing deserts, Sturt is attracted by the Darling, and he avers that, had he the wherewithal to follow it, he stood every chance of locating a fertile land: "the river itself had increased in size, and stretched away to the westward, with all the uniformity of a magnificent canal, and gave every promise of increasing importance; while the pelicans were in such numbers upon it as to be quite dazzling to the eye" (vol.I, p.100). The diminishing paradise continues to wane, yet it continues to beckon:

> The further knowledge that has been gained of the interior is but as a gleam of sunshine over an extensive landscape. A stronger light has fallen upon the nearer ground, but the distant horizon is still enveloped in clouds. The veil has only as it were been withdrawn from the marshes of the Macquarie, to be spread over the channel of the Darling. [vol.I, p.151]

The interior, despite Sturt's bitter experiences there, remains a symbol of Utopian aspiration as long as there are regions of it still to be explored. Although Sturt now acknowledges that the inland sea is only a pipe-dream, he claims that the "fact of a large river such as the Darling at the back of our almost inter-tropical settlements, gave a fresh importance to the distant interior" (vol.II, pp.1-2).

The mystery of the Darling provides the impetus for the second expedition which, as Sturt explains in the opening pages of volume two, must be seen as a direct consequence and continuation of the first. So the narrative of *Two Expeditions* continues virtually uninterrupted, initially along the "Morumbidgee" yet again, and then down the Murray. Sturt and his party make speed across the populated Goulburn and Yass plains, and then they are back in the familiar waste land which had prevailed during most of the first expedition.

They traverse a region which has been devastated by a hurricane, and Sturt reintroduces the notion of Australian nature as bizarre and somewhat inimical to its pioneering white inhabitants:

> Within that space, no tree had been able to withstand its fury, for it wrenched every bough from such as it had failed to prostrate, and they stood naked in the midst of the surrounding wreck. I am inclined to think that the rudeness of nature itself in these wild and uninhabited regions, gives birth to these terrific phenomena. [vol.II, pp.18-19]

However, as Sturt is now more inclined to interpret the landscape in which he has for so long felt alien, his experience, allied with his persistent hope in a Central Australian paradise, persuades him to anticipate the rewards of a Purgatory: "Amidst the desolation around us, the river kept alive our hopes. If it traversed deserts, it might reach fertile lands, and it was to the issue of the journey that we had to look for success" (vol.II, p.58). Increasingly, in the account of the second expedition, Sturt is allowing his own personality — with its ever-broadening Australian knowledge, unflagging optimism, and stoic perseverance — to add shades to the image of the land which develops out of his reportage. The prose is becoming less objective, less "photographic" insofar as he is increasingly prepared to invest his descriptions of the landscape with his own emotions, which derive from his experience in the country. As the environs of the "Morumbidgee" become more barren Sturt projects the melodramatic, almost gothic side of his personality onto the region as he renders it in prose:

> It is impossible for me to describe the kind of country we were now traversing, or the dreariness of the view it presented. The plains were still open to the horizon, but here and there a stunted gum-tree, or a gloomy cypress, seemed placed by nature as mourners over the surrounding desolation. Neither beast nor bird inhabited these lonely and inhospitable regions, over which the silence of the grave seemed to reign. [vol.II, p.59]

The gloomy cypress standing as mourner recalls a previous passage in which Sturt described the "Morumbidgee" plains (which in actuality are parched and sunbleached) as "dark and gloomy tracks" (vol.II, p.16). As his experiences wring his emotions, the portrayed country comes to reflect his own moods; he records the evidence supplied by his mind's, not his body's, eyes as they are supplied both with lived Australian experience and with English literary traditions containing such motifs of doom as gloomy cypresses. Perhaps the most striking image which Sturt conjures in response to his plight in the interior occurs when he writes of a rock formation along the banks of the Murray:

> At first, it did not exceed a foot in height above the water; but it gradually rose, like an inclined plane, and resembled in colour, and in appearance, the skulls of men piled one upon the other. The constant rippling of the water against the rock had washed out the softer parts, and made hollows and cavities, that gave the whole formation the precise appearance of a catacomb. [vol.II, pp.139-40]

Sturt is writing about an alienating environment just as the less subjective writers such as John White and David Collins had done before him, but he is *evoking* it by recourse to personal responses and literary motifs whereas the annalists' method entailed a more objective description of Australian characteristics. The annalists attempted to stand outside the environment; Sturt is beginning to internalise it, to interpret it, and in the process he anthropomorphises it to an extent, as his Australian experience and his English background interact to give rise to a more personal view of the country. Even while he senses the horror of the landscape, Sturt is beginning to empathise with it, as when he describes the "Morumbidgee" itself as an entity "struggling for freedom" through the "deep ravines and precipitous glens" of its course (vol.II, p.17). Similarly, as the Murray bears the party through the land of their trials, Sturt feels a special respect (as well as a certain gratitude no doubt) for the river:

> Had the country corresponded with the noble stream that traversed it, we should have been proportionately elated, but it was impossible to conceal from ourselves its inhospitable and unprofitable character, as far as we had, as yet penetrated. [vol.II, p.136]

If the stream is noble enough, perhaps it will lead Sturt to his promised land just over that horizon which he has not yet penetrated. His steadfast belief in the diminishing paradise colours his report.

At the same time as he is expressing an intense feeling of alienation in the desert country, he is also succumbing to a love of the interior despite the suffering it is causing him. This development is most apparent when he discusses the Aborigines, whom he respects for their integrity and their knowledge of the land: "I was happy in having. . .an opportunity of shewing the natives of the interior that I came among them with a determination to maintain justice in my communication with them, and to impress them, at the same time, with a sense of our love of it in them" (vol.I, p.143). The author and the readers are discovering that the Aborigines are essential aspects of the Australian environment and that English people are not necessarily the natural inheritors of this earth.

This realisation is part of the maturing process whereby the colonists become less "blinkered" in their attitudes to the country. They are learning for example that there are criteria for natural beauty other than the traditional English ones, and that the land and its native inhabitants must be construed as remarkable in their own terms. When Sturt is moved aesthetically by the landscape in the early stages of his book he is responding to an English taste for the Romantic and the picturesque. For example, when the party approach the "Morumbidgee" at the beginning of volume two, Sturt is cheered by the return of a beauty to which he is accustomed: "The scenery around us was wild, romantic and beautiful; as beautiful as a rich and glowing sunset in the most delightful climate under the heavens could make it" (vol.II, p.22). Only after a lengthy process of assimilation to the environment can Sturt come to recognise and evoke an additional, more terrible beauty in Australian nature, as in the passage cited earlier concerning trees standing as mourners in the waste land. Admittedly, the terms in which this latter sublimity is described are derived from a "foreign" taste for the gothic, but change has occurred insofar as the writer is now prepared to notice some remarkable features in the waste lands whereas writers before him (Barron Field and Thomas Watling for example) could perceive nothing but reasons to condemn the country as aesthetically negligible. Sturt can be seen to be in the process of adapting to the land even as he is involved in the colonial conquest by which the land is being wrought to the purposes of an English society.

As the narrative continues along the Murray River the party are carried across a plain that appears to have been "rent asunder by the river to allow of a passage for its waters" (vol.II, p.137). As Sturt realised earlier, they are investigating rude nature which is capable of giving birth to "terrific phenomena".

However, Providence is preparing its rewards. Although Sturt is still lured on by the mystery of the Darling, which he correctly assumes to be the river which joins the Murray from the north, the party are now committed to being borne along the Murray to whatever fate awaits them. The men are sick and exhausted, and Sturt himself is in the first stages of blindness. The river turns southward, away from the heart of Australia, into virgin territory which appears increasingly fertile. After such prolonged suffering the narrative of the journeys reaches a climax of joyous discovery. As the Murray carries them onward Sturt is moved to proclaim that "it would have been impossible for the most tasteful individual to have laid out pleasure ground to more advantage, than Nature had done" (vol.II, p.152). A "land of promise" lies "smiling before them" (vol.II, p.223). The Murray eventually flows into Lake Alexandrina which in the context of the overall narrative is simply idyllic. In his sense of joy and deliverance, he finds that:

> It is difficult to give a just description of our passage across the lake. The boisterous weather we had experienced seemed to have blown over. A cool and refreshing breeze was carrying us on at between four and five knots an hour, and the heavens above us were without a cloud. It almost appeared as if nature had resisted us in order to try our perseverance, and that she had yielded in pity to our efforts. [vol.II, p.162]

The final sentence is crucial. It emphasises a developing attitude to the attractive aspects of Australia. Sturt has come to an understanding about the continent. Paradise is not simply there for the taking. It is a lesson which he reiterates in his summary of his impressions of the "reward-land" around Lake Alexandrina:

> It contains land which is of the very richest kind. . . If its hundreds of thousands of acres were practically available, I should not hesitate to announce it one of the richest spots of equal extent on earth, and highly favoured in other respects. . . It is, however, certain that any part of the valley would require much labour before it could be brought under cultivation. [vol.II, p.182]

This is a departure from the standard paradisaic image: the land has potential, but it does not give up its fruits unasked. Here is a less naive image of Australia.

Sturt's avowed intention in *Two Expeditions* is to lead the reader into the "interior recesses" of the country (vol.I, p.lviii). On the literal level he achieves this simply by following the plot of the expedition; but on a metaphorical level he attempts to relate, through stylistic means, his own reactions to the continent as he comes to know it, to absorb it, throughout his lengthy and often harrowing experiences in the interior which developing myths had installed as a symbol of essential Australia. Most obviously Sturt's selection of imagery leads the reader into a very personal version of Australia, as the representations of the land become increasingly expressive of Sturt's own darkening mood until the luxuriance of Lake

Alexandrina rewards the travellers. This interpretation of the land of suffering and concomitant reward is reinforced throughout *Two Expeditions* in the writer's prose style. Michael Langley has observed that Sturt's writing has "little 'flesh and blood'"[32], by which he means that *Two Expeditions* is a very spare work with almost no depth of characterisation (unless the continent itself can be considered a character) and little dramatic conflict between individuals. Certainly, in the early stages of *Two Expeditions* there is a patent flatness of narrative as Sturt simply furnishes geographical and botanical description in an effort to comprehend the most basic aspects of the continent. Initially the author and the readers are alien to the environment, scrutinising it as outsiders, rarely detecting any spirit of place. In this sense Sturt's writing resembles the work of the First Fleet annalists. Where Sturt differs from them is in the fact that his experience of the land is more extensive and ultimately more endearing. Whereas John White and David Collins had neither time nor incentive to change from their feelings of alienation, and to change therefore their predominantly objective and distanced presentation of the land, Sturt finds reasons eventually to feel part of the Australian scene. He is able to express his Australian experience, whether he is evoking his sense of despair in the deserts before Lake Alexandrina or his sense of reward at the end of the passage down the Murray.

In order to emphasise that he has not attained a region of permanent beneficence at Lake Alexandrina, Sturt promptly reminds the readers that the party are now obliged to retrace their agonising route in order to return to Sydney: "our difficulties were just about to commence, when those of most travellers have ceased" (vol.II, p.176). The next stage of the narrative is most informative in terms of what is unstated rather than stated. In actuality, the return up the Murray comprised a major part of the expedition, in both time and effort. The party battled continuously against the current, against thirst, hunger, exposure and disease, and against incessant fear of native attack. However, within the format of *Two Expeditions*, Sturt's concern with literary form predominates over his preoccupation with historical veracity. In order that the sojourn at Lake Alexandrina should dominate the narrative pattern, Sturt does not allow the description of the return voyage to overshadow the lead-up and resolution which occurred during the downstream trip. He accounts for the upstream voyage comparatively cursorily. Quite simply, as the writer tells his tale he does not allow the dénouement to detract from the climax.

As a result of this arrangement of the plot, the main impression taken from *Two Expeditions* is one of optimism, as the "reward-land" of Lake Alexandrina is kept uppermost in the reader's mind. Indeed in addition to the description of the lake, Sturt asserts that just over the horizon, where he had not been able to investigate, he had glimpsed "beautiful country between the lake and the ranges" (vol.II, p.175). Hence the narrative's overall optimism is maintained and even enhanced by the prospects of further rewards not far from the known areas around the river mouth. In this somewhat projective conclusion to the plot, the notion of the diminishing paradise is still informing the purgatorial interpretation of the land.

As part of his project to delineate a detailed image of Australia Sturt has been concerned throughout *Two Expeditions* to convey a sense of the continuous panorama through which the party is progressing. The reader is never allowed to lose his or her orientation. One is always aware of the general character of the environment as it is bounded by the horizon. Sturt is adept at sketching a vista with a few rapid pen strokes:

> On the rich and picturesque grounds near the river the angophora prevailed with the flooded gum, and the scenery upon its banks was improved by the casuarinae that overhung them. On the latter, inferior eucalypti and cypresses were mixed together. The country was broken and undulating, and the hills stony, notwithstanding which, they appeared to have an abundance of pasture upon them. [vol.I, p.9]

This is a technique most in evidence whenever Sturt presents one of his 360° sweeps of the horizon, describing what he perceives to be the most striking features as he scans about him:

> The summit of the hill was barren, and beef-wood alone grew on it. The valley, of which it was the western boundary, ran up northerly for two or three miles, with all the appearance of richness and verdure. To the south extended the flat I have noticed, more heavily timbered than we had usually found them, bounded, or backed rather, by a hilly country, although one fast losing in its general height. To the W.N.W. there was a moderate range of hills on the opposite side of an extensive

> valley, running up northerly, from which a lateral branch swept round to the W.N.W. with a gradual ascent into the hills, which bore the same appearance of open forest, grazing land, as prevailed in similar tracts to the eastward. The blacks pointed out to us our route up the valley, and stated that we should get on the banks of the river again in direction W. by N. from the place on which we stood. We accordingly crossed the principal valley on the following morning, and gradually ascended the opposite line of hills. They terminate to the S.E. in lofty precipices, overlooking the river flats, and having a deep chain of ponds under them. [vol.II, p.36]

This kind of passage is frequent throughout the narrative, and it is used to specific effect. Apart from supplying the reader with a wealth of information which heightens the sense of the authenticity of Sturt's prose, the 360° "pans" serve to locate the reader within an enormous geographical space in which a human being's tininess receives constant emphasis. Perhaps for the first time in literature about Australia the idea of the enormity of the landscape, in comparison to the communities developing in it, receives consistent attention.

Finally, in relation to *Two Expeditions*, it must be noted that although there are considerable differences in the degrees of imaginative expression or interpretation employed by Sturt, on the one hand, and by the First Fleet annalists on the other, all of these writers are fundamentally similar insofar as they look to the land itself, rather than to imagination, to supply the images of their Australian experience. (This is in contrast to the works considered in the previous chapter, where writers were prone to draw their images of the country from fancy, not from first-hand experience.) Consider for example Sturt's representation of Lake Alexandrina:

> It was now sunset; and one of the most lovely evenings I had ever seen. The sun's radiance was yet upon the mountains but all lower objects were in the shade. The banks of the channel, with the trees and the rocks, were reflected in the tranquil waters, whose surface was unruffled save by the thousands of wild fowl that rose before us. [vol.II, p.166]

As the mind's eye is directed across the view of the lake, a sense of movement and life within the setting is evoked as the birds arise in the imagination, all as part of the composition of the scene. The description of the landscape is being used as the basis from which actions can be depicted and against which the narrative can be delineated. Another passage, from volume one this time, further illustrates the point:

> To have remained in our position would have been impossible, as there was no water either for ourselves or the animals; to have descended into the reeds again, for the purpose of carrying on a minute survey, would, under existing circumstances, have been imprudent. Our provisions were running short, and if a knowledge of the distant interior was to be gained, we had no time to lose. [vol.I, p.60]

As a result of this state of nature, the party and the narrative must press on. Therefore the very character of the landscape, the description of which is a primary concern, becomes an element in the narrative structure. The author scrutinises nature, extracts an impression from it, and explains the next step in the narrative accordingly. The narrative structure *becomes* the image of the land, and vice versa. Sturt's writing can be said to grow out of the land.

Two Expeditions into the Interior is a landmark (the pun in this case is not gratuitous) in English literature about Australia. It mapped out the way to a new perspective on the continent, making possible a valid composite image comprising the two seemingly irreconcilable interpretations of infernal Australia and paradisaic Australia which had been put abroad in the previous half century. Sturt presented a survey of an Australian Purgatory.

However, he did not resolve the question of what lay, literally and metaphorically, at the heart of the continent. The paradise with which he had been rewarded was coastal. The interior still beckoned. Much of the purgatorial image remained to be developed. Sturt himself was to continue the quest a decade later. Others were to respond more promptly.

Sir Thomas Mitchell: Triumphant in Australia Felix

Thomas Mitchell (born in Stirlingshire, Scotland, in 1792) volunteered for the army at the age of sixteen and participated in the Portuguese battles of the Peninsular campaign. Exuding the sort of self-confidence and assertiveness which officers notice, he was steadily promoted until in 1827 the young Major Mitchell was appointed deputy Surveyor-General of New South Wales. As fate would have it, his immediate superior, John Oxley, died the very next year, and the ambitious Mitchell was left in charge of a prestigious and rapidly expanding governmental department. Taking advantage of his authority during the next two decades, he appointed himself leader of four exploratory journeys into unknown Australia. The first three ventures are described in *Three Expeditions into the Interior of Eastern Australia* (1838). The *Journal of an Expedition into the Interior of Tropical Australia*, published in 1848, accounts for the fourth. In 1837 Mitchell returned to England for three years, during which time he supervised the publicaton of his first book, was knighted, and received an honorary Doctorate of Civil Law at Oxford. On his return to Australia he was appointed to the legislative assembly as member for Port Phillip. But it was to be a brief parliamentary stint, made tempestuous by Mitchell's refusal to follow a party line, and he resigned the seat almost immediately. Continuing in his post as Surveyor-General he took more extended leave in order to return home in 1847, in readiness for the publication of the second book. He died at his Sydney residence, Carthona, in 1855.

Three Expeditions into the Interior was favourably reviewed. The *Athenaeum Journal*, for example, proclaimed that "these are altogether the best volumes which have yet appeared on the subject of the interior of Australia".[33] Its popularity was such that a second edition was issued in 1839. Mitchell certainly stamps his personality on the book and presents in it a compelling and personal image of the land. It is ironic, in fact, that Mitchell dealt with his subject and themes so comprehensively in this work that he had nothing new to say when he published his *Journal of an Expedition into the Interior of Tropical Australia* in 1848. Despite the promising title, this is a prosaic and unimaginative work whose publication brought "no enthusiastic response"[34] from reviewers or the public. Accordingly, it is *Three Expeditions* which contains the "essential" Mitchell, dealing with all of his important themes and attitudes, and exerting a powerful influence on English peoples' impressions of Australia.

Extensive biographical information now leaves no doubt that Mitchell was in fact ruthlessly ambitious, a self-publicist not averse to distorting truth in order to heighten his esteem in the public assessment. J. H. Cumpston gives an example when he points out that Mitchell claimed celebrity for *discovering* Australia Felix, when in fact during 1834 and 1835 "there had been a great migration from Tasmania to Victoria, as a result of which... there were two hundred persons with 30,000 sheep and numerous cattle and horses" settled to the west of Geelong. Mitchell mentions only one settler, Robert Henty, whom he encountered at the southern extremity of Australia Felix.[35]

Mitchell's overconfidence in his own knowledge and abilities caused grave errors of judgment — logistic and navigational — particularly during the first expedition. There can be no denying also that throughout his career his ineptness at dealing with the Aborigines contributed to several violent deaths, of unnumbered natives and of three colleagues. For example, from an objective point of view, culpable tragedies — two members of the party slain by panicky natives — comprised the only notable outcome of an ill-considered first expedition. However, in Mitchell's own "mythicising" of his exploits, such facts are reworked and variously emphasised to produce a markedly different story. He manages to gloss over his mistakes as he directs the reader's attention to his more successful exploits. This is a strategy which Mitchell employs throughout his writing career, as he invariably creates for himself a persona which fulfils his own desires.

Three Expeditions can be interpreted as part of an established literary tradition. It presents the lengthy narrative of a quest after knowledge of the interior, over which "a veil of mystery still hangs".[36] The attraction of the interior stays with Mitchell throughout his life, and he attempts to explain its allure in the preface of his 1848 volume. He commences with a quotation from Robert Burns, and then elucidates:

> "Admiring Nature in her wildest grace", it has ever been the most attractive of the author's duties to explore the interior of Australia. There the philosopher may look for facts; the painter and poet for original studies and ideas; the naturalist for additional knowledge; and the historian might begin at a beginning. The traveller there seeks in vain for the remains of cities, temples, or towers; but he is amply compensated by

> objects which tell not of decay but of healthful progress and hope; of a wonderful past, and of a promising future.[37]

In *Three Expeditions* a great explorer pursues an ideal. The protagonist narrates a quest, and the first journey is simply "Part One" of the entire process. The expedition is mounted in response to a tale related by a convict named Clarke, alias "The Barber", who had "gone native" for several years after escaping captivity and who, on being recaptured, sought clemency by offering information about a great inland river which his native comrades named the "Kindur". Of course, this imaginary river is a variant of the mythical fertile land lying at the core of the diminishing paradise. Viewed in the context of the myths defining Australia in Mitchell's era, the Major's willingness to risk lives in order to investigate a desperado's tall tale must not be interpreted as ingenuous.

As Mitchell rides out to the north-west of Sydney he ruminates about his quest:

> It seemed that even war and victory, with all their glory, were far less alluring than the pursuit of researches such as these, for the purpose of spreading the light of civilization over a portion of creation as yet unknown, rich, perhaps, in the luxuriance of uncultivated nature, where science might accomplish new and unthought-of discoveries, and intelligent man would find a region teeming with useful vegetation, abounding with rivers, hills, and valleys, and waiting only for his enterprising spirit and improving hand to turn to account the native bounty of the soil. [*Three Expeditions* vol.I, p.5]

Cantering behind the Major are a group of convicts who form part of his team. For them, as for Mitchell, this is no ordinary journey: "All were ready to face fire or water, in hopes of regaining by desperate exploits, a portion, at least, of that liberty which had been forfeited to the laws of their country" (vol.I, p.16). With references to elemental trials of fire and water, the author deliberately evokes connotations of redemptive ordeals in a land of mystery where, as he admits later, "active fancy" leads a quester on into unsurveyed regions of anticipated splendour (vol.I, p.208).

The first expedition is described as the tribulation section of a purgatorial experience, as the party are "about to enter at length the *Terra incognita*" (vol.I, p.34). As Mitchell tells the tale, they are constantly beleaguered by inimical natives from the Darling River tribes, and two members of the expedition lose their lives to the "savages". The party are punished with heat, hunger, and thirst: "unable to eat, the cattle lay groaning, the men on their backs watching some heavy thunder clouds that at length stretched over the sky; the very crows sat on the trees with their mouths open" (vol.I, p.66).

Mitchell decides at this stage that the party must return to civilisation. But instead of accepting blame or admitting defeat, he manages to submerge the ill-begotten first expedition within the larger structure of the work's narrative pattern. After the suffering comes the reward. After the first journey come the second and third.

The second expedition sets out in 1835 to explore the course of the Darling River. In the light of Charles Sturt's speculation two years earlier that this river could lead to fertile expanses in the interior, it is apparent that Mitchell is still chasing the diminishing paradise. The party trek westward of Bathurst and encounter barrenness stretching for kilometres on both sides of the Darling. As they trace the river southward (towards its eventual junction with the Murray) they find that they "had, at length, emerged from these arid valleys, and entered upon an open and more promising country" (vol.I, p.167). The change of fortune prompts in Mitchell a pithy statement of moral:

> It is on occasions such as these that the adventurer has intervals of enjoyment, which amply reward him for his laborious days of hardship and privation. His sense of gratification and repose must be quite unknown to him whose life is counted out in monotonous succession of hours of eating and sleeping within a house, his food adulterated by salts, spices, and sauces, intolerable to real hunger — and whose drink, instead of sweet refreshing distillation from the heavens, consists of vile artificial extracts, loathed by the really thirsty man, with whom the pure element resumes its true value. [vol.I, pp.167-8]

Mitchell is learning the lessons of the land. In his understanding of the way of the bush, strength and joy arise out of adversity. The rewards of hardship are ample. In a Romantic fashion, nature blossoms and inspires:

> The evening was beautiful; the new grass springing in places where it had been burnt, presented a shining verdure in the rays

> of the descending sun; the songs of the birds accorded here with other joyous sounds, the very air seemed alive with the music of animated nature, so different was the scene in his well-watered valley, compared to the parched and silent region from which we had just descended. The natives whom we met here were fine looking men, enjoying contentment and happiness within the precincts of their native woods. Their enjoyment seemed derived so directly from nature, that it almost excited a regret that civilized man, enervated by luxury and all its concomitant diseases, should ever disturb the haunts of these rude but happy beings. [vol.I, pp.168-9]

The spirit of a *regenerative* nature vivifies the scene. After spending so much time as aliens in an unresponsive environment, the travellers have come through to a landscape which purifies the human spirit.

As a result of his experience, Mitchell is developing the ability to "read" the landscape. He can now make sense of the country where originally he stood as a baffled outsider:

> My ride along the mountain road presented no object worth describing here, but I have frequently found that the most dreary road ceases to appear monotonous or long, after we acquire a knowledge of the adjacent country. The ideas of locality are no longer limited like our view, by the trees on each side. The least turn seems to remind us that we are passing some "antre vast", or lateral ridge, occupying a place in the map, which thus determines our position. In crossing these mountains an extensive knowledge of the localities relieved the monotony of the road to me, and being inseparable from it in my mind, the digressions in this part of my journal, will, after this explanation, perhaps appear less objectionable. [vol.I, pp.154-55]

However, at this stage of the surveyance of the Darling and environs, the ultimate rewards have not yet been attained, and the narrative continues. Tracing the river further south, Mitchell's group encounter hostile natives, and tragedy strikes again as Cunningham, the party's botanist, wanders far afield looking for specimens and is murdered by the Aborigines. This event provides the motive, in Mitchell's account of the journey, for the return to Sydney and the conclusion of the predominantly arduous second expedition.

Because they have not verified unequivocally that the Darling does flow into the Murray, a third venture is instigated in 1836. The narrative in this section of the book labours for 120 pages describing a "melancholy waste" (vol.II, p.234) which is made doubly dreary by the fact that it is not new to either the author or the reader. In this region where the men bed down "burning with thirst and dreaming of water" (vol.II, p.51), there is neither the exhilaration of discovering new fertile expanses, nor the educative experience of new regions of deprivation. However, after reaching the junction with the Murray, the reader is brought to the climactic section of the entire narrative:

> We had now got through the most unpromising part of our task. We had penetrated the Australian Hesperides — although the golden fruit was still to be sought — [and] to trace the Murray upwards and explore the unknown regions beyond it, was a charming prospect, now that we could bid adieu forever to the dreary banks of the Darling. [vol.II, p.126]

Mitchell takes possession of a paradise, which he dubs "Australia Felix":

> We had at length discovered a country ready for the immediate reception of civilized man, and fit to become eventually one of the great nations of the earth. Unencumbered with too much wood, yet possessing enough for all purposes; with an exuberant soil under a temperate climate; bounded by the sea-coast and mighty rivers, and watered abundantly by streams from lofty mountains: this highly interesting region lay before me with all its features new and untouched as they fell from the hand of the Creator! Of this Eden it seemed that I was the only Adam; and it was indeed a sort of paradise to me. [vol.II, p.170]

Although Mitchell's reward-land is more overwhelming than Sturt's, there are remarkable similarities between the works of the two writers. Each presents his exploits as a quest for an ideal region in interior Australia; each interprets Australian experience by way of a narrative entailing suffering and eventual reward; and finally, each regards himself as "chosen", as someone whose successes are due in part to the positive involvement of Providence in his exploits. (Sturt's faith in abiding Providence has already been testified. One example of Mitchell's comes from

Three Expeditions (vol.I, pp.61-62): "I was truly sensible of the goodness of Providence, considering that this was to all appearances the only water within miles".) In fact they were both well aware that each man encroached on the other's exploratory and literary fields, and a bitter lifelong rivalry developed early in their concurrent careers. Their relationship is summed up in an anecdote cited by Michael Langley. Between 1847 and 1848 both men were in London preparing journals for publication. "By extraordinary coincidence," in this city of millions, "Sturt and Mitchell passed each other in the street; but, as Sturt records, 'he saw me. . .but hurried on without recognition'."[38]

At the same time as the two men have similar preoccupations, their differences are fundamental. They both interpret Australian experience as purgatorial, but their presentations of the manner in which redemption might be attained are markedly dissimilar. The distinctions are embodied in the authorial persona developed by each writer. The Sturt of *Two Expeditions into the Interior* is a patient, resolute man determined to survive in Purgatory until he has assimilated himself to the land, until he blends into it and attempts to understand it in its own terms. Mitchell, on the other hand, presents himself as an energetic conqueror, come to inherit the land in the interests of himself and the English nation. Whereas Sturt's narrative is structured according to the landscape, Mitchell's is propelled by his own energy. In Sturt's writing the landscape regulates all human action; Mitchell's narrative becomes a sequence of *events* which the author himself instigates and controls.

Mitchell portrays himself as a man of action. His frequent encounters with the Aborigines demonstrate his attitude toward the land. Whereas Sturt always approaches the native people with genuine respect, virtually seeking permission to pass through their land (see vol.I, p.109 and vol.II, p.209 of *Two Expeditions*), Mitchell appears as a man who seizes control in a confrontation. Early in the first expedition, just after the party have crossed the torrid plain where "the very crows sat on the trees with their mouths open", some natives challenge the intruders. As Mitchell relates the story, his own gallantry saves the day as he calls their bluff by charging them on his horse. It is a triumph of the English will over rude nature.

On another occasion, as Mitchell increasingly feels himself the inheritor of this earth, he hears natives in the distance:

> The calls of the natives, first heard at a distance in the woods, having become more loud, and at length incessant, I answered them in a similar tone; and having halted the carts, I galloped over a bit of clear rising-ground, towards the place from whence they came. [vol.I, p.210]

This image of Mitchell whooping, hollering and galloping his way across a landscape which may test him, but which he will eventually dominate, is apposite. Whereas Sturt becomes part of the environment and persists in it until he reaps its rewards, Mitchell ranges over it, makes it succumb to his energy, and eventually takes for himself his just deserts as he spurs his horse "into a gallop over the verdant plain" which leads into Australia Felix (vol.II, p.155). Once the trials of the desert have been overcome, the English sovereignty over the land is taken to be as righteous as it is inevitable:

> We now advanced with feelings of intense interest into the country before us, and impressed with the responsibility of commencing the first chapter of its history. All was still new and nameless there, but by this beginning we were to open a way for the many other beginnings of civilized man, and thus extend his dominion over the last holds of barbarism. [vol.I, p.36]

It is noteworthy that Mitchell's *Three Expeditions* is arranged according to a journal format, with regular dated entries. The effect is to heighten the sense of daily progress. Time is predominant, and the characters' awareness and *control* of it are emphasised. Mitchell's daily progressive chronology in which the party inevitably achieve objectives in a constant state of advancement provides a structure for the narrative. This is in contrast to Sturt's writing, in which the reader loses a sense of time, and perseveres in seemingly infinite geographical and narrative space until the Murray River itself carries the party to a land of promise.

Mitchell's vision of Australia is influenced considerably by his susceptibility to that "Old World diction" which had also controlled so many writers during the 1820s. Mitchell was a learned man; one of his projects in the years before his death was the translation and publication of a version of Camoens' *Lusiads*. (Such an epic celebration of imperialist conquest seems entirely germane to Mitchell's interests.) Paradoxically his erudition served to restrict the originality of his attempts to express his vision of Australian nature. Because he was steeped in traditional literature he was susceptible to those "reflex" responses whereby landscape is "automatically" described in pastoral terms. More so than with Sturt, Mitchell's vision of the Aborigine, for example, was shaped largely by his preconceptions, whereas Sturt attempts to view and describe the natives with reference to their own culture; Mitchell, on the other hand, perceives as remarkable only those Aboriginal characteristics which align with his own more classical, English criteria. Hence, he finds the natives particularly worthy of mention when they are thought to assume "such a figure as Neptune or Jupiter are usually represented to wear" (vol.I, p.238). From a similar cultural "reflex" comes Mitchell's praise of a "splendid valley" in Australia Felix which could be measured favourably against his standard English taste in landscape because it resembled "a nobleman's park on a gigantic scale" (vol.II, p.210).

Yet because he was also a scientist, he was not prepared to ignore what he perceived as the bleaker side of Australian nature. He was loath to distort his data to the extent of describing paradise where he did not encounter it. The solution which is evident in *Three Expeditions* is to avoid landscape description and to concentrate on the events enacted by himself and his colleagues, until such time as the party encounter territory which can be evoked in terms suited to his literary diction. As a result his prose blossoms only occasionally, when he describes verdant landscape. The reader is presented with patches of traditional fecundity, which are made especially attractive by virtue of their juxtaposition with a prosaic desolation. For example, in his description of the "new and untouched" Australia Felix cited earlier, the diction which is "triggered off" by the perceived fertility is drawn from *Genesis*. The land is another Eden, and Mitchell is a new Adam.

Once Mitchell had acknowledged that there were tribulations invariably associated with the land, he managed to underplay their significance by extolling the pastoral virtues of Australia Felix. It was a naive and/or deceptive view of Australia generally; and it could not prevail once authentic experience of the country became more commonplace.

During the 1840s writers became increasingly aware of the necessity of understanding the new continent in its own terms.

Mitchell's new land of old legend was attractive, but it was not verifiable. This could account for the failure of his 1848 book; by that time a more "down-to-earth" *Australian* interpretation of the land had been validated, and Mitchell's evocations of an Edenic Australia Felix seemed anachronistic. Ironically it was Mitchell's rival Charles Sturt who contributed to the further evolution of the more pertinent image of the continent.

Part Two
Sisyphus Survives:
Charles Sturt's Narrative *and E. J. Eyre's* Journals

Charles Sturt: Toward the Forbidden Centre

Although both Sturt and Mitchell had been granted the rewards of their purgatorial journeys, neither had discovered what lay at the centre of the land. Still lured on by the *terra incognita*, therefore, Sturt set out from his residence in Adelaide in 1844 (the second year of the great drought) on an expedition which would last almost two years and in which he would experience unprecedented horrors of deprivation near the still centre of an infernally desolate world. His *Narrative of an Expedition into Central Australia*, published in 1849, describes human experience in a virtually lifeless heartland, that focal point of all the dreams of people who had yearned to possess the diminishing paradise.

Similar in narrative format to *Two Expeditions*, Sturt's later work portrays a group of men struggling for survival in an awe-inspiring landscape unlike anything encountered before in history. The difference between this and his earlier work is of degree, not of kind. The intensity of the hardship which the party endure this time becomes the most significant aspect of the narrative. After a leisurely trek along the Murray, they follow the Darling through a deteriorating environment; then when the river begins to lead them east-north-east away from the interior, they leave it and head northward into adversity in a country of which even the Aborigines "spoke . . . in terror, as a region into which they did not dare to venture".[39]

"The country as we advanced became more open and barren", observes Sturt (vol.I, p.150). And this is only the beginning. The progress of the party has little to do with individuals' wills; rather the men simply attempt to exploit the whims of nature as they trek from water-source to water-source, moving from their previous sanctuary only when it appears that nature will provide them with sustenance for the journey: "Although slowly, we were gradually . . . working our way into the interior" (vol.I, p.207). However, with the heat averaging 110°F (43°C) in the shade and increasing as they head inland, Sturt's optimism evaporates, and he is left with a stoic resolution to persevere and to survive the trials awaiting him. The drought continues and the party are stranded at an oasis: "it became evident to me that we were locked up in the desolated and heated region, into which we had penetrated, as effectually as if we had wintered at the Pole" (vol.I, p.265).

They remain here for six months, occupying themselves with surveys of the nothingness surrounding the oasis. Their fate could be interpreted simultaneously as cruel and kind:

> Providence had, in its allwise purposes, guided us to the only spot in that wide-spread desert, where our wants could have been permanently supplied, but had there stayed our further progress into a region that almost appears to be forbidden ground. [vol.I, p.265]

Here, so close to the centre, they experience emptiness that is almost absolute, and quite ghostly:

> We were then in one of the most gloomy regions that man ever traversed. The stillness of death reigned around us, no living creature was to be heard; nothing visible inhabited the dreary desert but the ant, even the fly shunned it, and yet its yielding surface was marked all over with the tracks of native dogs. [vol.I, pp.277-78]

Human beings are completely alien to this environment. Nature seems aware of the incongruity of the party's presence, as is demonstrated in Sturt's description of the predatory kites which scrutinise the men's desert sojourn:

> These birds had a most formidable aspect, and were too numerous for us to have overpowered, if they had really attacked us. That they came to see what unusual object was wandering across the lowly deserts over which they soar, in the hope of prey, there can be no doubt. [vol.I, p.269]

It is a region characterised by negation:

> We had gradually been deserted by every beast of the field, and every fowl of the air. We had witnessed migration after migration of the feathered tribes, to that point to which we were so anxious to push our way. Flights of cockatoos, of parrots, of pigeons, and of bitterns, birds also whose notes had cheered us in the wilderness, all had taken some high road to a better and more hospitable region. The vegetable kingdom was at a stand, and there was nothing either to engage the attention or attract the eye. [vol.I, p.321]

This land, which had been the subject of dreams for so long, becomes nightmarish. After the drought is broken the party leave the oasis (following the funeral of one of their colleagues who died after months of incapacitation through scurvy) to trek into the Stony Desert, which is entirely devoid of life, even of soil. The horses and carts do not leave tracks as they clamber over the kilometres of flatland strewn with millions of stones. The desert seems interminable. At one stage they pass an artesian well, around which flocks of birds — the first life encountered in days — hover before plummeting deep underground into the darkness in order to allay their thirst. On consecutive cloudless days the silence of the interior is broken by an explosion, like the discharge of a great gun, emanating from beyond the horizon. Sturt can offer no explanation for the phenomena; he can only assert that they did occur (vol.II, pp.24-5). As the party come closer to the centre the heat increases until the thermometer, graded to 127°F (53°C), finally bursts (vol.II, p.90).

Sturt's relationship with the land reaches its nadir when he admits that "the idea of a detention in that horrid desert was worse than death itself" (vol.II, p.99). Confessing that he now has "no hope of any inland fertile country" (vol.II, p.130) he decides to return to the paradise which he is helping to create in Adelaide. Once the narrative of the disillusioning expedition is complete Sturt commences a lengthy and enthusiastic examination of the prospects of South Australia. This change of focus, away from the quest for a dreamland in the interior and toward the description of daily realities in South Australia, stands as a tacit admission that a reassessment of aspiration, a certain coming of age, is required now that the central secrets of the continent have been investigated to no avail. The colonists must now work with the certainties of their lived experience:

> When I went into the interior I left the province [that is, South Australia] with storm-clouds overhanging it, and sunk in adversity. When I returned the sun of prosperity was shining upon it, and every heart was glad. Providence had rewarded a people who had borne their reverses with singular firmness and magnanimity. Their harvest fields were bowed down by the weight of grain; their pastoral pursuits were prosperous; the hills were yielding forth their mineral wealth, and peace and prosperity prevailed over the land. [vol.I, p.39]

Whereas in the earlier works, Mitchell and Sturt had set off in search of a legendary land and did indeed finally come through to their own versions of paradise, in Sturt's later account, he *returns* to a happy land after intense suffering. Aware that starkly disappointing realities lie at the centre of Australia, Sturt can now be reconciled to reward-lands which he knows to exist in actuality.

Sturt himself assesses the significance of the experiences described in the *Narrative of an Expedition into Central Australia*. A new relationship between humanity and the continent has arisen. No longer can people assume that they will tame the Australian earth, either by way of Mitchell's energetic conquests, or through Sturt's earlier patient attendance of inevitable recompense. A new awe of land which can be mysterious and terrifying, as well as cornucopian, takes hold. English people must learn humility in this unique natural environment:

> Men of undoubted perseverance and energy in vain had tried to work their way to that distant and shrouded spot. A veil hung over Central Australia that could neither be pierced or raised. Girt around by deserts, it almost appeared as if Nature had intentionally closed it upon civilized man, that she might have

> one domain on earth's wide field over which the savage might roam in freedom. [vol.II, p.2]

Instead of being a symbol of the ultimate riches at the end of a quest, the interior now represents the awesome power of Australian nature, a mystery which human beings cannot expect to fathom.

Rewards in such a Purgatory need not be inevitable; nor are they necessarily material. For Sturt at least, the expedition into the continent has also become an exploration of himself. As he explains, the *Narrative* is written out of a desire "faithfully to record my own feelings and impulses under peculiar embarrassments, and as faithfully to describe the country over which I wandered" (vol.I, pp.34-5). Sturt is one of the pioneer surveyors of the "country of the mind" which is so prevalent in the Australian arts, obvious examples being the paintings of Sidney Nolan and the novels of Patrick White. With Sturt, the Australian environment begins to enter "into man's bone and tissue, into his mind and soul".[40] The image of the submissive landscape presented by Mitchell is no longer relevant as the land itself begins to transform the English people who attempt to comprehend it.

Edward John Eyre

> But something on foot, and burning, nudges us
> Past bitter water, sands of Exodus.
>
> Francis Webb, "Eyre All Alone" (1961)

During the time when Sturt was realising that desolation is part of the Australian experience, another traveller-author, Edward John Eyre, published his *Journals of Expeditions of Discovery into Central Australia* which suggested that outright horror can lie in wait for Australian dreamers.

Born in 1815, the third son of an English country curate, Eyre arrived in Australia in 1833 with a wanderlust in his soul which would propel him across the country, then to New Zealand, and around the world eventually to a tragic governorship in the insurrectionist West Indies of the late 1860s. By his own admission Eyre was obsessed with penetrating the "vast recesses of the interior of Australia, to try to lift up the veil which has hitherto shrouded its mysteries from the researches of the traveller".[41] Like so many traveller-writers before him he was lured on toward goals which, as J. L. Allen had pointed out, were "based less on what empirical knowledge was available than on non-empirical lore"[42]; he set out pursuing a myth, created history, and then gave the world a new myth in his published *Journals*.

Eyre left Adelaide in June 1840 intending to conquer the interior. As he progressed north he found the country impenetrable in the environs of Lake Torrens. From here he turned south-west and resolved to blaze a trail between Adelaide and the settled regions of Western Australia. The images of the landscape and the intensity of Eyre's experiences during his "arduous undertaking" accumulate in the narrative until *Journals* takes on epic proportions, with Eyre surviving and describing prolonged and ultimately horrific tests in the purgatorial deserts which are behind Australia's "blessed lands". It is a narrative in which very few "events" occur and in which characters other than Eyre and his native companion, Wylie, do not predominate. For these reasons the *Journals* becomes a prolonged construction of an image of nature; impression is piled upon impression and the mood of the environment forces itself upon the reader. Characters act and react in response to the landscape which is being described. Even more so than in Sturt's *Two Expeditions*, the environment "becomes" the literary structure.

As Eyre travels daily "further from the pale of civilization and from aid or assistance of any kind" (vol.I, p.24) nature's relationship to humanity becomes plainly inimical. As he begins to comprehend that the continent shapes people at least as much as people can control the continent, he begins to see the Aborigines as truly native products of their environment:

> The very stones lying upon the hills looked like the scorched and withered scoria of a volcanic region; and even the natives, judging from the specimen I had seen today, partook of the general misery and wretchedness of the place. [vol.I, p.63]

In fact, *Journals* can be seen as a chronicle of an Englishman's education in "Aboriginality" as the natives Eyre travels with and meets teach him survival techniques such as the practicality of "travelling light" and the vital expediency of well-digging and root-tapping for water. Eyre and the reader gradually develop a profound respect for Aboriginal character:

> It may be worth while to take a view of the conduct of the Aborigines of Australia, generally, towards the invaders and usurpers of their rights, setting aside altogether any acts of violence or injury which they may have committed under the influence of terror, naturally excited by the first presence of strangers among them, and which arise from an impulse that is only shared by them in common with mankind generally. I shall be borne out, I think, by facts when I state that the Aborigines of this country have seldom been guilty of wanton or unprovoked outrages, or committed acts of rapine or bloodshed, without some strongly exciting cause, or under the influence of feelings that would have weighed in the same degree with Europeans in similar circumstances. [vol.I, pp.166-67]

And Aboriginal lore is ultimately accorded respect as a truly pertinent, innate system of Australian knowledge:

> In estimating the facility with which a native can remain for a long time in a country, apparently arid and inhospitable, we must not omit to take into account his education and experience, and the general nature of his habits. The two former have accustomed him from infancy to feel at home and at ease where a European sees only dread and danger: he had thus the advantage over the European in the desert, that a swimmer has in the water over the man who cannot swim; conscious of his own powers and resources, he feels not the least apprehension, whilst the very terrors of the other but augment his danger. [vol.II, pp.246-47]

In the early stages of Eyre's trek, before he has been adequately "educated" by "Aboriginal" experience, he can see no encouragement in the deserts. To the north of Adelaide, rain does not fall; and even if it did it would be to no avail, for the land is saline to the degree of absolute sterility:

> In such a country, what accommodation could I expect, or what hopes could I entertain for the future, when the very water shed from the clouds would not be drinkable after a few hours on the ground? Whichever way I turned myself, to the West, to the East, or to the North, nothing but difficulties met my view. [vol.I, p.63]

The land described is the complete antithesis of the picturesque vistas which earlier writers such as Mitchell and Field sought out as conventionally beautiful and expressible in well-tested literary terms. On numerous occasions Eyre attempts to orientate himself and the readers in vast nothingness by presenting a 360° pan around the horizon:

> To the north were low broken hills similar to those around me, but less elevated, and immediately under these hills to the westward, were heavy red sandy ridges, such as we had crossed during the day. To the eastward and ten degrees north of east were seen Flinders range, with which Mount Deception and Termination Hills were connected, by long low spurs thrown off to the northward. In the north-east the horizon was one unbroken, low, flat, level waste. . . Wherever I turned, or whatever way I looked, the prospect was cheerless and disheartening. [vol.I, pp.87-88]

It is a landscape which seems to define "alienation"; it is an environment which breeds despair: "Hitherto, even when placed in the most difficult or desperate circumstances I was cheered by hope, but now I had no longer even that frail solace to cling to" (vol.I, pp.119-120). Yet it is also a land in which reason and conclusions drawn therefrom (such as Eyre's unequivocally justifiable despair) can be transcended, because all customary logical tenets seem somehow irrelevant there. For example, when Eyre arrives at the shores of Lake Torrens, he experiences a startling sense of disorientation:

> From the extraordinary and deceptive appearances, caused by mirage and refraction, however, it was impossible to tell what to make of sensible objects, or what to believe on the evidence of vision, for upon turning back to retrace our steps to the eastward, a vast sheet of water appeared to intervene between us and the shore, whilst the Mount Deception ranges, which I knew to be at least thirty-five miles distant, seemed to rise out of the bed of the lake itself, the mock waters of which were laving their base, and reflecting the inverted outline of their rugged summits. The whole scene partook more of enchantment than reality, and as the eye wandered over the smooth and unbroken crust of pure white salt which glazed the basin of the lake, and which was lit up by the dazzling rays of a noonday sun, the effect was glittering, and brilliant beyond conception. [vol.I, pp.111-12]

The new experiences in this environment can challenge the visitor's accepted view of the world, even if only for an instant. In this somewhat fantastic region, even though Eyre *knows* by now that a promised land cannot exist in the interior, he continues to see encouraging signs. The appearance in the desert of four wayward cockatoos is taken virtually as an omen: "had they come from some better country beyond the desert by which I was surrounded. . . how was that country to be attained, supposing it to exist? Time only may reply to these queries" (vol.I, p.124). He is aware of his illogicality, and he accepts it. In this world of inverted expectations, terror and desolation can possess a "romance" of their own, as in the vista of the precipitous coastline along the Great Australian Bight:

> Distressing and fatal as the continuance of these cliffs might prove to us, there was a grandeur and sublimity in their appearance that was most imposing, and which struck me with admiration. Stretching out before us in lofty unbroken outline, they presented the singular and romantic appearance of massy battlements of masonry, supported by huge buttresses, and glittering in the morning sun which had now risen upon them, and made the scene beautiful even amidst the dangers and anxieties of our situation. It was indeed a rich and gorgeous view for a painter, and I never felt so much regret at my inability to sketch as I did at this moment. [vol.I, p.327]

Where observers such as Mitchell or Field might have perceived only a waste land which was not counted worthy of depiction, Eyre is prepared to recognise some innate sublimity. Like Sturt, he begins to accept the country on its own terms rather than according to the aesthetic preconceptions drawn exclusively from his English cultural background. Admittedly he is only *beginning*, for he still evokes the weird beauty by using traditional images of picturesque battlements. Like Sturt with his images of "gloomy cypresses" and calciform skulls, Eyre is mapping out a literary ground where his new Australian experience and his English heritage are being forced to meet.

Aspects of Eyre's literary style serve to reinforce his composition of the image of the land as a symbol of Australian experience. Firstly, Eyre allows only himself and Wylie (whose importance to the whole work soon becomes apparent) to assume a personal identity. All the other members of the party are kept deliberately anonymous, including Eyre's overseer (actually named Baxter) who was a faithful employee of many years' standing. The result of this reticence is that the journey becomes an intensely personal experience. The reader is given the sense that events occur and that nature is significant only because of Eyre's own perception, and the reader is therefore forced to internalise Eyre's experience. No other opinions, sensations, or reactions exist. One is aware of the presence of Wylie, but even he exists only insofar as Eyre deigns to name him occasionally as a servant and adviser on bushcraft.

Moreover, the reader becomes intensely involved with the very landscape. The narrative becomes a chronicle of the most basic survival exercises, and the landscape is not merely something which Eyre (and the reader) passes through; it is the elements of life itself. The narrative and the characters continue only if the essentials of survival can be found. Every page is concerned with the water, the heat, the shade, the topography, the scant vegetation which constitute this waste land, and the sand which becomes a motif of constant torment (see vol.I, p.321). Eyre and the reader are compelled to scrutinise the land as an extension of themselves. If Eyre's relationship to the environment deteriorates in the slightest, he dies.

Journals presents a minimalist experience and a minimalist literary text, yet it is also intensely involving. It is the literature of survival. Life is everything, but it is also insignificant: "We were now alone, myself, my overseer, and three native boys, with a fearful task before us, the bridge was broken down behind us [i.e. no water or provisions to retreat to], and we must succeed in reaching King George's Sound, or perish; no middle course remained" (vol.I, p.306). Each decision becomes part of a dramatic conflict with death:

> After tying up the horses the boy lay down, and was soon asleep, happy in his ignorance of the dangers which threatened him. I lay down, too, but not to sleep; my own distresses were lost in the apprehensions which I entertained for those who were behind...It was questionable, even, if they would reach the distance we had already attained in safety; and it was clear, that unless I discovered water early in the morning, the whole of our horses must perish, whilst it would be very doubtful if we could succeed even in saving our own lives. [vol.I, pp.330-31]

In this context, where the explorer is shown to be so vulnerable, the personal experiences described in the minutest detail stand as all that he can claim as his own. As the self is virtually annihilated, its own state of "suspended animation" is all that can occupy the authorial persona's mind:

> After sitting for a few minutes to rest — and we often had to do this — it was always with the greatest unwillingness we ever moved on again. I felt, on such occasions, that I could have sat quietly and contentedly, and let the glass of life glide away to its last sand. There was a dreamy kind of pleasure, which made me forgetful or careless of the circumstances and difficulties by which I was surrounded, and which I was always indisposed to break in upon. [vol.II, p.40]

With such a tone prevailing, the "dated journal" format which Eyre chooses to employ produces an effect far different from that which is evident in Mitchell's *Three Expeditions*. Whereas in Mitchell's journal the daily advance is represented as a systematic progress which the author is controlling, Eyre's narrative presents time washing over him in great periods of sameness and relative inaction as the party move almost imperceptibly across the enormous continent. Each new day continues the struggle to survive, and as time progresses so importunately, as Eyre's minuteness against the backdrop of the environment becomes so intense, the autonomous personalities of the people struggling against the elements diminish in contrast to the awesome dimensions and importunity of the landscape.

After the image of the seemingly interminable waste land has been composed over days, weeks and months, Eyre sets up the climax of the narrative, and suddenly the reader is awakened most forcefully to the horror which is latent in this elemental Australia. After describing hundreds of days of attrition and deprivation as he trudges through space and time, often in dazed semi-consciousness (see vol.I, p.326), Eyre deliberately slows down the passage of time, on 29 April 1841. An ominous sense of expectation is evoked as the author begins to describe in detail a dramatic setting at a *specific* period of time, as he strolls around the camp during the evening watch:

> The night was cold, and the wind was blowing hard from the south-west, whilst scud and nimbus were passing very rapidly by

> the moon. The horses fed tolerably well, but rambled a good deal, threading in and out among the many belts of scrub which intersected the grassy openings, until at last I hardly knew where our camp was, the fires having apparently expired some time ago. It was now half past ten, and I headed the horses back, in the direction in which I thought the camp lay, that I might be able to call the overseer at eleven. [vol.I, p.401]

Time falters, then the readers are shocked as if from a daze. A gunshot is heard, and then Wylie comes running, screaming, "Oh, Massa, oh Massa, come here". The exclamation is dramatically startling, coming after 400 pages in which there is no direct speech and little sense of emotional depth in characters other than the narrator, and in which a distancing historical past tense has been predominant. Eyre follows Wylie back to the camp . . . "I was horror-struck to find my poor overseer lying on the ground, weltering in his blood, and in the last agonies of death" (vol.I, p.402). With these words, strategically, the publishers conclude volume one, metaphorically allowing dust to settle and shock to take effect before continuing the account. The ghastly event is thereby placed at the centre of the two-volumed *Journals*.

With the commencement of volume two the dislocation of the established time-sense is continued. After pausing to consider his plight, Eyre commences to reconstruct the murder in flashback:

> At the dead hour of night, in the wildest and most inhospitable wastes of Australia, with the fierce wind raging in unison with the violence before me, I was left, with a single native, whose fidelity I could not rely upon, and who for aught I knew might be in league with the other two, who perhaps were even now, lurking about with the view of taking my life as they had done that of the overseer. [vol.II, p.2]

Rapid thoughts, in short clauses, crowd in on him, and nature seems to react with pathetic fallacy. The "night of horrors" (vol.II, p.4) converts the *Journals* into a dramatic tale of an Englishman entirely alone in the continent; for, even Wylie is an aspect of disturbing Australian mysteries.

Eyre and Wylie now continue westward, across landscape similar to that which they traversed before 29 April. Most importantly, however, the journey is now haunted by the "night of horrors" as Eyre continues attempting to analyse what led to the overseer's death. (All is conjecture, of course, and the doubts simply promote his unease.) And the night has a retrospective effect also, because it encourages the reader to interpret all of the suffering which preceded it as a prelude to an Englishman's confrontation with the most forbidding spirit of Australia. The *Journals* emphasise the sense of death and autochthonous malevolence which had lain unnoticed behind the attractive exterior of mythic Australia.

After a month of following the bleak coastline of the Bight, the explorers are picked up by a French ship, the *Mississippi*, captained by an Englishman. They stay aboard for a fortnight, and then at Eyre's request he and Wylie are set down further along the coast so that they can complete their trek overland. On 7 July they reach Albany — civilisation and safety.

Eyre's *Journals* challenged people's attitudes toward Australia. It is noteworthy that reviews at the time of publication were hostile because of the "unsatisfactory results" of the quest.[43] Eyre's image of the purgatorial land did not comply with preconceptions. The critics' censure was immediate and vehement, but it was not necessarily unequivocal. The *North British Review*, for example, complained that Eyre's mission was a failure because he found no fertile garden, but the reviewer then conceded that "the sufferings, escapes, and spirit of endurance, make this narrative very interesting".[44] *Journals* did not satisfy established criteria, perhaps because it was in fact setting up new standards of writing about Australia.

Most importantly, the influence of the *Journals* has been enduring. Patrick White has acknowledged his debt to Eyre. *Voss*, he claims, was shaped during its long unconscious gestation by "memories of nights in my Ebury Street bedsitter reading Eyre's Journal as the bombs fell on London. A seed was sown in what had the appearance of barren ground".[45] Francis Webb is another whose understanding of Australia has been influenced by Eyre, as evidenced in his intensely moving and perceptive poem, "Eyre All Alone" (*Socrates and Other Poems*, 1961). After claiming that "Eyre's personal journal is infinitely more dramatic than this poem", Webb proceeds to retell the story of 29 April at the same time as he attempts to understand the instinct of survival in an environment seemingly designed to test humanity to its limits. The poem is too lengthy to be quoted here in full, but it is an unjustly neglected work which deserves recognition. It may be no less unjust to cite mere excerpts here, but a reader may gain an impression of Webb's (and perhaps Eyre's) literary preoccupations:

Wylie, where have you sprung from, what do you say?
I must go to a rare country with this stranger,
Cross an inhuman acre to sleep and forget.
O my warm gentle desert! — a squall threatens.
Well, Baxter, here you lie, bleeding and inert,
Across the yellow moon is drawn a curtain.

. . . You are dead. And two other parts of man have fled.
Is there life in my slack fingers to cross the ledger?

. . . Your pain and your great patience in the dream
Are working oddly over the Bight and gleaming.

One suspects that Webb, who spent lengthy periods of his life undergoing treatment for "mental illness", is not the first to read Eyre's journey as "suggestive of another which is common to us all".

Esau Selleth His Birthright

Sturt's and Eyre's 1840s journals provided information enough to take the image of Australia out of the Romantic era. After the explorers' experience, the naive expectation of an Australian paradise could no longer be taken seriously. Neither author denied that there were regions of the colony which were abundant and full of potential; rewards were available, but Australian nature could no longer be regarded as compliant and benign. Behind all the fertile regions — Sydney, the Bathurst plains, Australia Felix, and the Adelaide area — there lay bizarre dead lands which could be completely indifferent to something as negligible as a human society. If from the deserts prophets come, the message which Sturt and Eyre had to preach was cautionary: "fear the land".

The explorers' writing presents the culmination of the initial era of Australian literature insofar as the great animating dream of blessed lands in the interior had finally been invalidated. There was no longer any prospect of locating the diminishing paradise in Australian topography. The next development would entail another inward movement, to that country of the mind where the centre of the continent became a symbol of Australian aspiration and experience.

However, it would be a century or so before such a logical extension of the explorers' work was achieved. Instead of being immediately influential on the Australian ethos, the journals of Mitchell, Sturt and Eyre were "submerged" soon after publication, only to re-germinate in the popular imagination when writers such as Patrick White and Francis Webb recognised their "proto-mythic" potential and saw in them the seeds from which the elementary white Australian myths might grow. The reasons for the journals' submergence are many and complex, and are not strictly within the chronological and thematic scope of this study. But it can be contended that, although popular at the time of publication, the journals' effects on the representation of Australia were inhibited almost at the outset because soon after the publication of their purgatorial images they were swamped by the events and writings of the goldrushes in the 1850s, with the revival of fantasies of immense wealth and fertility in the Australian bush. As Coral Lansbury has demonstrated in *Arcady in Australia*, the spirit of the goldrushes has been prominent in the Australian consciousness, so prominent in fact that it obscured for too long the contradictory and experientially validated image of an Australian Purgatory which predated it. The explorers' vision of the country was not reinstated for so long mainly because the more alluring notion of the Australian golden age became too well entrenched for too long. The more chastening aspects of the explorers' writing were repressed (although still available at the level of memory and research) in the collective consciousness while the prospect of favourable material conditions catalysed one more attempt to realise an Australian golden age. Also, perhaps because of the peculiar nature of the writing — being part history, part myth, part reportage, part imaginative interpretation — critics have been slow to analyse it because it does not fall into the standard categories of creative literature. The more paradisaic image, being largely a product of fantasy, was better expressed in fictional forms such as the novels of Charles Reade, Henry Kingsley and Samuel Sydney, writings which were to some extent more easily analysed according to traditional critical methods. Accordingly, the post-1850s images have been "legitimised" more readily because they have received greater academic attention.

The insights which arose from the writing of the 1830s and 1840s were obscured before they could take immediate hold. But for a brief time before the goldrushes, the impact of the explorers' literature could be discerned in development. After the great explorer-writers had surveyed the pitiless interior, authors generally were wary of presenting any region of Australia as an unmitigated paradise. Paradise was being replaced by a Purgatory which eventually supplies its own rewards.

The "golden age" image of Australia, which was so popular in the 1820s, was still attractive. For example, Edward Bulwer Lytton painted a paradisaic picture in *The Caxtons*:

> Night in Australia! How impossible to describe its beauty! Heaven seems, in that new world, so much nearer to earth! Every star stands out so bright and particular, as if fresh from the time when the Maker willed it...Now and then a sound breaks the silence, but a sound so much in harmony with the solitude that it only deepens its charms...and the flowers hang noiseless over your head, as you ride through a grove of the giant gum trees. Now the air is literally charged with the odours, and the sense of fragrance grows almost painful in its pleasure.[46]

This painful pleasure bears no relation to that described by Mitchell or Sturt, and the harmonious bower has little to do with their actual Australia. Bulwer Lytton draws his images from a previous imaginary world. Significantly, however, his fancy is constrained somewhat by the new, grimmer attitudes to Australia. When Pisistratus, the protagonist of *The Caxtons*, goes to make his fortune in the colony, Lytton omits the first five years of the sojourn. The fiction requires that Pisistratus find wealth in bountiful Australia; plausibility demands that the rewards of the land are neither immediate nor automatic. The solution is to omit the early years in which tribulation ought to have occurred.

Lytton's fantasy was anachronistic. The attitude toward the country was plainly changing. As Thomas McCombie asserts in 1845, "the Colonies are the regions of stern reality; romance in the Colonies would not be tolerated".[47] The journal-writers had taught authors like McCombie to relinquish English pastoral criteria of beauty and to look anew at the land which had previously been ignored by so many writers who desired an Austral paradise. "Nay", he proclaims, "there is poetry in the vast weary plains from their utter desolation".[48]

This dual awareness of a stern reality and a poetic desolation proves enduring in the ever-complicating English image of Australia. The goldrushes were to gild the image once again but time could not completely erase the image which the explorers brought back from the interior. They encouraged other authors — English and Australian — to look directly at the land, to see its horrors and its beauties without relying exclusively on Old World vision. Because of Mitchell, Sturt and Eyre, Marcus Clarke could write his definitive "Australian aesthetic" in 1887:

> There is a poem in every form of tree or flower, but the poetry which lives in the trees and flowers of Australia differs from those of other countries. . . In Australia alone is to be found the Grotesque, the Weird, the strange scribblings of nature learning how to write. Some see no beauty in our trees without shade, our flowers without perfume, our birds who cannot fly, our beasts who have not yet learned to walk on all fours. But the dweller in the wilderness acknowledges the subtle charms of this fantastic land of monstrosities. He becomes familiar with the beauty of loneliness. Whispered to by the myriad tongues of the wilderness, he learns the language of the barren and the uncouth, and can read the hieroglyphs of haggard gum trees, blown into odd shapes, distorted with fierce winds, or cramped with cold nights, when the Southern Cross freezes in a cloudless sky of icy blue. The phantasmagoria of that wild dreamland termed the Bush interprets itself, and the Poet of our desolation begins to comprehend why free Esau loved his heritage of desert sand better than all the bountiful richness of Egypt.[49]

And the legacy of the travel-writers' experiences in Purgatory has prevailed in Australian culture until the present day. With the work of the explorers a new emphasis became established in literature about Australia. Whereas during the preceding decades writers had attempted to shape the image of the land according to their own traditional literary heritage, now the land itself was exerting its influence on literary forms and preoccupations. Imaginations once attempted to shape an image of the land; now the land was shaping imaginations through the agency of lived experience.

CHAPTER FIVE

Savages and Slaves:

IMAGES OF ABORIGINES

Why, a literature might be made out of the aboriginal all by himself. . .In his history, as preserved by the white man's official records, he is everything — everything that a human creature can be. He covers the entire ground. He is a coward — there are a thousand facts to prove it. He is brave — there are a thousand facts to prove it. He is treacherous — oh, beyond imagination! He is faithful, loyal, true — the white man's records supply you with a harvest of instances of it that are noble, worshipful, and pathetically beautiful.

Mark Twain, *Following the Equator* (1898)

We of this country, the richest in the world, just stand by and see our black compatriots wiped out. They'll be like the Noble Redman someday — noble when gone!

Xavier Herbert, *Capricornia* (1938)

You won't understand the country without understanding something of the original owners of it.

Xavier Herbert, *Poor Fellow My Country* (1975)

White Australians' attitudes to the Aborigines today are complex and ambivalent. There is nostalgia for a doomed heritage; disdain for a culture which will not or cannot readily adapt to modern urban existence; xenophobia in reaction to a race whose values are not identical to those of the suburban majority; and official patronage which purportedly protects and guides Aborigines in the modern world, but which often effectively alienates them from the rest of the Australian populace.

A similar blend of liberalism and bigotry can be discerned in the early English literature concerned with Australia. During the 1770-1850 period writers were slow to concur about the Aborigine. Some authors described a loathsome barbarian; others praised savage nobility; some could discern aspects of both character types in the one individual.

For a long time a double image of the native was set up; this complicated the image of Australia and served to reinforce the idea that the south land was a region of ambiguities and enigmas. It was only during the 1830s and 1840s that the contradictions began to be resolved. Inevitably, the development of the image of the Aborigine runs parallel to the progress of English understanding of the entire country. Australia itself has been the subject of vilification of an infernal gaol-colony, followed by extravagant praise of a new pastoral haven, until eventually a resolution of the two conflicting images was achieved in the representations of a purgatorial Australia.

The image of the Aborigine must be regarded as integral to, at the same time as it is emblematic of, any interpretations of Australia. An examination of the portrayal of the native in English literature can serve a dual purpose: one can analyse a distinctive aspect of the overall image of Australia at the same time as one "takes stock" of many of the attitudes which prevailed about Australia generally. A study of the depiction of the Aborigine can become a summary as well as a further investigation.

Part One
Savages

Prior to Captain Cook's voyages of discovery in 1770 and the subsequent English colonisation of eastern New Holland, the image of the Australian natives, like the image of the country itself, was being formulated under the two pressures of fanciful speculation about uncharted regions and discouraging first-hand reports of a daunting real world. At one extreme there was Pedro Fernandez de Quiros's vision of "Austrialians" who were "docible and easie of mannage"[1] and who would welcome the evangelistic Spaniards to an unspoiled paradise; at the other extreme there were William Dampier's proclamations that "the inhabitants of the Country [i.e. New Holland] are the miserablest People in the world. . .and setting aside their human shape, they differ but little from Brutes"[2].

When Daniel Defoe and Jonathan Swift responded imaginatively to the idea of the south land they focused on both aspects of the image of the native. They drew attention to a certain ambivalence by describing unwelcoming primitives in the known, barren areas of New Holland at the same time as they portrayed amicable and well-provided societies in the "fantasy-lands" of the unexplored south. In fact the ambivalence had prevailed since antiquity, when commonplaces pertaining to the antipodes led people to expect the bizarre in a region where the inhabitants walked upside down and the sun shone while Europeans slept. Such conjecture, allied with vestiges of the suspicion that antipodeans could not be of Edenic lineage, gave rise to disquieting connotations of mystery. No one knew quite what to expect as Captain Cook's *Endeavour* sailed within sight of the east coast of New Holland. Once daily contact was established with the Aborigines from 1770 onwards, the process of resolving the ambivalences was set in train.

The era 1770 to 1850 was one of radical speculation on the nature of humanity. Major influences — recent, present, or incipient — in the history of ideas at the time were: Rousseau's social philosophy; the French Revolution; Lyell's geology; Linnaean biology and tentative theories of evolution. It was an age in which James Burnet (Lord Monboddo) and Erasmus Darwin (grandfather of Charles) postulated theories of organic development which prefigured the more comprehensive work, to come two generations later, of Robert Chambers and Charles Darwin. Burnet regarded primitive man as positive proof of links between beasts and humanity. And Darwin contended that "all animals have a similar origin, viz. from a single living filament".[3] In fact he substantiated his claim by referring to his knowledge of New South Wales:

> The great variety of species of animals, which now tenant the earth, may have had their origin from the mixture of a few natural orders. . . Such a promiscuous intercourse of all animals is said to exist at this day in New South Wales by Captain Hunter. And that not only amongst the quadrupeds and birds of different kinds, but even amongst the fish, and, as he believes, amongst the vegetables. He speaks of an animal between the opossum and the kangaroo, from the size of a sheep to that of a rat. Many fish seemed to partake of the shark; some with a skait's head and shoulders, and the hind part of a shark; others with a shark's head and the body of a mullet; and some with a shark's head and the flat body of a sting-ray.[4]

Such unorthodox thinking affected not only the world of scientific scholarship. So, as Geoffrey Symcox has explained, circa 1770 "germinating ideas of biological evolution were being applied to society: a static model was being abandoned in favour of one which would allow for change and gradual development".[5]

This was a period of transition in which people attempted to align themselves between polarities of thought. The contention that all that is awry with the world could be imputed to ignorance of nature's simple and permanent laws vied with the opinion that human beings can establish themselves appropriately in the world only through a conscious transcendence of their base animal nature. The concept of the great chain of being became crucial to questions about the human condition. As Arthur Lovejoy explains it:

> [By] the late eighteenth century . . . the cosmical order was coming to be conceived not as an infinite static diversity, but as a process of increasing diversification. The Chain of Being having been temporalized, the God whose attributes it disclosed had been declared by not a few great writers to be one who manifests himself through change and becoming; nature's incessant tendency was to the production of new kinds; and the destiny of the individual was to mount through all the spires of form, in a continual self-transcendence.[6]

Inevitably, the analysis of "savage" humanity was pertinent to the entire metaphysical debate. Is pre-civilisation the most desirable state of being? Is it a condition of innocence from which reasoning people can progress? Is it simply depravity under the sway of ungovernable passions? Should civilised, rational people attempt to regain aspects of savage culture? Is "civilisation" a progression or a degeneration from "savagery"?

During these years the influence of Jean-Jacques Rousseau ranges through all literature, science and philosophy. Rousseau concentrated on the nature and nurture of humanity, and he legitimised interest in childhood and primitivism. He maintained that in the human constitution there is or has been potential for an ideal existence. Hence the Enlightenment concept of the noble savage. According to Rousseau's schema, modern humanity exists in the fourth stage of development, an era in which over-population and relative scarcity of food necessitate that human beings form social contracts and elitist classes. The supposed third stage of history — a stage which may have existed never, or only fleetingly — is envisaged as the best. It is imagined to be a period when people lived instinctively in a society in which laws and oppressive toil were not required. However, because of population growth this "golden age" is transient. Cooperative labour and trading become necessary to increase agricultural efficiency. Reason develops and is tainted with a competitive, egocentric impetus. Inevitably the collective consciousness becomes corrupted. Thus, to invoke Symcox again, "in the passage from the third period of development to the final stage of social inequality and conflict, Rousseau is in a sense secularizing and historicizing the myth of the Fall".[7]

The original golden age did not prevail because primitive, "natural" humanity was insufficiently "enlightened" by reason. And in modern times, "enlightened" people are estranged from the natural environment:

> The sweet voice of Nature is no longer an infallible guide for us, nor is the independence we have received from her a desirable state. Peace and innocence escaped us forever, even before we tasted their delights. Beyond the range of thought and feeling of the brutish men of the earliest times, and no longer within the grasp of the "enlightened" men of later periods, the happy life of the Golden Age could never really have existed for the human race. When men could have enjoyed it they were unaware of it;

> and when they could have understood it they had already lost it.[8]

Rousseau's implication was, "If only a society of uncivilized human beings were to exist today..." The possibilities were enticing to a person with knowledge and with a determination not to repeat the mistakes of civilised society. With the discovery and colonisation of new worlds, the noble savage ceased to be a mythical motif, and became an historical entity, conjectural but possible.

The exploration and settlement of the Americas so fired imaginations that many writers represented the Indian as a member of the ideal society. The precepts of Rousseau and the actual nature of the indigenous American were twisted in order to produce the image of the contemporary noble savage. However, it was not exclusively in America that writers located their admirable primitives. In P. L. Thorslev's words, the noble savage "began as a redskin and evolved to include Africans and South Sea Islanders, Albanians and Scotch Highlanders".[9] And his existence in the South Pacific seemed beyond contention after the publication and immediate popularity of Hawkesworth's *Voyages*, in which the Tahitians are especially praised by the various authors. It was a short and logical step from here to include the Australian Aborigine when considering "unfallen" humanity.

Rousseau did much to popularise debate on the admirable primitive, but the origins and development of the topic are obviously not restricted to the *philosophes'* salons. Fascination with primitivism had been part of the English literary tradition long before Dryden mused about being "free as Nature first made man/'Ere the base Laws of Servitude began/When wild in woods the noble Savage ran".[10] (The traditional English pastoral is an obvious precursor to this preoccupation.)

Once Rousseau had revived interest in this character from precivilisation, English writers discussed him readily, particularly with reference to the topical subject of the chain of being. According to contemporary theory, the natural hierarchy could be depicted as a linear pattern along which humanity progressed to an ideal state of rational enlightenment. To quote Richard Payne Knight:

> But still, as more society's refined,

Each native impulse less affects the mind;
Instinct to intellect is slowly brought,
And vague perception methodized to thought.[11]

Once the English began to colonise Australia, the Aborigine was bound to be tested against the criteria of popular concepts of noble savagery and human perfectibility. Was the Aborigine admirable or odious; perfect and unspoiled, or immutably degraded? A new progression along the chain of being was to be enacted and analysed as an uncivilised region became "methodised" (Alexander Pope's concept is recurrently pertinent) so that English people in the age of reason might understand and control it.

The earliest and least contentious post-1770 accounts of the Aborigines are by naval officers and scientists trained in the objective observation and description extolled by the Royal Society. When James Cook and Sydney Parkinson restricted themselves to writing in the scientific mode, they recorded "responsible" accounts of the natives as anthropological specimens. Parkinson, for example, does not offer personal opinions about the desirability or otherwise of the natives' lot. Rather, aware perhaps that observation must come before interpretation, he concentrates on describing the Aborigines' physical appearance, their diet, and their artefacts.[12] Similarly, Cook's *Endeavour* journal evinces detachment in assessment of the natives, although he does indulge in a degree of romantic primitivism when he declares that the natives seem "happier than we"[13] in their simple existence:

> The Natives do not appear to be numberous neither do they seem to live in large bodies but dispers'd in small parties along by the water side; those I saw were about as tall as Europeans, of a very dark brown colour but not black nor had they wooly frizled hair, but black and lank much like ours. No sort of clothing or ornaments were ever seen by any of us upon any one of them.[14]

By way of contrast, the rendition of this passage as it appears in the authorised publication of Cook's journals (edited by John Hawkesworth) is somewhat more subjective and suggestive. Concerned more with seizing the readers' imaginations (and their florins) Hawkesworth edits and emends to produce a rather more provocative description of savage existence. The writer's imagination predominates over the scientist's eye:

> All the inhabitants that we saw were stark naked: they did not appear to be numerous, nor to live in societies, but like other animals were scattered along the coast, and in the woods.[15]

The original subjects were the same for each account. The images presented, the hint of prurience in the description of "stark" nakedness, and the comparison of the Aborigines to animals serve to trigger off more "sensational" connotations of savagery than Cook's observations. (As Bernard Smith has pointed out, the image of the noble savage was often highlighted with a "strong erotic appeal".[16]) Two different types of literature: two different types of image in the making.

Despite Cook's attempts to establish an unequivocal image of the Aborigine, it was all in vain. A consistent pattern of observations did not appear. One obvious reason for the variety of representations is that Australia is of enormous size and diversity, and that Aboriginal groups were spread across its expanse. Even so, writers usually failed to acknowledge any variety of types among the natives. It is Hawkesworth who started the trend by interpolating this assertion in the *Voyages*:

> We also saw inhabitants upon parts of the coast very distant from each other, and there being a perfect uniformity in person and customs among them all, it is reasonable to conclude, that distance in another direction has not considerably broken it.[17]

Hawkesworth was aware that public interest in the Aborigine was considerable. It was to his advantage to present an image of a uniform type-character. If the public wanted exotica uncomplicated by scientific cavilling, they could be given just that. Joseph Banks's conclusions, drawn from his limited first-hand experience with the natives, are similar to Hawkesworth's. He is "struck with the uniformity of aboriginal material culture".[18] Moreover, the tendency persisted; as late as 1841 George Grey was generalising from his extensive knowledge of the Aborigines of Western Australia to claim that "we find. . . in Australia. . . the remarkable fact that the inhabitants of a tract of country nearly two thousand miles in breadth, are governed by the same institutions" of language, rites and ceremonies.[19]

Even the patent differences between the mainland groups

viewed as a race and the Aborigines of Van Diemen's Land were most frequently disregarded. One author speaks for the majority by asserting that it is merely on "superficial observation" that these Tasmanians seem "a different race" from the mainlanders.[20] In the eyes of many writers the only distinction that can be drawn is the fractionally more debased standing of the islanders on the chain of being:

> They are undoubtedly in the lowest possible scale of human nature, both in form and intellect. They have small hollow eyes, broad short noses, with nostrils widely distended, uncommonly large mouths, jaws elongated like the Ourang Outang, and figures scarcely more symmetrical. They are dark, short in stature, with disproportionately thin limbs and shapeless bodies, entirely naked.[21]

Writers tended to discuss "the Australian Aborigines" as consistent type-characters regardless of the fact that they were real people living in groups spread across an astonishingly various continent. For writers asserting the colonial rights of England it was best to describe natives of such lowly character that there could be no compunction about taking their land and destroying their culture. To humanitarians, of course, such an attitude was abhorrent, but it also seems to have been predominant for a time. Even with regard to religion, a weight of opinion condemned the natives. As Bernard Smith observes, "to the thoroughgoing evangelist, Aboriginals were pagan savages who (saving Christian conversion) were destined to perdition".[22] A cult of primitivism would prove influential, but it was not to be established without being challenged.

"an unimprovable, incapable, inert mass of brute . . ."

For many authors the position of the natives on the chain of being was beyond dispute. Writers employed by *Alexander's East India Magazine*, for example, were keen to justify English authority in Australia by implying that there was no point in championing the rights of a people who were barely human: "The New Hollander is the last link in the chain of humanity; with him it terminates; we grope in the dark, tracing aught beyond him".[23]

Similarly, the *Quarterly Review*, avowed opponent of the Whig *Edinburgh Magazine*, was not likely to be party to any sentimental philanthropy, for the creatures were clearly beneath respect:

> In this rank of beings, even the Hottentot is superior to the original native of New South Wales, who may perhaps be justly placed in the lowest division of the scale of human kind.[24]

Jeremy Bentham, somewhat peeved at the government's refusal to utilise his theories of the Panopticon prison at Botany Bay, was particularly severe on Aborigines in order to infer that convicts in a prison-colony could never be rehabilitated in this land where the natives, who were *free*, were barely human. Formulating his opinion from hearsay, he declared that the natives were a "set of brutes in human shape, the very dregs even of savage life".[25]

Moreover, disparagement was not the exclusive preserve of prosaic empiricists. Journalists and poets (so called) repeatedly described the native glowering at the far end of the scale of being. An anonymous pamphleteer of 1789 spoke of "Fauns and Satyrs living in hollow trees".[26] And as if to prove that hateful nature can be rendered in doggerel, George Morgan penned a prize-winning poem in 1846, when the stereotype of the base savage was obviously still current:

> And who is he who from the settler's gate
> Now timorous shrinks and now returns to wait;
> Whose narrow brow and vacant eye declare
> How faint the gleam of mind reflected there;
> Wild are his ways, unlike the ways of men,
> Child of the woods, Australia's denizen.[27]

From this point of view, Aborigines who have not been influenced by civilisation are as debased as human beings can be.

The crucial question, once the original condition of the Aborigines was portrayed, was one of potentiality. Regardless of how low they stood, were they capable of ascending the scale? If yes, then perhaps they were still worthy of a favourable literary image, because they could be described as the raw material of an exemplary new society. If no, then there was little point in treating them as human beings, given that they could never become the peers of the English people!

The majority of the disparaging commentators were adamant that the natives were incorrigible. For corroboration, there was the celebrated case of Bennelong, the first Aboriginal character to pass into white Australian folklore. As historians recount the events, Bennelong (a prominent member of the Aboriginal community around Botany Bay) became acquainted with Governor Phillip while living in the vicinity of the garrison when he was convalescing from a bout of the smallpox which had ravaged his people. He was communicative — an entertaining raconteur, in fact — and Governor Phillip was hopeful that he could be retained both as an adviser to the English settlers and as a test case of Aboriginal perfectibility. After six months, Bennelong absconded to the bush, shunning civilisation for approximately four months until he returned in September 1790 to join in an Aboriginal feast occasioned by the beaching of a whale on the garrison shorelines.

Contemporary journal writers interpreted Bennelong's "walkabout" as proof of his permanent degeneracy. However, the exceptionally liberal Governor Phillip refused to damn him as reprobate, and continued to offer friendship, even after Phillip was speared in the shoulder after a misunderstanding at the whale-feast. Indeed, in 1792 Phillip took Bennelong and another Botany Bay Aborigine, Yemmerrawannie, with him when he returned to England. Yemmerrawannie died there, but the more durable Bennelong adapted to the climate and to the games of social intercourse, and became something of a celebrity, although "curiosity" might be an equally apposite description.

The acid test of this experiment in educability came when in 1795 Bennelong returned to Botany Bay with Governor-designate Hunter. It is at this juncture that the journalists felt themselves vindicated. For, on his return, he cast aside his civilised garb and rejoined the native community. This action is open to countless interpretations. The majority of writers read it as proof of permanent native degeneracy:

> Whilst Bennelong, the Botany Bay chief, was in England, he was presented to many of the principal nobility and first families of the kingdom, and received from many of them presents of clothes and other articles, which a savage of any other country would have deemed almost inestimable. It was not so, however, with Bennelong; he was no sooner re-landed in his own country, than he forgot, or at least laid aside, all the ornaments and

> improvements he had reaped from his travels, and returned as if with increased relish, to all his former loathsome and savage habits.[28]

The "responsible" scientific language of genuinely experienced observers such as Captain Cook was not commonly utilised in the popular press. Journalists relied on their imaginations as well as their sources of information — more often derivative than first-hand — in order to express an opinion about the natives. The writer took the information, filtered it through his or her own prejudices, and aligned it with the bias of the editor and/or readers to produce an image which did not necessarily concur with the reality which existed some 18,000 kilometres from Grub Street. The journalists were writing for a market. In those early years of England's "great" colonial era, the percentage of people requiring an image of a savage who deserved to be subdued was considerable.

So morally and physically repugnant are the natives painted by the denigrators, that interbreeding cannot be considered seriously. This is deemed unfortunate, because "otherwise we might at least have looked for the springing up of a nation of half-castes, which, after the lapse of a few generations, might, perhaps, have scarcely proved inferior to the European settlers"![29]

Even when the *Alexander's East India Magazine* does concede that the Aborigine may in the future be susceptible to education, the ostensible optimism is couched in such negative terms as to render the proposition ludicrous. Perfectibility can paradoxically be ascribed to the natives because of their (purportedly) undeniable deterioration after interaction with the white convict society:

> What the New Hollander has become from contact with the refuse of British population is a further question. That with a larger evidence of his humanity, his fiercer and more malevolent passions have been called into action, there is no doubt. He has learned the language and the habits of the most dissolute of Europeans, but this is no argument against his capacity of improvement. On the contrary, it is a demonstration of the fact, setting to flight the hypothesis that he is an unimprovable, incapable, inert mass of brute, without an admixture of the qualities of human nature.[30]

The question of perfectibility was continually debated. Facts such as the existence of Aboriginal languages and art were undeniable and constituted proof that despite their apparent lowliness relative to the rest of humanity, Aborigines had at some stage progressed from being a collection of self-indulgent individuals and had become a society capable of communication and organisation. Even this admission of past development was grudging, for, it was reasoned, the improvement must have been instigated by superior beings. Richard Payne Knight outlines the process in general terms:

> Long unsuccessful did the savage try,
> In measured notes to articulate his cry;
> And e'en when some enlightened mind had taught
> To join the measured sound with measured thought,
> Long years elapsed ere yet one single horde
> Could make each sound and sentiment accord;
> Ere mimickry with memory combined,
> Could catch each note, and fix it in the mind:
> Instinctive mimickry, the guide of man![31]

Certainly in the particular case of the New Hollanders it was widely assumed that they were not capable of self-improvement. James Burnet (Lord Monboddo) considers the question when he wonders how it transpired that "the New Hollanders have the use of speech". He can "hardly believe that they have invented [their language]", and he assumes that they have "learned it by intercourse with some other nation".[32] It is significant, therefore, that innumerable authors comment on the natives' skills of mimicry, usually as demonstrative of what is seen as their clownish temperament, but also as corroborative of their lack of creative ingenuity. Moreover, the diversity of dialects in the Aboriginal language — called by Barron Field "the thousand Babel tongues of the New Hollanders and Van Diemen's Islanders"[33] — is taken as proof that the natives are incapable of refining and standardising their one humanising advantage.

For those with little faith in the Aborigines' perfectibility it seems sensible to "face the facts" as William Wickenden, for example, presents them:

> But not on man's enfeebled race who stray
> Amid these wilds has Nature poured the ray

Of light and sunshine o'er the darkened mind,
Or flowers of science round the spirit turned:
No — like yon cloud, tossed by the winds of Heaven,
Is his dark soul by storms of passion driven.[34]

Here is no idyllic primitivism. A typically derogatory image of the native such as that depicted by Robert Montgomery Martin refutes Rousseau's idealism:

> There may not be much in the appearance, still less in the manners of the New Hollander, to excite our sympathy, for assuredly if Rousseau had visited the aborigines of New South Wales. . .he would not have hesitated as to whether savage or social life is to be preferred.[35]

Similarly, Watkin Tench, ever the pragmatist aware that he is by profession an officer of a colonial peace-keeping corps, refuses to sentimentalise his opinion of the natives:

> A thousand times. . .have I wished, that those European philosophers, whose close speculations exalt a state of nature above a state of civilization, could survey the phantom, which their heated imaginations have raised: possibly they might learn, that a state of nature is, of all others, least adapted to promote the happiness of a being, capable of sublime research, and unending ratiocination: that a savage roaming for prey amidst his native deserts, is a creature deformed by all those passions, which afflict and degrade our nature, unsoftened by the influence of religion, philosophy, and legal restriction.[36]

Tench's imagination is ice-cool as he puts the natives in a place well below the enlightened Englishman and tacitly justifies English seizure of Aboriginal land at the same time as he subtly persuades his readers that a native is capable of any barbarity.

The "savage", "deformed by all those passions", is a prime subject for portrayal in gothic terms, especially to a writer like the young Winthrop Mackworth Praed, settling down to studies in civilised Cambridge:

A fiercer guiltiness, a fouler stain!
Oh! who shall sing the scene of savage strife,
Where hatred glories in the waste of life.
. . .The feast of death, the banquetting of blood,
When the wild warrior gazes on his foe
Convulsed beneath him in his painful throe,

WRECK OF THE ST

Horrib Treatment of T

LING CASTLE.

w by Savages.

A Copy of Mournful

VERSES.

YE mariners and landsmen all,
  Pray list while I relate,
The wreck of the Stirling Castle
  And the crew's sad dismal fate.
In an open boat upon the waves,
  Where billows loud did roar,
And the savage treatment they receiv'd
  When drove on a Foreign shore.

The Stirling Castle on May 16th,
  From Sydney she set sail,
The crew consisting of twenty,
  With a sweet and pleasant gale.
Likewise Captain Frazer of the ship,
  On board he had his wife,
And now, how dreadful for to tell,
  The sacrifice of human life.

Part of the crew got in one boat,
  Thinking their lives to save,
But in a moment they were dash'd,
  Beneath the foaming waves
And Mrs Frazer in another boat,
  Far advanc'd in pregnant state,
Gave birth unto a lovely babe,
  How shocking to relate.

And when they reach'd the fatal shore,
  Its name is call'd Wide Bay,
The savages soon them espied,
  Rush'd down, and seiz'd their prey.
And bore their victims in the boat,
  Unto their savage den,
To describe the feelings of those poor souls
  Is past the art of man.

This female still was doom'd to see,
  A deed more dark and drear,
Her husband pierc'd was to the heart,
  By a savage with his spear.
She flew unto his dying frame,
  And the spear she did pull out,
And like a frantic maniac,
  Distracted flew about.

The chief mate too they did dispatch
  By cutting off his head,
And plac'd on one of their canoes
  All for a figure head.
Also, a fine young man they bound
  And burnt without a dread,
With a slow fire his feet at first
  So up unto his head.

When you read the tortures I went thro'
  'Twill grieve your hearts full sore,
But now, thank HEAVEN. I am return'd
  Unto my native shore.
I always shall remember,
  And my prayers will ever be,
For the safety of both age and sex,
  Who sail on the raging sea.---BR.W.

1835 broadside about Mrs Fraser's shipwreck.

By permission of the British Library.

And lifts the knife, and kneels him down to drain
The purple current from the quivering vein.[37]

Scenes of death-feasts and blood-banquets introduce a new but inevitable aspect to the image of the barbarous Aborigine: cannibalism. Concerning this most provocative of topics some writers could in fact avoid overreaction. J. C. Byrne's opinion is considerably more generous than many: "A great part of the known Australian tribes practise cannibalism; apparently not from any wish for human flesh itself, but as an essential rite in their ceremonies".[38]

But cannibalism is not a subject which writers are likely to ignore, and at this time exaggerated reports persisted long after such sensationalism ought to have been discredited. (The question of Aboriginal anthropophagy is still a vexed one. Evidence of ceremonial cannibalism among certain tribes can be cited, but it is inconclusive.) Here was a topic with which authors could scandalise at the same time as they thrilled the reading public:

> According to the people of the Murray — who themselves kill boys for the sake of their fat with which to bait their fish-hooks! — the natives devour their children in times of scarcity.[39]

Or, for further variations on a theme:

> Examples have occurred of the father killing and eating his own offspring!. . .they have been seen to bleed themselves, make a sort of cake with the blood, and then greedily devour it.[40]

If some authors were prepared to consider the Aborigines as carnivorous animals, others had no compunction in portraying them as murderers lurking in the wilderness. Characterisations developed of hateful savages intent on "deadly revenge".[41] These natives' ferocity, reportedly, was not tempered by honourable bravery: "It cannot be said that they are a war-like people, as nearly all their enemies are killed by treachery, and scarcely ever in a fair and open fight".[42]

Richard Howitt and G. H. Haydon, the two writers quoted immediately above, are representatives of a significant group of traveller-authors who would spend a few years working in the grazing lands of New South Wales and Victoria — sometimes working for themselves on freehold land — and who would then return to England to write about their experiences for an

English public which was particularly fond of travel-literature. Inevitably such writers sympathised with the new squatter class of graziers who were developing their pastures by forcing the natives off their tribal lands. It stands to reason that the Aborigines should have reacted to this outrage with their own brand of violence; and it is also logical that writers who were in favour of the squatters' private imperialism should portray the Aborigines in as uncomplimentary a fashion as possible.

Moreover, it must not be forgotten that since 1779, with the death of James Cook in Hawaii, the murderous nature of natives from the Pacific region was readily credited, and was widely publicised in many an elegy and ode to the memory of the national hero, as well as in several paintings depicting either the slaying itself or the subsequent apotheosis of "the immortal Cook".[43]

The treachery of *Australian* natives in fact became so well "documented" that the figure of the homicidal native passed into folklore, into the broadside ballad and the sea-shanty. The versification may not be exemplary, but the message is explicit enough:

When first unto this new found place
O then that you come here
Everyone to labour you know he must repair,
To cultivate the land, all for to make it good,
But many of us our lives shall lose by the Indians
  from the wood...
So all you giddy lads remember this in time,
Lest you like unto us be forced in your prime
To leave your native land, and sail to Botany Bay,
Among the heathen savages for to become a prey.[44]

The Aborigine is here portrayed as the enemy, in opposition even to the convicts, the most oppressed and outcast of the whites in the colony. If there was any human being perceived to be lower than a Botany Bay convict, it was an Australian native.

All things considered, then, between 1770 and 1850 a plethora of literature portrays the Aborigine as the most ignoble of savages. Indeed, as Coral Lansbury has observed, the Australian natives must comprise, with the possible exception of the Jews, the most traduced race in all literature.[45] By slandering the

Aborigines and condemning them to the base of the human hierarchy, the English author could describe them as the archetypal wild people embodying all that is taboo and repulsive in the human condition. As Hayden White explains, the folkloric "wild man" "is conventionally represented as being always present, inhabiting the immediate confines of the community". Ever-threatening, he is "just out of sight, over the horizon, in the nearby forest, desert, mountains, or hills. He sleeps in crevices, under great trees, or in the caves of wild animals, to which he carries off helpless children, or women".[46] For the civilised English person contemplating New South Wales the representation of the Aborigine as a "wild man" served two purposes: (a) the native could become a comprehensible embodiment of the malevolence in the harsh Australian environment, and (b) he could stand as a constant reminder of what humanity can regress to. As White expresses it, the "wild man" can be seen both as a "nemesis" and a "possible destiny".[47]

The idea of the "wild man" as a possible destiny is especially relevant in reference to Botany Bay; writers were constantly aware of the degraded nature of the convicts who could be regarded as white, English savages. Certainly the white man could become a "wild man". The evidence was clear. However, by describing the Aborigine as especially heinous, writers were able to imply that not even the convict could fall so low. Therefore, the image of the native could also be used as a distancing device. Civilised people could feel contented that they had successfully eradicated savagery from their constitutions by comparison with genuine barbarity in a foreign wilderness.

The image of the savage was used to emphasise the relative merits of the English race. When English writers were not debasing the Aborigine, they could evince a commensurate effect by depicting the English person as inestimably high upon the scale in comparison to the "savage". Working from this opposite perspective, if the English were characterised as a race "born to rule" in Australia, the natives were definitely to be the subjects. When it came to a contest of merit, civilisation had to prevail. Charles Darwin, for one, has no doubts about who is best fitted to survive in the south land, when he proclaims that:

> Wherever the European has trod, death seems to pursue the aboriginal. We may look to the wide extent of the Americas,

> Polynesia, the Cape of Good Hope, and Australia, and we shall find the same result. . . The varieties of man seem to act on each other — the stronger always extirpating the weaker.[48]

Extinction perhaps is not only inevitable; it can be construed, in Judge Barron Field's way of thinking, as benevolent justice: "Perhaps it is better that their name pass away from the earth. They will not serve, and they are too indolent and poor in spirit to become masters".[49]

Might must prevail in Australia, as it did in recent history concerning that other English colonial venture: America. Whenever Richard Howitt writes of life and adventures in Australia Felix he does so with the following attitude influencing his opinions of the natives:

> The American Indians have waned away, and are become, as a people, less and less. So it must be with this inartificial and almost irreclaimable race. Rome is the dwelling of religious owls and bats — a race of dwarfs in arms, in civil and religious freedom. We are all that the greatest nations of antiquity have been, and infinitely more.[50]

England in all her glory is portrayed as rightful inheritor of the earth and its subjects. Even Rousseau's premise that the savage may have been the superior raw material of perfectible humanity is invalidated when the mettle of the Australian Aborigine is tested against the quality of the English person. The critic of primitivism, once again, is Watkin Tench:

> "Give to civilized man all his machines, and he is superior to the savage; but without these, how inferior is he found on opposition, even more so than the savage in the first instance." These are the words of Rousseau, and like many more of his positions, must be received with limitation. Were an unarmed Englishman, and an unarmed New Hollander, to engage, the latter, I think, would fall.[51]

In this era England was progressing to world domination, and national esteem reached its zenith in the 1830s. Patrick Matthew, for example, beat the drum loudly: "A change is at hand. The reign of Queen Victoria promises to be glorious for victory over barbarism and human misery — Colonization is the means".[52]

Such chauvinistic ardour gives rise to questions of evangelism. After the fervent missionary campaigns waged by the English among the natives of America, Africa, the West Indies and India, it is remarkable that accounts of missionary activity in early Australia are comparatively scarce. However, the reasons are logical enough. The Aboriginal population, which had always been small, was being ravaged by disease. The city-dwelling communities, afflicted by smallpox and alcoholism, were thought to be moribund. Also, opinions about immutable Aboriginal degeneracy were widely credited. Indeed when a poorly serviced Aboriginal school was established in 1814, writers were incensed that the pupils continually escaped over the walls of the compound to join their bush-dwelling brothers and sisters. The absurdity of an attempt to confine boisterous children of a nomadic race in an enclosed space and fixed routine, all in order to teach the Golden Rule and algebra, was not acknowledged. How could these children possibly reject such charity? To the "abused" English person there seemed little point in attempting to redeem such a small number of irrevocably lost souls, if indeed the natives had souls at all.

From a liberal point of view, also, evangelism seemed pointless. The authorial persona (the "emigrant mechanic") in Alexander Harris's *Settlers and Convicts* "feels inclined" to put aside all missionary efforts as "quite useless at present". In the mechanic's opinion, "there seems something so intrinsically absurd in the nation which is robbing another of its land and its means of subsistence soliciting that other to adopt its religion".[53] By way of an indictment of white society, Harris speculates about how an Aborigine would respond to an evangelist's attempts to convert him:

> "You!", he says, "you who tie one another up, and flog one another within an inch of life, for some little hasty word; you who begrudge one another enough to eat; you who deprive me of my hunting grounds, only to increase possessions for mere possessions' sake; you, a people divided into two classes the one hateful and the other contemptible, the tyrant and the slave. . .you teach me to be better! Me who walk the forest free, who appropriate no more than I need, who never fight but as a deeply injured man, who would not lay your bloody lash upon my dog, much less my brother".[54]

In Harris's opinion, the English had to set their own colony in order before they could presume to preach to the Aborigines.

Even in less liberal circles writers acknowledged the need for the colony to reform itself; the blackened souls of the convicts had to be reclaimed first. Only after the white community had been saved would it be possible for the pastors to expend energy on the natives. If the Aborigines happened to be improved by contact with the admirable sections of the white community, this was the best that could be done for them. Thus, in their sense of superiority, the English were being generous in domesticating the savages. Thomas Richards of the *Westminster Review* exemplifies this attitude when he describes "tamed" Tasmanian natives:

> These individuals were enjoying every comfort of civilized life, nay, they are a sort of pets with the inhabitants of Launceston, and were fully imbued with the importance of the interest which they created.[55]

The wonder, to borrow Doctor Johnson's wit, is not that the domestication is done well, but that it is done at all! Such is the condescending tone.

At their most clement, the English could be most damning. There is something more insidious about patronising toleration of incorrigible savages than there is about outright hostility and calumny. Regardless of which attitude prevailed, however, a large group of writers between 1770 and 1850 established one image of the Aborigines by depicting them consistently as objects of fear and loathing: fear because the Aborigines reminded these civilised people of a barbarous heritage; and loathing because nothing about savage culture seemed to conform to the criteria of English Christian civilisation.

"Caffres have black faces, but white hearts. . ."

Not all writers at this time are strictly condemnatory in their descriptions of the Aborigine. Nor are they all unreservedly adulatory of the English nation. Many interpret English society as so disconcertingly "fallen" that it is impertinent to regard an English colony overladen with convicts as far superior to the savages' community. According to this point of view, any corruption of the blacks ought to be accredited to the taint-by-association with the white society:

> On coming in contact with the whites, they [the blacks] seem speedily to acquire all their vices without one of those conservative virtues which mitigate their effects and render practicable the consolidation of society. There is obstinacy mixed with dulness [*sic*] in the savage, there is impatience mixed with overweaning pride in the civilized man.[56]

Sympathy for the native even changes occasionally to admiration as several writers wonder whether to extol an Australian noble savage. William Thomas Moncrieff is just such a cautious romanticist. In *Van Diemen's Land!* he utilises poetic licence to its limit, as he transposes the now-legendary Bennelong (called "Ben-ni-long" in the play) in time and space to become the oratorical spokesman for a group of Aborigines in Tasmania in 1818.

The Aboriginal sub-plot of the play supplements the two plots outlined in chapter three of this book. Ben-ni-long and his band of native followers, including an apocryphal sister named Kangaree, become increasingly involved with the white community as the play progresses. When romance develops between Kangaree and Darby Ballylaggan (the Irish convict), the native tribe begin to sympathise with the new settlers, in contrast to Ben-ni-long's earlier exhortations for "Caffre revenge". Darby marries Kangaree, sealing an honourable peace between the blacks and the newly arrived whites, and the Aborigines play a vital part in the climactic scene in which the bushrangers' murderous plan is foiled and justice and happiness are meted out in appropriate proportions.

Moncrieff's comparatively liberal attitudes are in evidence in his handling of this plot. Ben-ni-long is accorded the least prosaic language of any character in the play and is certainly represented as more sinned against than sinning. Just as Moncrieff sympathises to some extent with the convicts, naming two of the free settlers "Bolter" and "Scapetrap" in order to imply that more people than just those convicted are guilty of misdemeanours, so he sides with the natives many times when savage and civilised existence are compared. White society is criticised when Ben-ni-long recalls his experiences in England:

> What saw the untaught savage — the wild chief there? — this saw he! — he saw the white man, his neighbour, poor! — distressed! — shut him in prison! — make him poorer still to make him pay! — he saw the white man hang white men, like dogs, for stealing food to save them from starvation! — but for a wife, a daughter stolen, oh, bits of shining gold are ample recompense![57]

Moncrieff attempts to emphasise the message when Kangaree chants a clumsy paraphrase of the opening two lines of William Blake's "The Little Black Boy" ("My mother bore me in the southern wild,/And I am black, but O! my soul is white", in *Songs of Innocence*, 1789): "Caffres have black faces, but white hearts, but white men's faces white, their hearts black!" (p.37).

Also, Moncrieff's rendition of Ben-ni-long's return to the wilds after his sojourn in England differs from the more common, condemnatory interpretations of the actions of an unregenerate savage. In *Van Diemen's Land!* Ben-ni-long is obviously a character with whom the audience is meant to sympathise. His insights are to be regarded as cogent when he recounts his experiences:

> Ben-ni-long, savage as he was, found white men worse; he left his country, what found he here, when he came back? he found the white man chief! he found his lands all seized, and he, their prince, the white man's slave! He threw off the fine clothes the white man gave him — left their gay feasts — shut ear to their smooth words — took to his native skins again — his hunter's fare — and wars 'gainst white men now, as white men warred 'gainst him! [p.38]

From this point of view the savages' vengeance can be seen as righteous, and even commendable. Kangaree and the chorus dance as they sing:

> White man come with fire in hand
> Seize poor Caffre's native land,
>
> . . . Let him fear, Black man near,
> Him take dark revenge! [p.37]

Perhaps the most informative aspect of this plot is Moncrieff's evident confusion over his own attitude to the Aborigine. At the same time as he invariably portrays Ben-ni-long as a noble spokesman of serious themes, he also exploits the Aboriginal scenes in order to present diverting local colour. The natives are dressed flamboyantly; the stage directions specify Ben-ni-long's costume as "White shirt — short trunks — brown legs and arms — scarf — Indian head-dress", while Kangaree is to wear an "Indian striped dress". Also, when the tribe is not singing and cavorting like spirits of the forests, they are often planning "good works", like some antipodean approximations of Robin Hood's band of merry men. To add to the confusion, Moncrieff occasionally allows these scenes to become trite farce, as when Darby marries Kangaree and is immediately elevated to the status of "Chief Brien Boroo of Derry, chief of the Broken Head tribe" (p.42).

Moncrieff's play appears at a time when many writers concerned with Australia are exclusively condemnatory of the Aborigines; his desire to romanticise Ben-ni-long and the tribe is challenged by voluminous literature professing an opposite idea. As a writer Moncrieff is afflicted with many shortcomings, but he cannot be blamed entirely for his inconsistent attitude to the Aborigine, for the ideological climate in which he writes would confuse a better intellect than his. Moncrieff is aware that a balanced view of the relative merits of whites and blacks is required. Although Kangaree speaks of the white man's black heart, she also affirms that "some pale-face, good and kind! — better than Caffre" (p.38). Aboriginal courting worries her especially: "Pale-face take but one wife, that good — Caffre take two, that bad; — Caffre court girl with blows — beat her to make her love him, that bad" (p.38). (The courting customs are a popular topic with writers of the time. Possibly the most influential presentation of the distastefulness of Aboriginal "romance" comes in the 1803 edition of T. R. Malthus's *An Essay on the Principle of Population*, chapter three, "Of the Checks to Population in the Lowest Stage of Human Society". He refers to reports of cruel treatment of Aboriginal women and children, and he condemns such behaviour as an unacceptably barbaric means of population control!) As a result of her observations Kangaree is determined to marry a white man, and the audience is persuaded (albeit with a minimum of nuance and finesse) that each society is far from perfect.

A partial resolution of Moncrieff's puzzlement over the

comparative worth of civilised and savage communities in Australia comes at the denouement of the play, when Ben-ni-long engineers the capture of Michael Howe's bushranger gang. Inferring a moral from the marriage of Kangaree and Darby, Ben-ni-long proclaims that blacks and whites should co-operate rather than seek to destroy each other: "For your sakes, friends, I'll be at peace with England, will yield my lawful claims to this fair isle" (p.68).

Behind Moncrieff's confused characterisation of Aborigines in this generally confused play, there is a dissatisfaction with the simplistic portrait of the native as an entirely odious creature who crouches in degradation while the ideal English settler lives out an exemplary existence. The weaknesses of the play stem from the fact that Moncrieff is intelligent enough to realise that stereotypes of both whites and blacks in Australia are inadequate to the task of presenting the issues which are now pertinent to the English vision of the colony. But the play's flaws are also its comparative strengths. Had Moncrieff been a worse writer, the tensions and ambivalences in *Van Diemen's Land!* would not have been evident, and the problems of interpretation of the Aborigine, which the play highlights, would have been concealed by the application of well-worn but inflexible and flat stereotypes of the lowly savage and the righteous settler.

For authors like Moncrieff who are gifted with some self-critical faculties, the treachery of the natives is due not to untempered passions, but to a sense of just retribution and self-preservation. As Thomas Bartlett explains:

> It must not be forgotten, while we are meditating on the treatment of the natives of New Holland, that their country is occupied by force — that they attempted, but in vain, to beat off the English settlers. However much this question may be mystified, it is evident that New Holland is only held by the right of might. Therefore, it is not justifiable to assert that all the evils which have been brought on the Aborigines by the settlement of the whites in their country, have arisen from the inherent depravity of their natures.[58]

These writers are prepared to see good and bad in the Aborigine. They attempt to maintain a balance in their characterisations.

E. J. Eyre makes a similar point in the supplement to the second volume of his *Journals*. After describing his epic trek across the continent, Eyre devotes a portion of his book to an account of Aboriginal society. This section of the book is a fine study in social anthropology, in which Eyre avoids ascribing literary stereotypes to the Aborigines; rather he seeks to place the natives' behaviour in a broad historical context. He begins his inquest with an unequivocal declaration: "Could blood answer blood, perhaps for every drop of European's shed by natives, a torrent of theirs, by European hands, would crimson the earth".[59] From this perspective he then analyses the injustices perpetrated by colonial society, such as squatters' farming and policing methods which deny Aborigines access to their lands and water-courses; he criticises the apathy of colonial administrations with regard to native affairs, and he vehemently refutes the "unfair and unwarranted assumption" that the disappearance of the natives is "the result of the natural course of events; that they are ordained by Providence, unavoidable, and not to be impeded".[60]

Eyre, like Moncrieff, cannot accept the popular stereotypes of the natives. Unlike Moncrieff, he resorts to an avowedly non-fictional means of presenting his understanding of them. Much of Eyre's account consists of "scientific" observation drawn from personal experience as he details the physiques and physical capabilities of Aborigines; as he analyses native dialects and discusses the conflicts between European and Aboriginal tribal laws; as he meticulously describes hunting and fishing methods, weapons, diet and habitation; and as he earnestly examines (and tentatively approves) the new missions which were recently set up to put Aborigines on the long road to some degree of integration with white society. All in all, Eyre's work on the Aborigines is well balanced and truly innovative, fully meriting Geoffrey Dutton's praise of it as "not only a pioneering work but an eloquent and humane plea for the rights of native peoples".[61]

Works of equanimity and objectivity, however, are uncommon with regard to the Aborigine at this time, because Old World literature and language so often influenced people's vision. A tolerant and sensitive attitude towards the native people called for innovative thinking which would enable people to consider the Aborigine separately from a stereotype such as the fearsome wild man. Therefore, if writers were inclined to reject the image of the murderous savage, they were not likely to opt for a fictional rendition of the position which Eyre adopted and which Moncrieff almost achieved. Rather, they were more likely to remain "trapped" by traditional diction and literature, and to opt for the opposite stereotype of the ideal savage who roams the florid glades of a terrestrial paradise. Such writers were to set up the other aspect of the double image of the Aborigine.

"The very ideal of a wild man, with all the romance of his agility, ferocity, and love of daring..."

The favourable characterisation of the Aborigine is the result of several literary and artistic influences. To say that he is depicted as a "noble savage" is almost meaningless because that concept has been so variously interpreted and embellished. It is undeniable, however, that for many writers the native becomes a type of superman living outside the debilitating influence of civilisation, the male displaying the virtues and capabilities of all that epitomised contemporary praiseworthy masculinity. (The attitude to the Aboriginal woman is significantly different, notions of "primitive" femininity being located outside the codes of "noble savagery". These issues will be treated later in this chapter.)

There was a large stock of images and characters which writers could derive from classical legend as well as from Edenic and arcadian traditions. Also the visual arts exerted a strong influence on the literary portrayal of the Australian native. Publishers' engravers were constrained by certain tenets of taste, which required that the appearance and the actions of human figures in a landscape must be as inspiring as the picturesque landscape in which they were (almost inevitably) set. One of the original formulators of this enduring sense of taste was Sir Joshua Reynolds, who had proclaimed that any human subject depicted in a painting "ought to be of some eminent instance of heroic action, or heroic suffering" so that the portrayal "powerfully strikes upon the public sympathy".[62]

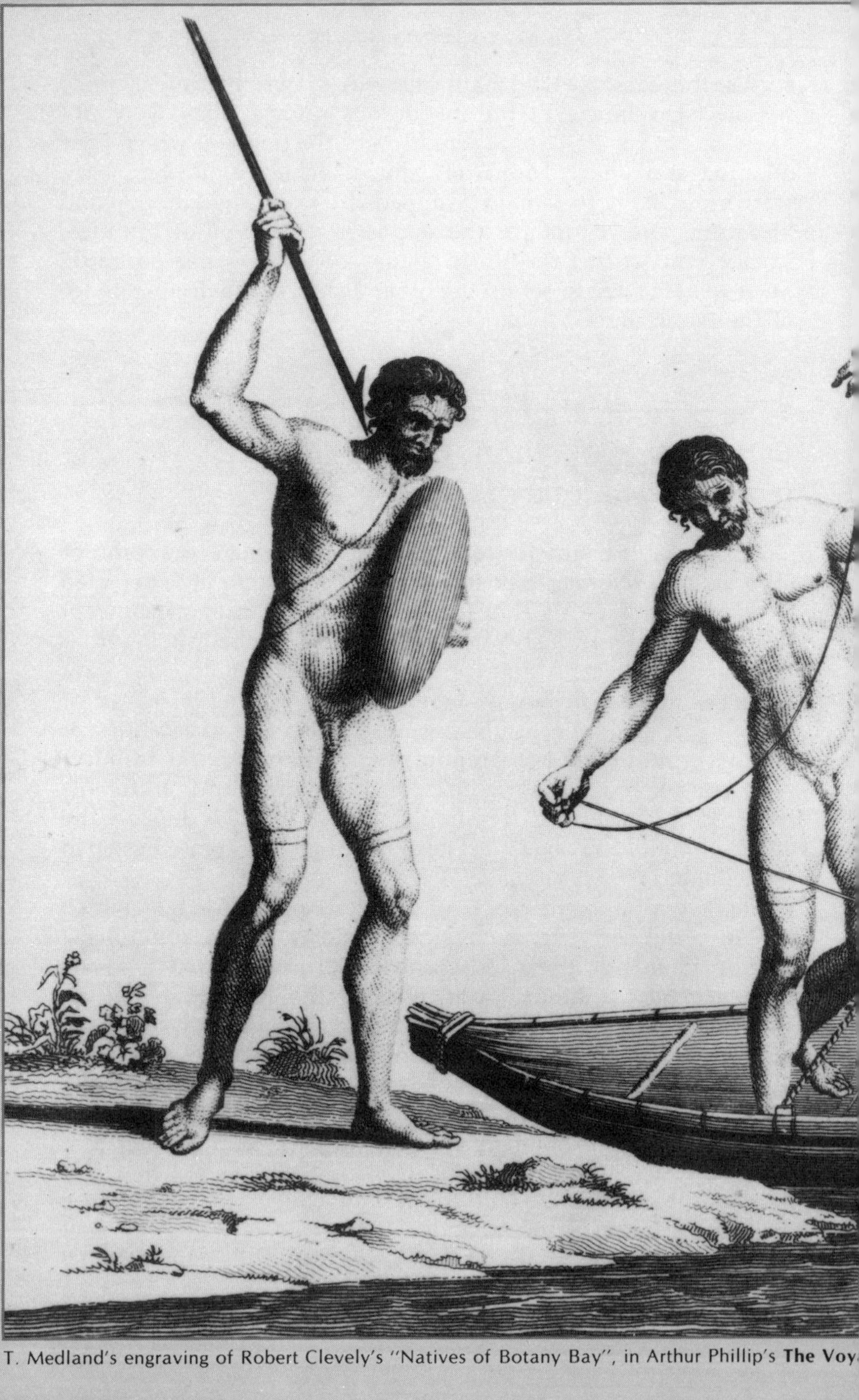

T. Medland's engraving of Robert Cleverly's "Natives of Botany Bay", in Arthur Phillip's **The Voy**

overnor Phillip to Botany Bay (1789). *By permission of the Fisher Library, University of Sydney.*

Such thinking held sway until well into the nineteenth century. As Bernard Smith has remarked, pictorial representations of lowly savages could offend propriety: "publishers, it seems, while utilizing original natural-history illustrations drawn on the spot, rejected similar drawings of native people. The rejection was due, doubtless, to a question of taste".[63] Certainly the lithographed images which often accompanied the literary representations of the Australian native predisposed readers to expect verbal descriptions of an admirable primitive performing heroic or exemplary actions in a felicitous environment. And certainly there were several writers prepared to corroborate the expectations of the market.

In the literary characterisation of an exemplary native, courage is a prerequisite. In one of the early "ennobling" texts, Hawkesworth's Captain Cook marvels at the fact that two warriors greeted his landing party steadfastly in the face of overwhelming numerical odds:

> They brandished their weapons, and seemed resolved to defend their coast to the uttermost, though they were but two, and we were forty. I could not but admire their courage.[64]

As the image is gradually formulated, such valour is repeatedly aligned with a sense of honour and gallantry which places the Aborigine in a literary mould similar to that of a classical warrior. Adversaries respect one another as Hector did Achilles, and in the tradition of so many sons of Mars, the Goddess Venus can waylay them ruthlessly. As David Collins affirms:

> Friendship and alliance were known to subsist between several that were opposed to each other, who fought with all the ardour of the bitterest of enemies, and who, though wounded, pronounced the party by whom they had been hurt to be good and brave, and their friends.[65]

Similarly Watkin Tench writes of Colbee, a Botany Bay Aborigine: "Love and war seemed his favourite pursuit; in both of which he had suffered severely".[66] Also, in this vein, Moncrieff's Ben-ni-long is a warrior whose just vengeance matches his eloquence: "Aye, let the colourless strangers fear! that have usurped our plains, and would fain extirpate our race! let them beware the Caffre's just revenge".[67]

Far from being predominantly warlike, however, the idealised Aborigine is without malice. When discussing the Aborigine's

Chambers' engraving of Sydney Parkinson's "Two of the Natives of New Holland advancing to
mbat". *By permission of the Mitchell Library, Sydney.*

character *before* the advent of the Europeans the *Alexander's East India Magazine* paints a typical portrait tinged with sentimentality:

> The New-Hollander is a savage, without the faintest tincture of the cruelty of the savage. The first impulses of his nature have ever exhibited themselves in kindliness. . . But he is a savage in the paucity of his wants; he has no desires, no call beyond the gratification of his present hunger and thirst.[68]

As in Arcady, here is the imagined society of the ideal Aborigine, "mine" and "yours" are meaningless words. These people own nothing and everything, as George Barrington asserts:

> That happiness is obliged to result from property, is by no means true, for few savages have less to call their own, than those of New South Wales, and yet they are perfectly happy; this arises from only seeking what is requisite to satisfy nature, and any thing more they will not keep.[69]

Taking the fantasy of the perfect culture to its logical conclusion, Sir Thomas Mitchell earnestly evokes visions of Eden when discussing white people's transgressions on native territory:

> [The Aborigines] prefer the land unbroken and free from the earliest curse pronounced against the first banished and first created man. The only kindness we could do for them, would be to let them and their wide range of territory alone; to act otherwise and profess good-will is but hypocrisy. We cannot occupy the land without producing a change, fully as great to the aborigines, as that which took place on man's fall and expulsion from Eden. They have hitherto lived utterly ignorant of the necessity for wearing fig leaves or the utility of ploughs. . . We bring them the punishments due to original sin even before they know the shame of nakedness.[70]

Moreover, despite E.W. Landor's contention that they are the "most light-hearted, careless, and happy people in the world" and that they subsist on the produce which "happens to fall in their way"[71], the model Australian savages are nothing like indolent hedonists. When survival requires exertion in the wilds the idealised Aborigine can be as ingenious, tireless and harmonised with nature as the Deerslayer character which James Fenimore Cooper was portraying in America in the 1820s:

> The person of the Australian is singularly athletic, flexile, and strong. He bounds along the earth with the fleetness of the deer; the resilience of his limbs is almost fabulous; no dangers repel him; no fatigues subdue him; inured to toil, to the daily chase for a dinner, and to the perpetual companionship of the forest tribes he presents the very ideal of a wild man, with all the romance of his agility, ferocity, and love of daring.[72]

Although native ferocity is not denied, it is presented as part of a natural violence, in accordance with the interaction of the species. When he is free from the contingencies of subsistence, the admirable savage is a gentle man with child-like desires and inclinations. Even Watkin Tench remarks on the "gentleness and humanity of. . .disposition" of an Aborigine in the presence of children.[73] Such ideally portrayed natives are in complete harmony with their environment. When Thomas Mitchell becomes adulatory, he is extreme. The singing of native women and children seems to him to be the "overflowing of the animal spirits". Free in their Edenic land, the Aborigines are "so contented and happy, that the overflowings of their hearts [are] poured forth in song! Such is human nature in a wild state!"[74]

All through the 1770 to 1850 period such admirable natives roamed the imagined Australian landscape. They sang and danced at the same time as other writers' Aborigines murdered and pillaged and committed unspeakable rites on the fringes of colonial settlements. One of the images could not survive. The noble Aborigine was bound for extinction, but also for a canonisation of sorts.

"to speak in the most favourable terms of the aborigines, whose degraded position in the midst of the white population affords no just criterion of their merits. . ."

In 1848 Thomas Mitchell was praising the Aborigines just as enthusiastically as Captain Cook had done when noting in his journal on August 1770 that "they are far more happier [*sic*] than we Europeans" because they "live in a Tranquillity which is not disturb'd by the Inequality of Condition: The Earth and sea of their own accord furnishes them with all things necessary for life".[75] However, in the progress of time the alternative image of the treacherous native came to be credited as current and factual.

In much the same way that the conflicting images of Australia as hellish and paradisaic were compromised in the image of an Australian Purgatory, so the divergent attitudes about the native were resolved to a certain extent during the 1830s and 1840s. The idealised Aborigine became a nostalgic figure of lost innocence, a character who was presently suffering humiliation and degradation under the influence of colonial society now that his golden age of dominance in the Australian environment had waned.

By this time in England, "savagery" was no longer a vogue. In H. N. Fairchild's words, the "history of the Noble Savage from 1810 to 1830 is in the main the history of a dying convention".[76] Science presents a harsh picture of nature, and, as Fairchild continues:

> [it] becomes more and more difficult to think of her [i.e. nature] as a kind mother...And the evolutionary conception of man likewise makes it more and more difficult to regard primitive beings as ideal. Hence the Noble Savage, deprived of his philosophical significance, becomes a mere outworn fad, and gradually gives place to other aspects of the romantic spirit.[77]

In an atmosphere of scepticism, reports of the Aborigine's degeneracy could gain more credence. By the 1830s the black Australian population had been decimated. Contact with the whites had introduced the natives to smallpox and alcohol, against which they had no conditioned resistance. Moreover, the advance of civilisation meant the violation of the black peoples' land, with which they had a deeply spiritual relationship. By occupying and clearing the land, the colonists tore the very soul from a proud race. Such an outrage had a more murderous effect than arsenic or gunpowder and lead, all of which were also utilised efficaciously.

As a result, when the Aborigines were encountered in civilisation, they were frequently bewildered and cowed, diseased or alcoholic. To the English observer the urban Aborigine sprawled at the base of human hierarchy, blinking through bestial eyes. Moreover, because any *favourable* description of the Aborigine almost invariably located him in a wild setting, uncorrupted by white people and city-life (the new horror of the nascent industrial age), and because the advance of civilisation rendered the rural native more and more scarce, the idealised Aborigine came to be regarded as an historical relic at the same time as the "fallen" native in the cities was increasingly conspicuous. Ironically, then, as Bernard Smith has remarked, just as the overall image of Australia was improving now that prosperity was eliminating some of the taint of convictism, impressions of the contemporary Aborigine were deteriorating irrevocably.[78]

In the 1830s and 1840s therefore, with more towns becoming established throughout the colony, evocations of the Australian noble savage take on elegiac tones. Mitchell, for example, observes the passing of a paragon:

> The half-clad native finds himself in a degraded position in the presence of the white population: a mere outcast, obliged to beg a little bread. In his native woods, the "noble savage" knows no such degrading necessity. All there participate in, and have a share of, Nature's gift.[79]

Colonisation was progressing, and the completely "uncivilised" Aborigine was disappearing. The image of the Aborigine was being reassessed: perhaps the idealised savage actually did exist in Australia once upon a time, but not in the present.

By 1838 Thomas Mitchell could reminisce about the days before the fall, when the true Aborigine roamed all the land:

> My experience enables me to speak in the most favourable terms of the aborigines, whose degraded position in the midst of the white population, affords no just criterion of their merits.[80]

The idealised Aborigine by now exists in another time, or in another place, decades and kilometres away from the developing cities. It is only in the bush that these model Australians have a chance of leading their exemplary lives. Out there,

Augustus Earle's "Natives of N. S. Wales" (circa 1827). *By permission of the Mitchell Library, Sydne*

George Street

Mitchell continues, "they are never awkward; on the contrary, in manners and general intelligence, they appear superior to any class of white rustics that I have seen".[81]

Out in the bush, one could lead the pastoral life *par excellence*. This is a contention which Alexander Harris emphasises in *The Emigrant Family*. While continuing his attacks on the self-satisfied colonial society Harris administers the unkindest cut by comparing the civilised whites unfavourably with the wild blacks. The author makes his point when "new chum" Willoughby Bracton converses with an "old hand" who had gained the knowledge of experience:

> "The natives appear a very degraded race," observed Willoughby.
>
> "About the settlements, they are undoubtedly: but in their primitive state I have always felt inclined to think them far less vicious than the mass of civilized society."[82]

By adopting such an attitude, much to the detriment of the remaining Aborigines, writers could validate both aspects of the double image of the native. The surviving urban blacks were confirmed as being of the lowest caste, regardless of how ideal their ancestors may have been. The surviving rural natives were no longer representative of their race because their numbers were negligible and ever-diminishing. There was no way for the Aborigines to regain their previous felicity. Their land was lost to the whites and their prelapsarian innocence was gone forever. The existing natives were assumed to be despicable and irretrievable. The admirable Aborigines were now virtually extinct. As the writers presented the situation, the natives had been usurped as possessors of the land by the more energetic whites.

Significantly however, many characteristics of the ideal savage and his culture could now be extolled as innately Australian. The Aborigine had been part of pristine Australia, and his spirit still appealed to those who sought to identify an Australian ethos. Industrialisation in England was drawing people away from rural life and capturing them in unplanned, unhealthy cities. The prevalence of miserable urban conditions ensured that nostalgia would conjure memories of self-sufficiency in verdant countryside, kilometres away, outside the factory walls. Noble savagery was still an attractive theme, but it could no longer be attributed to primitive man. Therefore, "to replace the eighteenth century's black noble savage the nineteenth century produced a white one: the noble frontiersman".[83] Fenimore Cooper's Natty Bumppo, half white man, half Indian, fending for himself in a challenging new terrain, is an obvious example drawn from across the Atlantic. But Wordsworth's rustics such as Michael (or even himself as a child in *The Prelude*), investigating their own personalities and their immediate environments, can be said to have been exploring frontiers much closer to home.

With regard to Australia, although the native becomes a traduced and neglected figure in the colony, and although he is portrayed in English literature as a sadly inferior type of contemporary man, the imagined best features of a former Aboriginal culture are still relevant to an image of the colony. The noble Aborigine's outdoors activity, his virtues of stamina, independence, bravery, and communion with nature are all combined in the beginnings of a bush ethic (and perhaps also in its later corollary, the sporting ethic). Alexander Harris's admiration for the Australian version of the frontiersman is typical:

> A good hand at making his way in the bush is called a good bushman — A man is not entitled to the appellation until he has acquired a sort of tact of going right instinctively. The infallible accuracy with which some men will hit a point several miles off in a dark night, and all the way through thick forest, is quite astonishing.[84]

According to such a definition a bushman is harmonised with nature to the extent that he can be seen as a new member of Rousseau's select group of human beings who hail from a golden age which is separate from the debilitating, artificial or "contractual" life of civilisation.

Russel Ward touches on this subject in *The Australian Legend* when he quotes from a travel-book by Clement Hodgkinson (1845), in which the white bushman is favourably compared with two stock figures from the gallery of noble savages:

> The bushman of Australia, unshackled by the customs and constraint of civilised communities, may roam through the grassy wilderness, with his horse, gun, and kangaroo-dogs, with a

> thousand times more freedom than the wildest chiefs of the African deserts, or American savannas.[85]

The attractions of frontier-life in the Australian bush became the subject of several journal articles, novels and travel-books in the late 1840s. In E. W. Landor's *The Bushman* (1847), for example, the narrator and his two brothers leave England in search of a "simpler and less artificial manner of living than that which has become the essential characteristic of European civilization".[86] The narrator seeks health and happiness after being "condemned to death" by three eminent physicians in England, while the elder brother is simply "desirous of realizing the pleasures of rural life", and the younger, escaping a cloistered future in Oxford, packs up his Virgil's *Bucolics*, fits himself out with "Lowland plaid and a set of Pandaen pipes", and dedicates "himself to the duties of a shepherd" (pp.9-10).

With such aspirations they embark for Australia with notions (recognised retrospectively by the narrator as somewhat naive) of a country "very much of the same character as that so long inhabited by Robinson Crusoe" (p.10). They arrive at Fremantle anxious "to begin the primitive life of a settler as speedily as possible" (p.41). They strike out for the bush immediately — in a chapter entitled "First Adventures" — and live off the land by shooting black swans and catching mullet in the streams. Establishing themselves on a favourable tract of land they become successful graziers by dint of hard but exhilarating labour. As the narrator comes to know and love the bush, he admires the natives and is conscience-stricken that he had no moral justification in overrunning their lands. He acknowledges that the Aborigine was something of a lord in his own environment and that only a special type of white man — the bushman — can match the native:

> When once a man begins to believe that he is lost in the wilderness, he feels as helpless as one who is blind-folded at the game of blindman's buff. . . Those who are used to the bush steer their course with almost unerring precision by the sun, and a few known objects, but there are numbers who never acquire this power. The natives appear to know by instinct the direction of every spot they wish to reach; and many white men seem to possess the same faculty. [p.93]

In the environment which once belonged to the admirable native, an exemplary community comprised of remarkable Anglo-Saxon people was perceived to be developing. H. W. Haygarth, in *Recollections of Bush Life* (1848) saw the beginnings of a self-sufficient egalitarian society:

> Few places can show so strange a mixture, and yet so complete a "fusion", of the heterogeneous materials of its society, as "the Bush" of Australia. It is curious to see men differing so entirely in birth, education, and habits, and in their whole moral and intellectual nature, thrown into such close contact, united by common interests, engaged under such circumstances of perfect equality in the same pursuits, and mutually dependent on each other for all the good offices of civility and neighbourhood.[87]

In the land which was once the preserve of the noble Aborigine, a new idyll might now be enacted, as a writer from the *London Journal* affirms:

> For roaming, adventurous, and fiercely energetic dispositions — for men wearied by the carking cares of civilised life — and for those who are disgusted by the sacrifices it is necessary to make to hollow conventionalisms, who, swimming and struggling bravely against the stream of fortune, grieve and grudge at expending hard-earned gains in luxuries and ornaments they do not enjoy, but are compelled by custom to use — bush life has the charm of healthy independence[88];

and as Edward Bulwer Lytton declares as he turns away from civilised Victorian England:

> No one can tell how clear the memory of the wild Bush life becomes to him who had tried it with a *fitting spirit*. How often it haunts him in the commonplace of more civilized scenes! Its dangers, its risks, its sense of animal health, its bursts of adventure, its intervals of careless repose.[89]

The white bushman, who lives by instinct, knowledgeable of Australian nature, tracing the same paths and sleeping beneath the same skies that the noble Aborigine knew during seventy years of literary representation, becomes the new paragon of the English writer's Australia. Whereas in 1827 William Wickenden was imagining that "playful children" of blissful

Aborigines plaited "fairy wreaths of flowers" as they sat "with frolic glee" beneath "the orange bowers"[90]; by 1850 journalists were averring that it was the offspring of exemplary white pastoralists who "may be seen decorating themselves with flowers, or dragging a creeper to beautify the horses".[91] The trappings of an ideal Australian life remained the same; only the racial heritage of the fortunate participants was now different.

With a brutal irony, the surviving Aborigines who inhabited the squalid outskirts of the cities came to be regarded as all that remained of Australian humanity once the ennobling aspects of a bush ethic were completely negated; in fact they came to exemplify all that was "un-Australian". It was the "extinct" noble Aborigines who retained a degree of respectability in white Australian culture, as they were enshrined as models in the development of an Australian ethos, as prototypes of the figures of "the drover, the rouseabout and shearer" who eventually became, in Coral Lansbury's words, "the knights errant of Australian literature".[92]

Thus the problematic figure of the Australian native began to be integrated into the English image of Australia.

Part Two
Slaves

> "You be careful, Miss Mary. Women can find themselves in ugly harness, out here in these god-forsaken colonies. Worse harness than any you've ever kicked against."
>
> D. H. Lawrence and M. L. Skinner, *The Boy in the Bush* (1924)

The English image of the Aborigines can be seen to have influenced more than the developing Australian attitudes to the natives themselves and to the bush. It is possible to argue that the portrayal of women in Australian culture derives in part from a complex interplay of English images pertaining to savages, convicts and slaves.

As I will attempt to demonstrate, during the years 1770 to 1850 certain "connections" were set up between groups of people such as Aboriginal men and women, convict men and women, and "free" white Australian women. The "links" between writers' representations of such people were provided by concepts of "savagery" and "slavery", which were perceived at the time to be somehow common to all the abovementioned classes of people.

Continuing this line of thinking, one can then argue that, as the Aborigines and convicts began to be excluded from Australian society, the white Australian women were left to endure various prejudices underlying the representations of outcasts set up by writers during the colony's early decades.

"contemned by the males, as beings of an inferior order. . ."

Of those writers who praised the Aborigines, virtually all were opinionless about the women, for noble savagery is essentially a code of "masculine" vitality and virtue. Of the writers who unequivocally located the natives at the base of the chain of being, some felt in no way constrained to discuss the females of the species, the implication being that no further insights would be gained by considering them. Notably, however, many others cited the character of the women as the most cogent proof of native degeneracy, and because of the laudatory writers' reticence about native women, such citations went virtually unchallenged. In terms of the shaping influence of English opinion, the attitude to the female sex in Australia had unfortunate beginnings in literary representation.

If Aboriginal men were the very dregs of humanity, then the women, according to those writers who expressed an opinion, could be of dubious biological status:

> If their intellectual functions, then, are. . .far above debasement, how is it that the abject animal state in which they live, and their great and glaring deficiency in all the useful mechanical arts. . .should place them at the very zero of civilization, constituting in a measure the connecting link between man and the monkey-tribe? — for really some of the old women only seem to require a tail to complete the identity.[93]

Writers who sought to vilify the native women were pleased to observe that Aboriginal society seemed discriminatory in the extreme, roles being rigidly prescribed so that the males were the "leisured class" always on call for hunting and warfare while the females performed the daily toil which kept the community supplied with the essentials of life. These "facts" were seized upon as corroborative of opinions about native females' debasement. As the writers describe the state of affairs, the Australian environment can be harsh, and the savage life arduous; this is not a place where (presumed) female frailty can be in the ascendancy:

> Among savages, strength and boldness are the only valued qualities: in these qualities females are miserably deficient; and for that reason are contemned by the males, as beings of an inferior order.[94]

A woman without a man in a savage society is presented as a pitiable figure. Such is the sentiment of a poem entitled "The Aboriginal Mother", written by Eliza Hamilton Dunlop. The author was an Irishwoman who did know Australia at first-hand by virtue of the fact that she accompanied her husband in his vocation as Protector of Aboriginals at Wollombi and Macdonald River between 1839 and 1847.[95] Dunlop's poem was composed during the controversy of the Myall Creek massacre in which white stockmen slaughtered a community of twenty-eight natives. It was first published in the *Australian* on 13 December 1838, and it then appeared in the London *Australian and New Zealand Monthly Magazine* in 1842.

The tone of the poem is sympathetic. The Aboriginal mother mourns her warrior husband who has just died in a battle with the English. She addresses her child:

> For thy young life, my precious, I fly the fields of blood,
> Else I had, for my chieftain's sake, defied them where they
> stood;
> But basely bound, my woman arm, no weapon might it wield,
> I could but cling round him I love, to make my heart his shield.
>
> . . .To flee, my babe! but whither, without our friend our guide?
> The blood that was our strength is fled, *he* is not by my side,
> Thy sire! Oh! never, never can Toonboohra hear our cry,
> My bold, my stately mountain bird! I thought not he could die.[96]

Left alone in the wilds, without the protective male to guard them, the mother and child are rendered pathetically vulnerable.

Especially noteworthy is Dunlop's implication that the Aboriginal woman's plight is in fact simply an extreme version of the condition of women the world over. The mother's persona is distinctly "civilised" English as she expresses her sense of helplessness at the loss of "the blood that was [her] strength". The differences between the lives of "civilised" and "savage" women are to be seen as questions of degree rather than of kind. The black woman is especially desolate at the loss of her husband because in the wilds the strength of a "basely bound...woman arm" is inadequate for survival. Dunlop accepts uncritically the notion that a woman is physically vulnerable and therefore ought to be subservient to a man. The greater the exigency, the greater is the disparity between the sexes. The "Aborigine question" is utilised as a test-case for themes which are unequivocally European. The very *image* of the natives becomes colonised.

Aboriginal women's putative inferiority is often depicted in accounts of the social and "domestic" interactions within and between native communities. The women are invariably represented in traditional, sex-determined roles of servitude and submission: as wives and mothers. The husband/father is lord and master, as in this description by George Barrington:

> The women are kept in the greatest subjection by the men. If a tribe is travelling and meets any of our people, the women are made to retire to a distance, from which they are not suffered to advance till ordered; and on any occasion the slightest offence given to the husband is punished with the blow of the club, which never fails to cause a stream of blood, and very often a fractured skull; yet this inhuman practice appears rather to strengthen the wife's attachment than weaken it, and the very wounds are shown as marks of honour.[97]

The courting custom is a popular subject. As it is presented, it entails the seizure by physical violence of any woman whom a warrior desires for a mate. It is all part of a romantic ritual of dominance and surrender:

> The women of Australia exhibit a remarkable fidelity to their husbands, and are fond and affectionate mothers...The first act

> of courtship, savage as it seems, is generally a mere ceremony, to which the women submit not unwillingly. The savage has no time for long courtship, and knocks his mistress down, and carries her off by force, that her virtue may appear unimpeachable, and her resistance great. After this cruel ceremony she is not generally ill-treated.[98]

Indeed in the opinion of most authors the one aspect in which these native women might be considered admirable is their acceptance of subservience. There may be an exception in Moncrieff's Kangaree who prefers to be wooed by a white man rather than suffer the violence of an Aboriginal betrothal. However, in this case also the prospective bride is desirable because of her capacity to serve. Kangaree extols to Darby her own virtues as a wife: "She climb gum trees, like opossum, for you — get you honey — dig yam for you — make you fern cake, and sing low sweet song".[99] Of course, it is an offer Darby cannot refuse, and he readily marries into Aboriginal aristocracy.

Supplementing this image of women as the drudges of Aboriginal society, there is a widespread description of them as merchandise rather than as sentient beings, as cattle for male consumption:

> Women are treated in the most inhuman manner, wives being procured from adjacent tribes by stealing on the encampment during the night, beating a young girl on the head till she falls senseless, when her future spouse drags her off through the bushes, as a tiger would its prey.[100]

While "savage" passions prevail, respect for human dignity cannot be expected. As Aboriginal life is portrayed, the women are sexual objects. Certainly, it is cruel, but it is also presented as the "way of the bush":

> Those who delight in sentimental love tales, will probably be disgusted with the male natives of New South Wales, for their conduct to women renders them considerably inferior to brute creation.
>
> ...Strangers to the finer passions, they seek only the gratification of their brutal desires.[101]

It is significant that discussion of miscegenation is virtually non-existent. Regardless of its actual prevalence, interracial congress is too indelicate a subject for refined Christian writers and their readers. Black women's dalliance with convict men is discussed discreetly, disapprovingly, but only because the degradation of sinners ought to be held up as a lesson to all readers and because convicts are often regarded as another class of degraded savage. The women's behaviour is damnably lascivious, regardless of whether they are consorting with their native or their convict partners, and disease is part of the wages of sin, as Peter Cunningham asserts: "From their natural filthiness the [Aboriginal] women soon become diseased with gonorrhoea, and propagate this infectious malady among the convict servants who cohabit with them".[102] Even though the venereal disease which was epidemic in the colony was actually introduced by the new settlers, the Aborigines, particularly the women, were most often blamed for its propagation. While there were scapegoats, the guilt could easily be ascribed to them. "Sexual objects" or "damned whores", it was so often simply a question of classification with regard to Aboriginal women.

The English literary image of Aboriginal women at this time renders them so subservient, in terms of their survival capabilities, their roles as menial workers, and their sexual function, that many writers choose a particularly evocative and controversial term to describe the female native condition. Louisa Meredith, writing in 1844, is representative of many authors:

> These poor unhappy wretches are *slaves*, in every social sense, and are not even permitted to feed but at their husband's pleasure, and off the offal he may choose to fling them, although on them devolves the chief care of providing the materials for the repast.[103]

Even when writers concede a certain nobility in the male savages there is a damning consensus concerning the women, as George Angas indicates:

> The men walk along with a proud and majestic air; behind them, crouching like slaves, and bearing heavy burdens on their backs, with their little ones astride on their shoulders, come the despised and degraded women.[104]

Edward Eyre agrees: "Like most other savages the Australian looks upon his wife as a slave".[105] But certainly it is Richard Howitt who is most eloquent when comparing the native men ("the lords of nature") with the "miserable women" ("their peasantry, their slaves")[106]:

> I have never seen more graceful figures of many of the Australian blacks; the men, some of them vulnerable-looking, with quite Roman-like nobility of contour; bold, strong, well-rounded limbs and fine countenances. The lubras [women] as I have said, are not very beautiful; many of them are wretchedly put together...There is no necessity to go to Tartarus for a Fury: more wild and fantastic heads of hair, in elf-locks pomatumed with earth and whale grease, were never seen. Fear, Hate, and probably Revenge, would, meeting with these people, wish to change heads...Both men and women, lords and their slaves, are, though lamentably situated, and low as human nature can descend, human creatures.[107]

Even though Howitt is concerned to represent the native as degraded and deserving of usurpation by the squatters, the stock image of the noble Aborigine attracts and "controls" him momentarily at the beginning of this passage. Ultimately, however, he is brought back to his purpose by describing the "lubras".

The comparison of the Aboriginal women to slaves ties in with the portrayal of convict women. In this age of William Wilberforce and the abolitionists, the plight of the slave was widely publicised. Writers recurrently referred to a most pitiable persona, such as Charles Lloyd's "poor slave! Misfortune's harass'd child!/Who liv'st to weep, and breath'st to sigh", who is "from every friend exil'd,/And hid from Pity's melting eye".[108] In such an ideological climate, many authors compared the African's servitude to other forms of exile, and were reminded of the "inmates" of the gaol-colony at Botany Bay. George Loveless, one of the Dorchester "martyrs" transported for political activism in organising trade unions, is predictably bitter about conditions in the penal colony:

> England has for many years been lifting her voice against the abominable practice of negro slavery; numbers of her great men have talked, have laboured, have struggled, until at length emancipation has been granted to her black slaves in the West Indies. When will they dream of advocating the cause of England's white slaves?[109]

The convicts, exiled in what Alexander Harris calls "this system of white slavery"[110], are just as much outcasts as that most denigrated of the pariah groups, the native women. At Botany Bay a prisoner is condemned "like a negro to labour all day".[111] Depending on whether he or she is assigned to "a kind or . . . a hard-hearted master", the convict, "like a slave", can be trapped in "bondage — galling bondage" in Botany Bay.[112]

Moreover, another literary stereotype pertaining to convict women — that of the transported prostitute — reinforces the image of Australian women in slavery. In Robert Southey's *Botany Bay Eclogues*, Elinor describes herself as "the slave/Of vice and Infamy", who, for her sins, has been exiled to the "pathless woods,/Where the rude native rests his wearied frame/ Beneath the sheltering shade". This white woman's oppression is everlasting in this sorrowful land where even the indigenous inhabitants must struggle to survive. She can only turn incessantly to her "daily toil" in the hope that she may expiate her guilt and shame and thereby avoid condemnation as "the mercenary tool/Of brutal lust".[113]

In the same way that the Aboriginal women are described as sexual objects for the native men, so the female convicts can reportedly be procured at will, like merchandise. In Moncrieff's *Van Diemen's Land!*, the free settler Scapetrap ponders the convict ship as it sails into the harbour:

> Well, heaven grant the next cargo of condemned livestock our mother England sends to bless us with may be females. I'd fain make an honest woman of one of them. My store terribly wants another mistress.[114]

And J. C. Byrne affirms in 1848 that the practice is a lasting one:

> At all periods during the progress of the colony, and up to the present time, single men could obtain wives, on application, from amongst the female convicts, at the chief depot in Paramatta.[115]

Such attitudes ought to have been expected in a colony set up by a government which (according to Helen Heney) rebuffed Governor Phillip's objections to the squalid and insecure shipboard conditions provided for female transportees by asserting that "the conditions found successful for Negro slaves would do very well for women convicts".[116]

The issue of slavery is not the only connection between the English images of Australian blacks and convicts. Just as the Aborigines evoked favourable and condemnatory treatments from writers during the 1770-1850 period, so the convicts were envisaged, favourably and censoriously, as types of savages. From one point of view they could be romanticised as renegades who have rejected the squalid and evil urban society of abhorrent imprisonment. According to such sentiments the most admirable convicts were those who threw caution to the wind, and became bushrangers who communed with unspoiled nature and conducted themselves according to codes resonant of the Robin Hood legends. David Burn is an early contributor to this literary tradition which has persisted until modern times and has caused the ghost of Ned Kelly to ride through the expanse of Australian culture for over a century.

David Burn (born 1800) emigrated to Van Diemen's Land in 1825. Three years later he returned to Britain with a preparatory draft of a play, which he completed while living in Scotland and which was performed at the Caledonian Theatre, Edinburgh, in 1829, under the title of *The Bushrangers*. In 1830 he returned to Van Diemen's Land to reside for another eight years before coming back to England in 1838. The rest of his life was spent in Sydney and in New Zealand, where he died in 1875 after a prosperous career as a newspaper editor.

The Bushrangers (of which the only known copy, a manuscript in two different hands, is kept in the Mitchell Library in Sydney) concerns the exploits of a band of renegades led by Brady who is a freedom-loving gallant willing to risk death in his outlaw life so long as he is encouraged by the knowledge that he has "slavery behind, and liberty before". Aptly described by Leslie Rees as "a Tasmanian Robin Hood"[117], Burn's version of Brady continually rejoices in the "stirring life" of the bush, and he never forgoes an opportunity "to do a good action and prevent some hellish cruelty". In fact, Brady closely resembles another noble bush character from another theatrical Van Diemen's Land of the time; except for the skin colour, he could stand as the twin of W. T. Moncrieff's Ben-ni-long.

Brady's status as "chief" of the romantic bush-convicts is emphasised sixteen years later by Richard Howitt when he describes a now-legendary character:

> The more gentlemanly of them [that is, the bushrangers] in Van

> Diemen's Land are there what Robin Hood and Rob Roy were in Britain. . . Of these famous robbers, none are so much talked of for their generosity, their invariable respect and tenderness for women and children, as Mike Howe, and more especially Brady. Their life is one of reckless daring, of hourly peril, for they are always liable to be shot or hung; yet out of all this, they seem to draw a fearful satisfaction, a stormy pleasure.[118]

The similarities between such characters as Howitt's Brady and Mike Howe (a very different character from Moncrieff's murderous bushranger) and the laudably independent figure of the noble Aborigine are patent.

Concomitantly, of course, there are characterisations of convicts as the lowest caste of the hierarchy of white humanity. Escapees are reported to seek a kind of amnesty among native communities. Such action defines convict nature damnably, as J. Ross asserts in the *London Journal* in 1846:

> No civilized person would voluntarily join the savages except a man of bad character, a libertine, either idle or passionate, or both, and possessed of little or no understanding.[119]

Such convicts readily sink to degradation identical to that of the lowest members of the human race. John Lort Stokes recalls a story he had heard while His Majesty's Ship *The Beagle* had been berthed in Sydney:

> During the eleven years [a particular escapee] had passed in the bush, without coming in contact with any other European, he had entirely forgotten his own language, and had degenerated into a perfect savage. . . He received his pardon and went to Hobarton but such was the indolence he had contracted that nothing could be made of him.[120]

Furthermore, at this time tales of cannibalism among bands of escaped Van Diemen's Land convicts wandering the inescapable island were repeated often enough to become the grisliest elements of white Australian folklore. In J. C. Byrne's fairly typical opinion, far from displaying any qualities of mateship such convicts-as-savages are more likely to "tear, crush, and mutilate the bodies of their very comrades, and revel in the infliction of additional torture on those around them".[121]

Just as some writers discerned parallels between the idealised Aborigines in the bush and the romanticised bushranging convicts, a great many more authors found similarities between savages and degenerate convicts; and by extension, a convict woman is comparable to any Aboriginal woman in terms of degradation.

"the issue of 'dominion'"

When the portrayals of Aborigines and convicts are examined together, a web of images can be discerned forming around Australian women, "trapping" them historically in typecast roles as the most servile and unregenerate characters in the colony. Aboriginal women are described as poorly adapted for survival; they are supposedly dependent on males for protection, and therefore they are also inevitably represented as servile; they are slaves, in fact. Moreover, as writers describe the courting customs which prevail in the bush, the native women are described as sexual objects to be procured and "used" by the males.

Similarly, the convict women are regarded as the sexual merchandise of the men of their class and of their free white masters. This sexual subservience, allied with the convicts' employment as free labour for the colonists causes the convict women's status as slaves to be established unequivocally. And finally, the frequent comparison of convicts to savages serves to complete the representational "web" which ensnares white convict women along with their native counterparts. Convict women are denigrated in literature as the most despicable of white savages. In many respects this is also how they were actually regarded in the colony. In the convict society, where individuality and independence were forcibly negated, dominance over one's peers was the only means by which one might achieve a sense of self-esteem. The most readily exploited class among the prisoners was the women, slaves of slaves, physically, economically and numerically powerless. As Miriam Dixson elaborates:

> With convictism, the issue of "dominion", that is of *dominance*, came to bulk larger and eat more deeply into personality than it did among the free casual poor, a convict would tend to need his woman to be just *that* much more wretched than did the male of the free casual poor.[122]

The shaping influence of English literary opinion until 1850 served to reinforce an attitude to women which was bound to develop because of the original social organisation of the colony. The influence of the defamatory image was to linger so that future generations of women would be afflicted as well. Several writers accepted the premise that female Australian character was especially debased, and concluded that the future elevation of such fallen women was almost as difficult as the improvement of savages, even in this Australian Purgatory. Once again the commentator is J. C. Byrne:

> Young, tender, fair and beautiful, the daughters of Australia present a choice ground in which might be implanted the principles of morality and religion, but such alas! is not their lot; before childhood dawns into maturer age and womanhood, the book of vice and sin stands open before them, with all its thoughts, longings and desires revealed. The impassioned feelings of woman, born beneath the bright and sunny skies of southern climes, need but little to excite them; and if the body does not soon become as polluted as the mind, want of opportunity, in most cases is the only cause.[123]

For these daughters of Australia, the sins of their mothers were to be visited upon them, and the prospects of women's attaining respect in the community became even less encouraging. As Miriam Dixson explains, the heritage of Australian women presents daunting obstacles to people concerned to improve their status in contemporary society:

> Convictism, a form of slavery which performed a unique and still imperfectly-explored function for emergent capitalism, meant that women served as outcasts (when Aboriginal women were absent). Our founding mothers, the convict women, imprinted on our moral economy the vision of woman as outcast. Essential to the function of the outcast group is that it enables projection of negative feelings, of hatred and contempt away from the dominant group.[124]

Of course, the stereotype of the woman as slave and base savage is only one of several which have served as models by which Australian womanhood has been shaped, or rather, distorted. The others, such as the "God's police" character analysed so effectively by Anne Summers, or the stoic "drover's wife" heroine depicted by Henry Lawson, have been developed predominantly "from the inside", by Australians as they have sought to understand and to formulate their own ethos. It was from the outside that possibly the most pernicious stereotype came. Australian women inherited the side-effects of English writers' racist images of Aborigines, and became type-cast to some extent as reprobates divested of independence and moral responsibility.

The development of the English image of the Aborigine in many ways epitomises the growth of the larger image of Australia. In each case, two contradictory views were set up early, and writers eventually began to resolve the inconsistencies until arriving at a compromise wherein both views were made to interact to form aspects of a new image.

With regard to the natives, nostalgia for a bygone, arcadian way of life which was ostensibly indigenous to the south land came to be embraced in the bush ethic when the afflictions of the "defeated" urban Aborigines of the 1830s and 1840s became all too obvious. Out of the vestigial sentiments of patronisation and even loathing for the blacks there came a complex and harmful attitude toward women in this "land of the savage, the convict and the slave".[125]

By the middle of the nineteenth century a "blueprint" or pattern for an Australian ethos had slowly been formulated after previous versions had been tested and adjusted. This "blueprint" would itself undergo alterations in the process of time and experience, but the imprint of ideas about the Australian Purgatory, the disappearing noble Aborigine, the emergent white bushman, and "slavish" Australian women would still be discernible in Australian culture more than a century later.

CHAPTER SIX

Preconceptions and Perceptions:

TWO NOVELS BY PATRICK WHITE

> "Here we are talking about our country as if it did not exist until now. . .Or as if it has now begun to exist as something quite different."
>
> Mr Bonner in Patrick White's *Voss* (1957)

The year 1850 marks the end of the first stage of Australian history. In the second half of the nineteenth century, Australian society was to be subjected to the evolutionary pressures of the sudden prosperity and population growth stimulated by the discovery of gold in several regions of the continent. New layers were thus added to the image which had been developed prior to 1850: there was to be the new golden age of the 1850s; later would come the embryonic radical nation of the 1890s; then the myriad complexities of the twentieth century society. But as each new portrayal arose, the basic structure of the image of Australia as a Purgatory, which involved aspects of felicity and torment, remained influential.

When the goldrushers' tales of inestimable wealth in Australian earth gilded the English image of the colony, people were distracted from the more cautious attitudes which had been validated in the explorers' literature during the previous two decades. Moreover, the influx of migrants changed Australia's social composition so that the colony suddenly developed a population large and varied enough to begin to support its own literature; and it had an economy prosperous enough to encourage in the colonists a new sense of separateness from England. As a result, the formative pressures on national identity changed during the 1850s, from external to internal. That is to say the influence of English writers in formulating an Australian image was mitigated by the existence of many more Australians who were prepared to analyse their society for themselves. It was a time of rapid development in terms of cultural identity as well as economy, and the colony's future appeared so malleable and immediate that the problematic and somewhat sobering past could be regarded, temporarily and erroneously, as *past*.

Because the 1850s saw the burgeoning of an indigenous sense of Australian identity, there is still a tendency to overemphasise the importance of that decade and thereby to underestimate the impact of the foregoing eighty years during which English opinions about the colony had been so influential. Similarly much attention is paid to the 1890s as a formative era of Australian nationalism and political maturity, as the period in which the issues which led to federation in 1901 were crystallised and the nation "found its voice", with the publication of major works by such important figures as Henry Lawson, A. B. "Banjo" Patterson, "Price Warung" and the *Bulletin* writers.

There can be no denying the importance of the writing — creative and critical — which draws its inspiration from the goldrushes and the 1890s, but the earliest years of the colony cannot be ignored, for the artists, mythologists and historians continually trek back past 1850 to solve the riddles of the Australian present.

One of the purposes of this book has been to redress the balance so that we can acknowledge the enduring literary significance of the Australian image as it underwent a series of transformations prior to 1850. From a modern standpoint it is essential to understand how the earliest English literature concerning Australia has influenced current attitudes about the country, and it is hoped that the concepts of this book can lead to fresh insights into the work of modern Australian writers.

By way of demonstrating how English attitudes from the pre-1850 period have permeated Australian literature and culture, and in order to show how an awareness of these attitudes can enhance an understanding of modern Australian writing, I would like to present a reading of the work of a contemporary Australian author. This final chapter can be seen as a conclusion at the same time as it points to some enticing loose ends which trace back to unextricated patterns in the works of several Australian writers and artists. So, the conclusion may be a new introduction.

If one is to select a writer who exemplifies the interaction between English culture and "native" Australian experience and preoccupations, the choice of Patrick White would seem logical. This is not to say he is the only artist whose work is readily analysed with reference to the pre-1850 literature. Several factors have combined to validate a new awareness of the thematic and formal concerns of the literature dealing with Australia before the goldrushes. Influences such as an ever-complicating economy, the self-referentiality made possible with the ageing of white society, the domestic and international traumas of two world wars and at least one temporary seizure in the capitalist system (the nineteenth century "ethic" on which so many naive Australian dreams were founded) have all set the scene for writers of the intelligence (and perhaps the courage) of White, Francis Webb, Thomas Keneally and Judith Wright to reinstate the unconscious (though still motivational) drives of painful reassessment of our dreams. Traditions run through a culture, emerging, submerging, re-emerging as the times and economic circumstances (and perhaps artists) dictate. Writers like Patrick White, operating as both sensors and motors of contemporary ideas, are able to isolate the more pertinent concerns (such as the purgatorial process of "rationalising" Australian dreams) by plumbing and re-assaying the well of national history.

Patrick White's background places him amidst English and Australian traditions. His Australian connections date back to the 1820s, when his grandfather settled in the colony and began to establish the family as landowners. Yet the major part of White's formal education was conducted in England (at Cheltenham and at Cambridge where he read modern languages); and until he returned in 1948 to live permanently in Australia he had spent approximately twenty of his first thirty-six years away from his homeland. It would seem obvious that any analysis of White's work must examine the conflicts and integrations associated with the duality of being an Australian — a product of a unique natural and social environment — and being steeped in the English and European attitudes which are the inevitable legacy of his education.

The interaction is complex, but it cannot be discounted. White is an Australian author. This is not a simple statement. It means at least three things: (a) he writes from personal experience of a unique native land; (b) as a white Australian whose cultural and genetic roots lead back to Europe, he writes against a background of the great traditions of European literature; (c) being a twentieth century Australian he writes in a society whose characteristics have been influenced by the reception, during the colony's formative years, of English opinions and myths about Australia. It is the third factor which I wish to consider in order to supply another perspective on White's art specifically and on Australian literature generally.

Even if one disregards White's biographical background, it remains obvious that his writing requires examination in conjunction with the material treated in the rest of this book because so many of his thematic and formal characteristics are demonstrably derived from the pre-1850 literature, notably from the works of the great explorer-authors, Mitchell, Sturt and Eyre.

It is worth remarking that his only two historical novels have been set in the late 1830s (*A Fringe of Leaves*) and the 1840s (*Voss*). Historical novels, by definition, involve the examination of past experience. As Georg Lukacs explains, such a retrospective view allows an author to select and analyse more objectively the "essential aspects" of the social life of a community; this is in contrast to a chronicle of the contemporary scene, where one is always in danger of becoming lost "in a whirlwind of details of apparently equal significance, for life has not done its selecting through the test of practice".[1] Of course the novel's relevance to contemporary life depends greatly on the pertinence of the chronological setting chosen by the author. To invoke Lukacs again, the writer ought to select a period in which "extreme possibilities" of aspiration and action are open to characters whose choices are determined by the decisive development of a society which is in the process of becoming "modern".[2] If the novelist deals with a period in which events occur which clearly shape the progress of a society until the present day, then the novel can be adjudged contemporary at the same time as it is historical.

White's choice of the 1830-1850 period in his historical novels indicates that he regards these decades as fundamental to the development of an Australian ethos. Of course, it may be objected that it is merely coincidental that the two actual incidents (concerning Eliza Fraser and Ludwig Leichhardt) which form the skeletons of *A Fringe of Leaves* and *Voss* occurred during the period. Even so, the facts remain that White was attracted to these incidents which occurred during these specific decades; he recognised them as somehow significant, and he consciously chose to adhere roughly to the chronology of the events even though he was at liberty to "fictionalise" any aspects of history.

By choosing this historical period and by working in similar fields to those surveyed by Sturt, Mitchell and Eyre in their "proto-mythic" texts, White invested the explorers' time, works and personalities with legendary status. He excavated the submerged images of the 1830s and 1840s and demonstrated their enduring pertinence to modern Australian society.

Part One
Voss *and the Diminishing Paradise*

As well as being an historical novel *Voss* is also part of the "explorer's literature" genre. On more than one occasion White himself has acknowledged his debt to Eyre's *Journals* and to the story of Ludwig Leichhardt.[3] The influences of explorers' writings abound in the novel. As J. F. Burrows has rightly discerned, for example, there are obvious similarities between Eyre's *Journals* and *Voss*, particularly in each protagonist's "half-comprehended and obsessive determination to make a futile journey rather than none at all".[4]

From the point of view of historical veracity in dealing with the 1840s, it is logical that White should concentrate on an explorer, for characters such as Leichhardt, Mitchell, Sturt and Eyre were the celebrities of their day. From an aesthetic perspective, the decision to structure the novel around the quests of a foreigner obsessed with comprehending the continent is appropriate to White's intentions and preoccupations in *Voss*. As a literary type, the explorer is similar to the detective in serious crime literature. Each character-type is an investigator searching for truth about a mystery which requires elucidation; and as a protagonist, each character leads the uninitiated reader into the workings of a disturbing and fascinating world. In *Voss*, the protagonist is the "guide" who absorbs dreams based on foreigners' expectations of the land, and who then tests them against the realities of experience in an Australia which is on the point of developing a sense of independent identity.

Hopes and Dreams

In chapter eight of *Voss*, just after the explorers have left the Jildra property of the aptly named Brendan Boyle and have set out for the Australian interior, the German rides forward singing, in his vernacular, of a soul who moves toward a "great blueness".[5] The song underscores the action most appositely because Voss is approaching a region as immense and mysterious as the sky or the sea, where affairs of the soul — damnation and regeneration — will be highlighted. As the novel progresses, the narrative is directed constantly toward the centre of Australia, where spiritual mysteries might be uncovered. Contributing to the tradition of the "diminishing paradise", White is preoccupied with the heart of the land. From one point of view in the novel, Central Australia is of purely mundane interest; such smug materialists as Mr Bonner and Mr Pringle are curious about the profits which would ensue should the party find "a veritable paradise adorning the interior" (p.62). But to more enlightened personalities such as Voss and White, and of course the reader, the fascination with the interior may be of a "purely metaphysical" character (p.62).

The journals of Sturt, Eyre and Mitchell caused the interior to be regarded as the ultimate stronghold of Australian secrets, as if "Nature had intentionally closed it upon civilized man that she may have one domain on earth's wide field over which the savage might roam in freedom".[6] Similarly in *Voss*, White depicts the interior as a theatre in which the inadequacies of alien European civilisation may be exposed, and in which some "native" knowledge about how to survive and flourish in the strange new world may be revealed to the white newcomer.

The established Sydney society represented by the Bonners is not fitted to the Australian environment. This is made clear in the first section of the novel, which contains a collection of satiric tableaux of genteel society which are comparable to those in Jane Austen. Voss is justified in his vexation with Sydney society when he pontificates to Laura about the colonists' lack of exploratory enterprise: "A pity that you huddle...Your country is of great subtlety" (p.11). Because the transplanted English bourgeoisie which is Sydney society is ludicrous in this expansive and unrefined setting (take, for example, the Pringles' picnic amongst the heat and rocks and glare), Voss's trek into the interior represents an escape into a seeming chaos which is daunting but also Australian and which must be confronted if European people intend to persevere in the continent. In the same way that in later novels Mrs Hare will "discover what is at the centre, if enough of [her] is peeled away"[7] and Mrs Hunter will arrive at the still point in an Australian storm by exposing herself to the natural elements[8], Voss and his party (and the reader) travel away from comfortable established society toward the centre of Australia in quest of an alternative to colonial life. By fleeing the stultification of that life in which people are thought dull when they "cease to talk about things" tangible (p.104), the explorers pursue an Australian dream.

John Docker, in his *Australian Cultural Elites*, argues persuasively that White can be located in a "Sydney intellectuals'" tradition which "tries to reject society as such, and looks to concepts of nature for an alternative reality".[9] Generally speaking, such a tradition is related to the veneration of the "noble bushman", that stock character who was popularised during the 1830s and 1840s when English writers combined their distaste for convict society with their nostalgia at the passing of the fictive ideal of the noble Aborigine, and sentimentalised an Australian version of the rustic swain. In the case of *Voss*, White does look to Australian nature hopefully. This is not to say that he has a naive trust in its bounty. At the same time as White is critical of the spiritless colonial society, he is also concerned to warn that Australian nature can ignore human endeavour most cruelly. Even so, despite its grimness, nature has much to offer people who manage to modify their European prejudices. As Peter Beatson has remarked, once Voss's party enter the desert in Central Australia the reader is not presented with "the barren wilderness one might expect. It has a teeming population of animals, aborigines, earth-spirits and ghosts", all of whom are intimately related in a "totemic, animistic religion" which gives meaning to Australian existence.[10] It is indeed a "country of great subtlety". Provided an explorer can survive the ordeal of learning about the environment, it is possible that the "chaos" which the party encounter in the interior's "approaches to hell" (p.336) can be appreciated in *Australian* terms. The garden of rational, refined civilisation may prove inferior to the natural desert. *If* one can survive the ordeal . . .

Accordingly, Voss and his party ride away from civilisation toward a confrontation with Australian nature; but the journey does not represent a flight from *all* society. The party comprises a microcosmic society (including the spirit of Laura Trevelyan who rides with Voss) which struggles to survive in an unknown environment and which deliberately gravitates away from established society towards an alluring (initially) and formless (increasingly) interior. Just as it is feasible to interpret the crew of the *Pequod* in Herman Melville's *Moby Dick* as America-in-miniature afloat in the unknown, so Voss's party may be young Australia searching collectively (though confusedly) for an alternative to Sydney's English civilisation: there is Judd, the emancipist convict; childlike Harry Robarts and the truculent Turner, who are employed as unskilled labourers; Mr Palfreyman, the ardent Christian and professional scientist; Frank LeMesurier, the mystic artist; and Ralph Angus, a member of the emergent "landed gentry". Furthermore there is the interaction between the white men and Jackie and Dugald, the Aborigines who are to guide the newcomers into the continent. The Aborigine in this situation is left with little choice but to attempt to adapt to the increasing European hegemony, to "expiate his innocence" (p.394), as White paradoxically describes the ultimate tragedy of Jackie's association with Voss. And finally there is the problematic significance of the Laura-personality who accompanies Voss throughout much of his journey. Laura, with her ambiguous sexual appeal to Voss and with her supplications to love, compassion ("a feminine virtue", p.213) and humility, represents for Voss, or more precisely, represents *in* Voss, a figure of sensibility which counteracts the traditional "male" values of pride, self-assertion and reckless independence.

On the literal level the explorers seek to cross the continent for an assortment of practical reasons. (Angus, for example, hopes to extend his pastoral property; and Harry Robarts simply idolises the charismatic German and will follow him anywhere to be in his presence.) On the allegorical level, a breakaway society gravitates toward the centre of Australian experience in search of a number of rewards, one of which, in this land of the convict, is "expiation". The Sydney community can never deny its guilt-ridden, "Botany Bay" background. It is a society founded on power and oppression, a community where unwilling people are "expiating their sins by force" (p.141). If Australia is to become a nation which does not simply duplicate the evils of that European civilisation whose shortcomings brought the gaol-land into existence, the expiation must be complete. It is the abiding concern of so many of the characters of the novel. Turner, for example, comes willingly to Australia to escape an unspecified sense of guilt which arises from his "vague record of vice" (p.287) in a lodging house in Kentish Town; Palfreyman later acts as nurse to the scorbutic Turner because the scientist regards the invalid as a "means of expiation" (p.287); even the self-righteous Mrs Bonner is moved to protect the orphan of her emancipist servant "as an act of expiation" (p.369).

If the expiatory journey to the centre is to be worthwhile there must be hope of atonement. Despair would render Australia an absurd Hell, but if there is promise of reward the land is endurable as a type of Purgatory. Indeed there are several signs of encouragement. The landscape itself evinces a remarkably regenerative life-force. Spring sunshine after flood-rains can draw forth the "green promise of a good season" in such proliferation that even the hardened explorers can flatter "themselves. . .that all the goodness which emanated from the earth was for their especial benefit, that it was even the fruit of their suffering" (pp.331-32). A rain-shower in the desert can "drown many doubts", for immediately afterwards greenness "masses" "in intensity" (p.259). Admittedly, since there is always the prospect that the earth "might absorb further punishment" (p.282), White never asserts that rewards in Australia are permanent. As Frank LeMesurier sombrely intones while surveying the "spears of grass massed distinctly in the foreground" after a rainstorm, "paradise may well prove to be a mirage" (p.260). However, the crucial fact is that, mirage or not, there are continual vivifying glimpses of paradise. As Frank himself realises later, there can be "love and poetry, as is only right, between the spasms of suffering" (p.286).

In the words of the authorial persona, it is possible for a few "stubborn" people to "blunder on, painfully, out of the luxuriant world of their pretensions into the desert of mortification and reward" (p.74). The fact that mortification and reward are here considered concomitant is crucial to an understanding of the journey into the interior. As Voss himself proclaims while inveigling LeMesurier to join the expedition, "To make yourself, it is also necessary to destroy yourself" (p.34). (R. F. Brissenden has rightly discerned here echoes from Goethe's aphorism, "'Stirb, und werde!' — 'Die and become!'".[11])

Because suffering is seen as an inevitable aspect of the regenerative process, it must be embraced readily. The quotation from Mahatma Gandhi which White used for the epigraph of his first published novel, *Happy Valley*, expresses a conviction which White has held during four decades of writing: "It is impossible to do away with the law of suffering, which is the one indispensable condition of our being. Progress is to be measured by the amount of suffering undergone . . . the purer the suffering, the greater is the sense of progress". This is not proclaimed with a masochistic sense of indulgence, but with expectation of the joy which accrues to inhabitants of Purgatory. According to the Helvetian epigraph from White's second novel, *The Living and the Dead*, it is the influence of *le plaisir* and *la douleur, l'un à l'autre* which can lead a person to discover the simple principles on which the order and felicity of the moral world are founded. As Laura declares to Voss, the "moments of severest trial are surely the obscure details of a design that will be made clear at last — if we can endure till then" (p.240). Purified substance emerges from a crucible.

I have spent some time outlining these preoccupations because it must now be acknowledged that so much of White's concern with stolid society and "formless" nature, with guilt and expiation, and with suffering and reward is directly related to the opinions expressed by the English writers who attempted to understand the new land during the early years of the colony, when European sensibilities struggled to comprehend the continent in its own terms. In the words of Judith Wright, much of White's writing is concerned with "a matter of death — the death of the European mind, its absorption into the soil it has struggled against".[12] By extension, taking into account White's fascination with the mutations of the European consciousness as it transcends chaos at the centre of Australian experience, one can argue that White is writing within a tradition established particularly by Charles Sturt, Thomas Mitchell and Edward Eyre. It is a tradition concerned with reconciling aspirations for a happy life in a new land, on the one hand, with the grimmer actualities of real Australia, on the other. It is a tradition which White invokes throughout *Voss* by way of his continual references to Central Australia as a land of dreams.

Early in the novel, when Voss has extricated himself from the Bonners' household after his first meeting with Laura, the German wanders into the botanical gardens, restlessly biding his time, "hoping soon to enter his own world, of desert and dreams" (p.26). One connotation of "dream" is "aspiration"; this is apposite here. The interior of Australia represents for Voss a region in which he might fulfil his self-assertive yearnings for freedom from mundane society. Often while planning his expedition Voss enters "in advance that vast, expectant country" (p.137). Like many writers during the colony's first eighty years, Voss projects his own desires on to the uncharted interior. As the authorial persona observes, "Places yet unvisited can become an obsession, promising final peace, all goodness"; a distant location can be invested "with those graces which one hopes to find at the heart of every mirage" (p.126). If dreams are credited with enough ardour they can shape lives. Palfreyman explains this to a sailor who thinks himself not guilty of adultery because he transgressed only in his drunken imagination: "If it happened in a dream that was not distinguishable from the life, it is still a matter for your conscience...*You wished to live what you dreamed*" (p.97, emphasis mine).

The party ride inland (guided by Jackie and Dugald who are about to revisit the realm of the Aboriginal dreamtime) and they are described as being "obsessed by their dream of distance and the future" (p.241). Temporarily, the escape from the torpor of Sydney buoys the party's hopes, as all of them, even the animals, seem cocooned in their fantasies: "All night the beasts were glutting themselves on dew and grass, but in the dreams of men the waves of grass and the waves of sleep were soon one. Dogs curled in the pockets of the grass, shivered and bristled as they floated in their own dreams" (p.165).

"Dream" has another meaning which also applies here; it can signify mere fantasy, as in "pipe-dream". And just as Sturt and Eyre quickly had to come to terms with daunting facts about Australia's dead heart, so the dreams of Voss's party are inevitably disturbed as they press on into the interior:

> The white men continued westward through *what could have been their own perpetual sleep*... Several days from there they came to a ridge, of hills even, at which a brigalow scrub *whipped their flesh back to waking*. Mules began to buck. The udders of those goats which had kidded were slashed and torn by twigs, and the glassy eyes of the most rational of all animals were seeing far too clearly as they advanced into chaos. [pp.210-11, emphasis mine]

In his examination of "The Place of the Imagination in the History of Geographical Exploration", J. L. Allen remarks that first-hand accounts of journeys into unknown territory almost invariably progress to a "point at which [the explorers'] preconceived image begins to break down" and they must gradually compromise their "pre-exploratory knowledge" drawn from "non-empirical lore" in order to comply with the facts of their actual experience.[13] Certainly such is the case in the journals of Sturt and Eyre, in which it soon becomes obvious that the interior is not the paradise anticipated through centuries. Similarly in *Voss*, once the land of the diminishing paradise is no longer *distant* it is no longer a land of *dreams*. Experience tests what Wordsworth once called "the deeper joy/Which waits on distant prospect".[14]

Experience and Compromise

This is not to say that dreams and their creative possibilities are summarily dismissed by White as he probes further into Australian experience. Through the relationship between Voss and Laura, White examines the workings of myth as he attempts to demonstrate that preconception and/or fantasy interact with experience in a constantly developing symbiotic process out of which emerges a national ethos which is in fact a means of survival.

Voss and Laura become acquainted stiffly, formally, as the result of "several cold conversations and one heated argument" (p.215). However, the relationship becomes truly passionate only when the two "lovers" are out of each other's reach, after Voss has written to Laura with his proposal of marriage and his request "to *join me in thought*, and exercise of will, daily, hourly, until I may return to you, the victor" (p.153, emphasis mine). Hereafter all the romance occurs within each person's imagination. The letters that they write are either never sent or never reach their destinations. Neither knows the other's mind exactly. The yearnings of each are projected on to a fantasy version of the other. After the proposal and acceptance, Voss carries with him a Laura of his own creation; and Laura conceals a Voss who satisfies her expectations. Each inhabits the dreams of the other. To this effect Laura writes Voss a letter, which he will never receive:

> I do truthfully believe that you are always lurking somewhere on the fringes of my dreams, though I seldom see your face, and cannot even distinguish your form. I only know it is you, I *know*, just as I have sat beside you beneath certain trees, although I could not describe their shape. [p.238]

Similarly Voss muses by the campfire and conjures up the Laura of his yearnings:

> From where he was standing, he could watch the secret place at the nape of her neck, of infinite creaminess, and the swathe of greeny-white veil round the hard, dark crown of her hat. He had never yet dared to touch, except through those formal gestures society expects, or else, the formless, self-explanatory liberties of sleep . . . And here was the little fire that he had made. How it flickered on the smile of this girl, or woman, as she was becoming. Her throat and shoulders were both convincing and convinced. He could not see the eyes, however. Because, she

> said, you cannot remember. It was true. He remembered her chiefly by the words and ideas they had offered each other, and by a certain poignance of her Italian hand. So that her form remained indistinct. While suggestive of hopefulness. [p.192]

The secret lovers benefit initially from the "insulation" from actuality which dreams can engender. For example, Laura can close her eyes, and she and her dream-Voss can ride as "two visionaries" "northward together between the small hills, some green and soft, with the feathers of young corn ruffled on their sides" (p.163). This is a "period of great happiness for Laura Trevelyan, her only known happiness, it seemed" (p.164).

In this same sequence, however, White emphasises that actuality invariably challenges the validity of the excitement and hopefulness of dreams: "Of course, the other side of her eyelids, there were many possibilities waiting to harm her" (p.164). On one level of interpretation White is analysing the process by which rather derivative dreams of simple happiness in uncharted Australia (note the pastoral verdure and fertility of the fantastic landscape through which Laura and her dream-Voss ride) are continually compromised by the intractability of so much of the real landscape which is encountered. This seems a close parallel, on a fictional basis, to earlier themes which emerged from the explorers' journals of the 1830s and 1840s. Just as Sturt and Eyre would finally be obliged to discredit the excessively "fantastic" literature produced about Australia prior to their own experiences, so Laura must eventually face the facts about mundane Australian realities.

Inasmuch as Voss and Laura both "invent" their respective "dream-lovers", White is employing the Doppelgänger motif. Each character is the complement of each other. Or, to put it differently, each creates her or his most complementary other. All in all, as Laura herself indicates, she and Voss "face each other, almost as in a looking-glass" (p.185). Together Voss and Laura comprise a "complete" personality unifying to confront and adapt to the new land. But how, precisely, does each character complement the other in the quest to arrive at the centre of Australian experience?

For Laura's part, when she accepts Voss into her imagination she begins to overcome her apathetic, foreigner's "huddling" attitude to the country. At the beginning of the novel Laura is still ensconced in the "luxuriant world of. . .pretensions" which dominates Sydney society (p.74). She is first seen attempting to impose "some order" on every aspect of life in the tidy Bonner household (p.7 and p.12). It is from such stultifying, conservative attitudes that Laura must "blunder on" toward Australian knowledge. She has already taken the momentous step of refusing to believe in the Bonners' genteel, Sunday-morning God; and she is prepared to shock her torpid family by asserting over Sunday lunch and steaming apple pie: "Everyone is still afraid, or most of us, of this country, and will not say it. We are not yet possessed of understanding" (p.28). She perseveres, announcing: "I have been afraid. . .And it will be some time, I suspect, before I am able to grasp anything so foreign and incomprehensible. It is not my country, although I have lived in it" (p.29). Now that she has met Voss, however, she has commenced her journey toward understanding.

Like the society which is establishing itself in Australia, Laura is an orphan who does not really belong innately in her environment. It is therefore necessary for her to understand and to adapt to her adopted land. Hers is to be a process similar to that which occurred so often in the writing of the early chroniclers of the colony. As White himself has contended, the writer in Australia must at some stage begin "to see things for the first time".[15] Laura must embark upon a mission which will enable her eventually to write to Voss proclaiming, "Finally, I believe I have begun to understand this great country, which we have been presumptuous enough to call *ours*. . .I could now lay my head on the ugliest rock in the land and feel at rest" (p.239). The presence of the questing Voss-spirit in her impels her to reject the materialist society in quest for some spirit of the land, in search for one version of the diminishing paradise.

Concomitantly Voss begins to understand Australia once his overreaching personality is progressively modified by the presence in him of the Laura-spirit of compassion and humility. Voss commences his quest without an appropriate respect for Australian nature. Initially his attitude is similar to Thomas Mitchell's haughty self-confidence. Voss rides out to conquer the land, determined to force the future and the continent to submit to his will (p.68). (A note about Voss's name is pertinent at this stage. The fictional Johann Ulrich Voss has a roughly contemporary historical namesake. Johann Heinrich Voss,

1751-1826, was a German poet, philologist and translator of, among others, Homer. The fictional Voss's name is therefore appropriately connotative of a character concerned with language, foreignness and "Homeric" ambition.) Laura is most perspicacious when she declares to Voss, "this expedition of yours is pure will" (p.69). And Voss himself sums up his initial attitude by haranguing Laura: "The humility! the humility! This is what I find so particularly loathsome" (p.90).

Even so, Voss finds himself attracted to Laura, and he is described most resonantly by the authorial voice as a man "who could have been trailing some humiliation" (p.26). After his proposal to Laura, Voss carries within him a slowly developing germ of humility. As the narrator informs us humility "was amongst the conditions she had made *in the letter* [of acceptance] *which was now living in him*" (p.199, emphasis mine).

Laura's influence is a call to love and survival in the Australian environment. If she and Voss are to continue their involvement, he must firstly return, and secondly and concomitantly, he must have learnt humility and compassion. He must have realised, as did Charles Sturt and Edward Eyre, that human beings must adapt to the continent and that they cannot expect to conquer Australian nature without themselves undergoing conquest and change. Voss is hesitant and reluctant in his progress toward humility. He is loath to relinquish his rather simplistic dreams of dominating the continent, of shaping it to whatever purpose he chooses.

As the novel progresses Voss never willingly embraces humility; but the indomitability of the Australian environment makes his compliance inevitable, and his arrogant personality must die by degrees. His will must bend to the spirit of the land. However, he does not embrace humility voluntarily. He is not prepared to become merely human. This is the significance of his death at the hands of Jackie. As William Walsh observes, the Aborigines should be seen not as murderers but as "priests of some other and incomprehensible god".[16] This spirit of the land may be meting out judgement for *hubris*.

Voss finally has humility thrust upon him, when he has no other choice. At the last he is "humbl*ed*" rather than humble (p.389). Whereas Laura has gained some "native" knowledge by heeding the Voss-spirit in her, by looking past the conservative colonial society, Voss pays the penalty for not changing his own preconceptions about himself and the land. He takes insufficient notice of the Laura-spirit of humility. Whereas Laura vivifies her existence by crediting myths about absorbing the land, Voss participates in his own death by refusing to allow the realities of his human frailty and the enormity of the land to temper his personal myths about the power of his own will. Unlike Laura, he fails to attain a balance between myth and experience.

The Country of the Mind

The expedition into the interior is in part a quest after the diminishing paradise. Literally, the story examines the practical possibility that the explorers might find rich and profitable grazing country. However, because the diminishing paradise exists predominantly in the imaginations of the questers, and because the interior is so often portrayed as a land of dream, the account of the journey is also manifestly an allegory of self-discovery. Each member of the party explores his own imagination. Each is forced to recognise his own delusions and to face the truth about his personality. For example, Judd, Turner and Angus find that they are all practical men (to varying degrees of laudability) who cannot continue to live on dreams and who must therefore abandon the quest; Voss begins to suspect that he will not attain the infinite, even though he continues his overreaching; and Jackie comes to realise that the white people cannot be exorcised, even though individuals can be killed: this is part of the knowledge that sends him mad. Australia is a testing-ground for hopes and dreams.

There is also a social aspect to White's explorer's tale. Insofar as the party can be regarded as a microcosm of the Australian colony, the social allegory is the psychic journey of each character expanded to a collective scale. Members of the new colony, dreaming of wealth and freedom (of paradise, perhaps) confront actual Australia and are forced to compromise their expectations and thereby to modify their collective consciousness. The journey outlines the progress of a society learning to adapt to the land, learning to "understand" (to use Laura's term) the spirit of the place. *Voss* details the way a society's myths impel its history, and the way history in turn causes modification to the myths as the process oscillates eternally. As White himself has suggested, there "is the possibility that one may be helping to people a barely inhabited country with a race possessed of understanding".[17]

The setting of the novel is Australia, especially the interior. Because Australia generally, and the interior particularly, have been as much dream-lands as geographical entities, the novel is inevitably set, to some extent, in the imaginations of the characters *and* of the readers. In a real sense *Voss* examines "the country of the mind".

Close examination of one passage from *Voss* demonstrates how White sustains the many layers of allegorical significance: literal or geographical, the psychological or personal, and the mythic or social. Early in the novel Voss rides out to Judd's property to meet the convict for the first time. The German is stimulated and disturbed by the encounter because he senses that Judd has already developed an understanding of the colony:

> Voss, who was looking down all the time upon the man's [that is, Judd's] massive, grizzled head, could not feel superior, only uneasy at times. It was necessary for him to enjoy complete freedom, whereas this weight had begun to threaten him. So he was chewing his moustache nervously, his mouth quite bitter from a determination to resist, his head spinning, as he entered in advance that vast, expectant country, whether of stone deserts, veiled mountains, or voluptuous, fleshy forests. But his. His soul must experience first, as by some spiritual *droit du seigneur*, the excruciating passage into its interior. Nobody here, he suspected, looking round, had explored his own mind to the extent that would enable him to bear such experience. Except perhaps the convict, whose mind he could not read. The convict had been tempered in hell, and, as he said, survived. [pp.136-37]

Voss instigates the expedition partly because of a need to "enjoy complete freedom". This idea of Australia as a land of individual liberty is one of the preconceptions that Voss nurtures as he continually enters "in advance" the "expectant country". The ambiguity of the last term is deliberate. Australia is a country constructed of expectations. But also, it is a country with expectant feelings because of the hopes of the people who comprise it; it is an anthropomorphic entity. Voss's Australia exists because human expectations exist, and for this reason it is appropriately described in human, "fleshy" terms. It is his own personalised country. *But his*. Ambiguity is used again to crucial effect in the sentence which follows: "His soul must experience first, as by some spiritual *droit du seigneur*, the excruciating passage into its interior". The sentence, indeed the entire passage, hinges on the ambiguity of the word "its". Does the pronoun refer to the "expectant country" or to "his soul"? In effect it refers with equal emphasis to both. Voss must pass, painfully, into the interior of the expectant country and into his own soul. By causing the reader to consider initially which concept the pronoun refers to, White forces an acknowledgement that the country and Voss's soul are one and the same. (This realisation sheds light, retrospectively, on Voss's remark when he was recruiting LeMesurier: "I have every intention to know it [that is, Australia] with my heart" p.33.) The journey into Australia is an exploration of each individual's "own mind". Then with the next sentence the word "experience" reverberates back through the paragraph. The journey into the expectant soul-country will be an experience difficult to bear; but also "such experience" as will be encountered in actual, geographical Australia will be challenging to the minds of all of the questers. Finally, Voss's consideration of the extent to which the other members of the party, and of the colony generally, have already explored their own mind-countries alerts the reader to the fact that a group of individuals, a society, is in fact projecting its collective consciousness onto the country.

The expedition therefore traces the path to Australian knowledge. As Voss muses to his dream-Laura, the expedition is concerned with "our other journey" (p.217), away from tangible certainties, into dream-land. "Australia" can therefore symbolise emotional, intellectual and spiritual experience. For this reason, images of the Central Australian landscape are employed by White to evoke states of mind, emotion or spirit. Take, for example, the scene in which Mrs Bonner and Laura finally achieve communication during Laura's illness: "These two people, looking at each other at intervals, in hope of rescue, had begun to realize that their whole lives had been a process of erosion. Oases of affection had made the desert endurable, until now the fierce heat of unreason threatened to wither any such refuge" (pp.357-58). Similarly, Laura assesses Voss as a character who offers "prospects to be explored" (p.19). And she describes him elsewhere in terms of Central Australia: "You are so vast and ugly . . . I can imagine some desert, with rocks, rocks of prejudice, and yes, even hatred. You are so isolated" (p.87).

The use of the Australian topography as a symbol is a recurrent concern in White's work. In his most recent novel, *The Twyborn Affair*, an image drawn from Central Australia is applied when Edith Trist blunders, miserable and alone, from a London restaurant, "looking in her bag to see whether she had the change to spend a penny or tip the taxi — or simply looking for reassurance as she crossed a desert plain".[18] Central Australia has become a symbol in literature. Once writers came to understand the continent, once they no longer needed simply to describe it, Australia could be used to symbolise despair, and/or Utopian aspiration, and/or ideas of purgatorial redemption, suffering and reward. From description through interpretation to symbol, the image of Australia has been carried by several writers. White is working in an advanced stage of its progress, but he could not have begun unless previous writers, particularly the First Fleet annalists and the explorers of the interior, had not surveyed much of the route already.

Life after Death by Torture

Humility and a willingness to reject the formality and materialism of colonial society are central concerns in *Voss*; and it has been established that pursuing such concerns is likely to entail suffering. In her notorious garden-party aphorism Laura rightly proclaims that knowledge "was never a matter of geography. Quite the reverse, it overflows all maps that exist. Perhaps true knowledge only comes of death by torture in the country of the mind" (p.446). English pride and prejudices must die before a more innate, "Australian" understanding can influence the mind.

Laura is the first character to sense that she has truly adapted to the land. She experiences something akin to an epiphany during the funeral service for the emancipist maid, Rose Portion. A violent storm suddenly blows across the city and rages round the mourners. The authorial voice describes events:

> Laura was calm rather than cold, as, all around her, the mourners surrendered up their faces to fear of anonymity . . . After the first shock of discovery, it had been exhilarating to know that terrestrial safety is not assured, and that solid earth does eventually swirl beneath the feet . . . she began to experience a shrill happiness, to sing the wounds her flesh would never suffer. [p.235]

Rose Portion had died as the result of giving birth to her "currency lass" child, Mercy, whom Laura will adopt as her own. Laura, the orphan English woman who is attempting to understand the country in which she has previously felt an alien, accepts Mercy, the "illegitimate" (in traditional terms) "native" fruit of convict suffering in Australia. As Rose is interred in the continent, Australian nature thunders in to impress upon Laura her own human frailty. With a sense of liberation she realises that she is in no way a superior being. She is simply a creature at the mercy of, and belonging to, the Australian environment.

Laura has come to understand that she must respect the land, just as Sturt and Eyre realised that they must compromise their ambitions to conquer the continent. She is now "blessed" both with humility and with her preparedness (provoked by the dream-Voss in her) to reject the materialist Bonner-society in order to strike out in search of something transcendent. This may mean that she is left with no security, with the solid earth swirling beneath her feet, but she is now completely adaptable and can allow the spirit of the land to begin to shape her. She explains her transformation (or is it beatification?) to Voss, in a letter that will never reach its destination:

> The material part of myself became quite superfluous, while my understanding seemed to enter into wind, earth, the ocean beyond, even the soul of our poor dead maid. I was nowhere and everywhere at once. I was destroyed, yet living more intensely than actual sunlight. [p.239]

She is learning to communicate with the spirit of the land.

Voss appeared initially as the explorer who was expected to guide the reader to knowledge at the Australian centre, but because of his *hubris* he is incapable of fulfilling this task. The lot falls to others. Laura is one. Frank LeMesurier is another. It is Frank who unwittingly corroborates Laura's sense of the redemptive understanding which arises from humility and from self-effacement even to the extent of embracing chaos, suffering and the "low-life" of convict guilt. Like Laura, Frank experiences an epiphany during a storm:

> The rain came, first with a few whips, then with the release of cold, grey light and solid water, and he was immersed in the mystery of it, he was dissolved, he was running into crannies, and sucked into the mouths of the earth, and disputed, and distributed but again and again, for some purpose, was made one by the strength of a will not his own. [p.249]

As with Laura, the knowledge which Frank absorbs from the storm entails both a feeling of one-ness with Australian nature, and an intense sense of humility in submission to a power greater than his own. He begins to record his discovered truths in poetry: "Humility is my brigalow, that I must remember; here I shall find a thin shade in which to sit. As I grow weaker, so I shall become strong" (p.296).

The poet surrenders to the mysteries of new, Australian forms: "O God, my God, I pray that you will take my spirit out of this my body's remains, and after you have scattered it, grant that it shall be everywhere, and in the rocks, and in the empty water-holes, and in true love of all men, and in you, O God, at last" (p.297).

Frank's view of Australian experience is similar to Laura's, and by virtue of the fact that these two visionaries concur, the reader is persuaded to accept their formula for understanding: one must acquire humility and maintain an awareness that the established Old World forms of behaviour and society must be changed because they are not entirely appropriate in Australia. It is a formula drawn from the oldest days of the colony, when English writers began to realise firstly that the continent ought to be understood and expressed in its own terms and not by application of English criteria, and secondly, that the discoveries in the interior did not open up a fantastic paradise. Therefore the emphasis was placed on the existing societies in Australia as regions in which a new life could be consciously constructed. After probing the interior, Sturt and Eyre had returned to South Australia where an experiment in an alternative Australian society free of convict guilt and prejudice appeared to be succeeding. Similarly, as Veronica Brady has explained, "unlike *Moby Dick* or *Adventures of Huckleberry Finn, Voss* does not end projectively. The frontiers are closed; what demands attention is what is objectively given".[19] The end of the quest is to be sought in the quotidian questions of survival and innovation in the society that has already begun to establish itself around the ridges of the indomitable inland.

The great heroic figure of Voss and the tragic romantic poet who is Frank LeMesurier may be the "stars" of the *dramatis personae,* but the fact remains that the novel does not end with their deaths. The final section of *Voss* concentrates on the people who have prevailed. How did they survive? And how do they live now?

A major survivor is, of course, Laura. She is perhaps a more important character than the two dead visionaries, for although she continues to feel alienated from the smug Bonner-society which she must inhabit, she perseveres with her "explorer's" knowledge, and attains a position — respected teacher and minor celebrity — in which her understanding might be passed on.

The other major survivor is Judd. Even before the expedition has begun Judd has come to understand and assimilate basic aspects of Australian experience, for he has survived convict life and has emerged "a union of strength and delicacy, like some gnarled trees that have been tortured and twisted by time and weather into exaggerated shapes, but of which the leaves still quiver at each change" (p.133). Having "risen from the tomb of that dead [convict] life" (p.133), Judd is an "improviser" who is "commendably adaptable" (p.22). Ultimately, he is a practical man who opts for life when he realises that Voss's goal is chimerical and necessarily fatal. "I cannot dream dreams no longer", he informs Voss, and turns back for civilisation (p.340). He is imbued with the nobility of a man who knows his own nature and is prepared to live content with it. Therefore, "[since] his own fat paddocks, not the deserts of mysticism, nor the transfiguration of Christ, are the fate of common man" (p.345), Judd turns for home.

In the final analysis, Judd's survival must be offset against Laura's. He has been gnarled to the extent that he cannot be "[reduced]. . .to dreams of the future" (p.243). Ultimately he does not have enough questing courage or the desire to seek new forms. Rather, he opts for the colonial *status quo* when he decides to return to his second-rate farm (almost literally in the shadow of the grander domains of Rhine Towers and Ralph Angus's property), to settle for what had dissatisfied him in the first place. Moreover, his prudence is not rewarded in the Australian environment. When he finally returns to civilisation he finds that his property has been sold, and his wife and sons have died: his tidy material world has disintegrated. Implicitly, one must be humble without losing the hope and determination to break the old moulds of a phlegmatic and spiritless materialism.

The Rhine Towers interlude is another aspect of *Voss* which is concerned with the development of successful means of surviving and thriving in Australia. Coming as it does at the very beginning of the trek into the interior, the description of the party's brief sojourn at the Sandersons' property forms a kind of prologue to many of the themes which will be elucidated as the party continues toward the centre. Rhine Towers is situated on the edge of known Australia, far from "fallen" Sydney. It is a model community (another Australia-in-microcosm) maintaining self-sufficiency in a decreasingly alien environment. Like Australia itself Rhine Towers is the product, in part, of Utopian expectations. For example, Voss participates in hopeful fantasies as he rides toward this version of the expectant country:

> Places yet unvisited can become an obsession, promising final peace, all goodness. So the fallible man in Voss was yearning after Rhine Towers, *investing it with those graces which one hopes to find at the heart of every mirage,* entering its mythical buildings, kindling a great fire in the expectant hearth. Its name glittered for him, as he rode repeating it to himself. [p.126, emphasis mine]

Continuing the analogy between this property and Australia, the narrator notes that Voss approaches the Sandersons' community "exalted by hopes of *regeneration*" (p.125, emphasis mine). Like Australia generally, Rhine Towers can be seen as the product of suffering as well as dreams. To this effect, the spirit of the community is symbolised by the pottery which is created from the soil on which the model society is constructed:

> If the clear colours and honest forms of their pottery had, in the one case, run, in the other, been distorted by the intense heat in which that had been tried, its poignance had increased.
>
> That was the quality which predominated in the dining room, in the whole homestead at Rhine Towers, a quality of poignance, for heights scaled painfully, or almost scaled. Incidental failure did not rob the Sandersons of success. It was perhaps the source of their perfection. [p.131]

Although Rhine Towers is merely part of the real world of heat and flies and daily routine (Frank promptly realises on arrival that the "serpent has slid even into this paradise", p.129), it is as close to paradise as any Australian region might be. It has progressed through all the stages of Australian experience, and has survived, encouragingly, to become "self-supporting" (p.131). It is a world in which yearning has been tempered by pioneers' suffering to produce a regenerated society which is a successful compromise between the initial dreams and the worst of Australian experience. Dreams are not completely dispelled; rather they are still credited sufficiently to be a positive benefit. Even Voss begins to luxuriate in the "healing air", as when he awakes one morning: "For a while the man lay there, trying to remember what he had dreamt, but failing. Irritated at first, he then remembered that it is enough to have dreamt. So he continued to lie, and the faded dream was still part of him" (p.140).

The experience at Rhine Towers is also a kind of overture to the discourse about legend and history which dominates the final section of the novel (and which always underscored the writings of the original explorer-writers of the 1830s and 1840s). The question of the interrelationship between dreams and the world which people perceive and construct, is taken up again at the conclusion when the survivors attempt to assess Voss's importance now that he has passed into myth as well as history. When Voss and his dream-Laura "rode on above the dust, in which they were writing their own legend" (p.367) they were involved in a process of influencing the way people interpret the continuing Australian experience, a process which Mitchell, Sturt and Eyre had instigated a century before White created Voss.

White examines the process in the scenes involving Colonel

Hebden, the English military officer who mounts an (unsuccessful) expedition in order to sift through the traces of history to find the truth (p.413), as if that can be the end of the matter. In Hebden's opinion, speculation about Voss is of no consequence; only the conclusive evidence of historical truth is "acceptable" (p.413). This contrasts with Laura's tendency to think of Voss in terms of myth (p.329). For her, Voss's significance can be assessed in any way she chooses, as long as the interpretation is "true" to the world as she perceives it. For this reason Laura challenges Hebden's empiricist teleology: "It is all lies. While there are men, there will always be lies. I do not know the truth about myself, unless I sometimes dream it" (p.413). Indeed Hebden is being "cruel" (p.413) by attempting to shatter Laura's faith in myths with inconclusive snippets of fact, as if the effect of believed illusion can be replaced by . . . nothing.

Even Judd, whose "eternal craving for material evidence" (p.430) had once so infuriated Voss, is shown finally to be living according to myth, now that his solid pragmatic world-view has been invalidated by the loss of his wife, his sons and his livelihood. He opts instead to believe in the legend of Voss as the Christ-figure who died with a spear in his side so that his spirit might permeate and placate the hostile continent. Judd's dream-Voss died so that others might be saved. Indeed Laura and Judd concur in their interpretations of Voss's lasting importance: Judd informs Laura and Hebden that the "blacks still talk about him [Voss] to this day. He is still there — that is the honest opinion of many of them — he is there in the country, and always will be" (p.443); and Laura's last words (spoken to an ingenuous English newcomer) echo those of her fellow survivor: "Voss did not die . . . He is still there, it is said, in the country, and always will be. His legend will be written down, eventually, by those who have been troubled by it" (p.448).

Certainly Laura is "living off [her] imagination" (p.325), as Lieutenant Radclyffe has accused her earlier in a discussion concerning Voss, but in her case it is an effective way of imparting meaning to her life. She is a visionary, like Frank LeMesurier, like Voss himself, and, to a lesser extent, like Judd; to quote from one of Frank's poems, such people "enjoy the immense freedom of dreams, in which nobody [but the dreamer] believes" (p.295). On a broader level, a nation can also enjoy such freedom if it takes heed of its legends. The dream-Voss who came to understand the spirit of the land may never be empirically verifiable, but his myth can help vivify the national ethos. The dream-Voss who was sacrificed to the new land is more potent than the actual Voss, and his spirit can only be found by examining the environment itself. Thus, the "air will tell us" the answers to Australian legends.

Language and the Australian Experience

In his oft-quoted autobiographical sketch, "The Prodigal Son", Patrick White describes the process by which he, as writer, had to come to terms with Australia when he returned to the country after his long "exile": "Writing, which had meant the practice of an art by a polished mind in civilized surroundings, became a struggle to create completely fresh forms out of the rocks and sticks of words".[20] As Voss advances toward the interior of the country (of the mind and of actual topography) he and the reader come to realise that comprehending the land and developing an Australian variant of the English language are concomitant processes. And for the use of words to change, old attitudes and criteria must be challenged. Minds must adapt as new experiences occur.

A journey into geographical Australia, once described, is also a journey toward the frontiers of one's language, and the attempts to express what is encountered on the physical journey therefore map out an investigation of the writer's and the reader's own minds. Wilson Harris develops this point in his fascinating article on *Voss*: "A mental landscape *is* a field of authentic discovery — a field where 'new' things are 'seen' as though language itself is the ground of an interior and active expedition through and beyond what is already known".[21] Without transcending "what is already known", writers cannot express Australian "newness". This is a theme which White returns to in *The Twyborn Affair*, most explicitly in the novel's epigraph from David Malouf's *An Imaginary Life*: "What else should our lives be but a series of beginnings, of painful settings out into the unknown, pushing off from the edges of consciousness into the mystery of what we have not yet become".

Just as English writers of the early colonial years were bound by their own literary styles and criteria when they attempted to express Australia, so Voss feels impeded by his own linguistic heritage as he, this "kind of foreign man" (p.7), begins his quest. Invariably in Australia he finds himself "resenting bitterly the foreign language in which he [is continually]...thrown back...precipitately" (p.55).

Voss's German heritage is simply an extreme degree of that condition of alienation experienced in early Australia by every non-Aborigine in that foreign land. English may be the dominant language of the colony, but it is certainly not innate. Who would dare say that Mr Bonner, by virtue of his command of the English language, is better equipped than Voss to understand the continent? Voss, at least, is aware that his language is foreign and must therefore be modified before the expedition begins to "mean" anything. Voss's early confrontation with Mr Bonner elucidates the point:

> "You are quite certain you are ready to undertake such a great expedition?" he [Mr Bonner] now dared to ask.
>
> "Naturally," the German replied.
>
> He had his vocation, it was obvious, and equally obvious that his patron would not understand.
>
> "You are aware, I should say, what it could mean?"
>
> *"If we would compare meaings,* Mr Bonner," said the German, *looking at each word as if it were a round pebble of mystical perfection, "we would arrive perhaps at different conclusions."* [p.20, emphasis mine]

Voss, like his historical counterparts, Sturt and Eyre, does attempt to understand the land. His words do have a "mystical errand in the silence of the grey bush" (p.143) even though he knows that his own language is ill-adapted and that once he has passed Jildra and is surveying the unknown, the "words [of his German song] have no meaning. Senseless!" (p.190).

Voss expresses this opinion to Dugald, one of the two Aboriginal guides who set out with the party. The Aborigines' presence as advisers to the microcosmic society is crucial. It is through them, and especially through Jackie, that some of the keys to Australian understanding are to be grasped. The Aborigines are seen as custodians of Australian knowledge.

They are, quite simply, native Australians. White shares with Sturt and Eyre a profound respect for Aboriginal lore. All three writers have looked to the native culture for advice about surviving and understanding the rigours of Australian life. In White's novel it comes as no surprise to find that so much of the insight which Laura, Voss and Frank gain from the interior complies with the Aboriginal lore and language which Jackie explains while commenting on the drawings which the party find in the "providential caves" (p.276).

The scene involving Jackie's "tuition" of the party represents the climax of the "language theme" of the novel. On entering the caves Jackie is moved instinctively to explain that "Blackfeller belong by these caves", and he commences "murmuring, but in his own tongue". It seems that the place is "full of a good magic". Then Voss discovers the drawings:

> "What do these signify, Jackie?" he asked.
>
> The boy was explaining, in his own language, assisted by a forefinger.
>
> "*Verfluchte Sprachen*!" cried the German.
>
> For he was doubly locked in language.
>
> As the boy continued unperturbed, the man had to recover from his lapse. He was looking.
>
> "Snake," Jackie explained. "Father my father, all blackfeller."
>
> "*Gut*," added the boy, for the especial benefit of the German, and the word lit the whole place.
>
> The man was yielding himself up to the simplicity of the drawings. Henceforth all words must be deceitful, except those sanctioned by necessity, the handrail of language. [p.274].

These drawings *do signify*; they do communicate ideas, as is evidenced by Jackie's readiness to explain. The fact that Jackie's explication is couched initially, automatically, in his own language indicates that the meaning is inherently "native". Voss, doubly locked in an "accursed" alien language, must yield to Jackie for enlightenment, which Jackie can in fact give, even to the extent of translating the message into one most significant German word. The meaning of the drawings can be expressed, and not only in one language, provided language is governed by necessity, guided by that which the speaker is seeking to express, guided in this case by the spirit of the land itself. If one word can light up a cave, an entire novel might elucidate a continent.

Voss continues to examine the drawings, genuinely hopeful of learning from them. Jackie then explains a drawing of metaphysical import, concerned with the Aborigines and their spirit-world:

> "Men gone away all dead," the boy explained. "All over," he waved his arm. "By rock. By tree. No more men," he said, beginning to comb the light with his dark fingers, as if it had been hair. "No more nothink. Like this. See?" He laid his cheek upon his hands, seed-shaped, and his eyelashes were playing together. "Wind blow big, night him white, this time these feller dead men. They come out. Us feller no see. They everywhere." [p.275]

This Aboriginal lore expounds the same knowledge which Laura and Frank comprehend and which Voss approaches. Frank's most evocative poem is written after he had experienced a "wind blow big, night him white" storm similar to that depicted in the drawing; and the knowledge that Frank absorbs from the experience coincides with Jackie's explications, in which the spirits of the dead are said to be everywhere in the land. Frank prays in his poem that his spirit will be taken from his body's remains and scattered everywhere, "in the rocks, and in the empty waterholes" (p.297). Similarly, Laura learns from a storm, during the funeral of Rose Portion; she learns that one must allow one's spirit to die into, or become part of, the very elements of Australian nature (pp.237-39). Finally, even Harry Robarts comes to embrace an Aboriginal world-view, as evinced in his reaction at the burial service of Palfreyman, who died in a kind of martyrdom to an Aboriginal tribe:

> In the case of Harry Robarts, however, truth descended upon ignorance in a blinding light. *He saw into the meaning of words, and watched the white bird depart out of the hole in Mr Palfreyman's side as they lowered the body into the ground.* [p.344, emphasis mine]

White's novel traces a journey away from Old World attitudes toward a more "native" Australian world-view. Using Central Australia as a symbol of personal and national aspiration, he elaborates the concerns which Mitchell, Sturt and Eyre had begun to crystallise a century earlier. During the first eighty years of Australian colonisation, the sources of Australian images developed from fantastic speculations founded in ignorance and yearning, through quantitative reports derived from bitter experience, until writers began to sense a relationship forming between themselves and the country which could now be perceived as both a materially immanent environment and a symbol of the spirit of a burgeoning society. *Voss* stands as a culmination of this first journey toward Australian knowledge. Having experienced versions of Hell, and having yearned for an imaginary, "literary" paradise, the major characters of the novel come to interpret the land as did the great explorer-writers of the 1830s and 1840s: as the explorers implied and as White elucidates, Australia is a unique kind of Purgatory, where *le plaisir* and *la douleur* are inseparable, and where "it is impossible to do away with the law of suffering".

Part Two
A Fringe of Leaves — *Toward a New Society*

In *Voss* Patrick White draws on and develops the genre of explorer's literature and the motif of the diminishing paradise, both of which were predominant in English writers' responses to Australia prior to 1850. In *A Fringe of Leaves,* White elaborates on another subject which fascinated the earliest English chroniclers: the Aborigines. Once again he takes his cue from a tradition established by English writers during the first eighty years of the colony. He examines the intricate connections between images of Aborigines, convicts and women with respect to the positions which these groups are forced to assume in a rigidly stratified Australian society (past and present) based not so much on the politics of economic classes as on unchallenged concepts of propriety, dominance, and the righteousness of established authority.

As many commentators have indicated, *A Fringe of Leaves* was written against a background of increasing feminist controversy in Australia, whereby the issue of women's subservience in society was being criticised and gradually explicated. White's deliberate examination and manipulation of long-standing images of the Aborigines and the convicts must be seen as inseparable from his preoccupation with the role assigned to women in Australian culture. The novel can be read as an examination of the subtle yet influential connections between the attitudes toward white women in contemporary Australian society and the images of Aborigines, convicts and women which were popularised by English writers prior to 1850.

The benefits of such a reading can be two-fold. First it is possible to demonstrate that White's interpretation of one woman's plight in Australia owes much to the English chroniclers who were writing about the colony 150 years ago. Secondly, by using the works of the early English commentators as guidebooks, a modern reader may arrive at territory within the novel which has not yet been surveyed.

A Dominant Society

Although *Voss* did not confront the question directly, it was concerned to some extent with a male-dominated society striving to establish itself in the new colony. In *A Fringe of Leaves*, partly in answer to the challenges of the burgeoning feminist movement in Australia in the 1970s, White has developed this inchoate theme by presenting an analysis of the attitudes which have led to the acceptance of the basic systems of dominance and coercion which became established before 1850 and which, implicitly, still pertain today.

The colonial society which White portrays in *A Fringe of Leaves*[22] is rigidly stratified according to the rights of dominance which one group of people can exercise over others. The group which invariably establishes itself at the top of the colonial "pecking order" is the non-convict white males. White seeks to expose the assumptions which support the hierarchy. In order to immerse the reader in the subtle processes of dominion which prevail, White chooses to narrate the novel from the perspective of a character, necessarily a woman, who experiences the oppression of every social system represented in the novel.

There are several such systems outlined throughout *A Fringe of Leaves*: the rustic community of West Country lass Ellen Gluyas; the Chippendale refinement of the Roxburghs of Cheltenham; the colonial society of convicts and masters; and finally, and crucially, the "savage" society in which Ellen (and the reader) achieves enlightenment induced by her most obvious suffering. Within each of these systems there are attitudes which prevail, mostly taken for granted by the characters involved, which facilitate the continuance of a *status quo* of male dominance.

For example, in the very first sentence of the novel White raises the question of "duty". This is not to say that he is concerned to extol the necessity of such a moral precept; rather he seeks to highlight how, in the highly formalised society of colonial gentility, "duty" is invoked by men as a panacea in moments of disquiet when the established order might be disturbed. On the opening page of the novel, when Mr Stafford Merivale taps the back of his wife's hand and remarks that they have done their duty, he is absolving himself from any further necessity to ponder on the perturbing Mrs Roxburgh (p.7). Similarly Austin Roxburgh restores his own peace of mind after the distressing scene in which Ellen's newly born infant dies and is disposed of at sea. He strokes his wife's cheek with genuine (though misguided) compassion, and assures himself that Ellen is "one by whom he thought he had done his duty in every sense" (p.203).

For the male characters of the novel, "duty" tends to be a code of symbolic yet ultimately noncommittal gestures which support the *status quo* by virtue of their deliberate ineffectiveness. "A sigh or two, a click of the tongue, and he had done his duty" (p.201): so Austin Roxburgh extricates himself from mourning the death of Oswald, the cabin-boy. The male concept of duty has an efficacy based on a negative response to any behaviour which challenges what is already established as right and proper. Within such a system the concept of *female* duty operates additionally in a positively repressive sense. Whereas a man's duty complies with a deliberately nebulous code of "decency", a woman, while never challenging such propriety, must also actively cater to her "betters". Female duty involves practical service. Hence, rather than justifying actions after the event, after the man has done what has suited him (as in both of the examples above), a woman acts positively, beforehand, using duty as her guideline. The man is in control of duty; the woman is slave to it. Ellen explains her situation when she is still the unenlightened and oppressed Mrs Roxburgh: "In a sense I am under obligation, but choose to serve someone I respect — and love" (p.198). Therefore at the end of the novel when Mrs Roxburgh finds herself embroiled once again in colonial society on board the ship taking her back to Sydney, she and Miss Scrimshaw positively comply with the demands of that society: "'Let us go below,' [Mrs Roxburgh] decided. 'We have said goodbye. I have done my duty, I hope, by everybody.'" (p.361) Only when she is outside of restrictive civilisation does she ever admit that she has a "graver duty towards herself" (p.249).

Ellen is constrained by the female roles which are "allotted to her" (p.25) throughout the novel. She is shackled by "that female passivity wished upon her at birth and reinforced by marriage" (p.237). Her early life as a servant farm-girl has bred into her a lack of independence and a belief that a man is necessary to her as an embodied sanctuary (p.119). For this reason and for the no less considerable one of her economic insecurity, "a crude and bewildered girl" like young Ellen, "alone and bereaved on a moor, could hardly have rejected Mr Roxburgh's offer" of marriage (p.119). She is "blown as passively" as if in a windstorm, from one form of servitude to another (p.119). Accordingly, in the character-roles of Ellen Gluyas in Cornwall and Mrs Roxburgh in Cheltenham and the colonies, her "constant aim" is to "please and protect" men (p.67), and the "whole of her uneventful life" seems to be "spent listening to men telling stories, and smiling to encourage" (p.139).

A most effective aspect of women's subjection in this "civilised" society is the fact that they actively participate in their own plight. Miss Scrimshaw exemplifies this point. She is the very embodiment of passivity and propriety, who has managed to suppress her most immediate and potentially assertive desires. Dry and manipulated as the carved whalebones that her name signifies, Miss Scrimshaw is gradually being whittled away in her passivity. Her life is an innocuous pastime, and she fulfils a merely decorative role in lieu of exercising her autonomy or exploring past the boundaries of her restricted life. Having sublimated her sexuality, into an admiration of "large men, handsome officers in His Majesty's Services, and those other officers of the cloth, if large too, and destined for purple" (p.350), she has spent her life in a state of dedicated inaction, awaiting the discreet proposal of marriage from "a certain bereaved bishop" and luxuriating in the poignant memory of her former fiancé, "a naval lieutenant who died of a fever at Antigua" (p.350). It is entirely appropriate that Miss Scrimshaw should now be living in colonial Australia. She almost explains, in a statement which comes perilously close to an expressed opinion in mixed company: "It is what some — not all of us — have chosen. To live in this country. Suffering is often a matter of choice" (p.20). By volition and by coercion, dutiful women accept their plight.

In White's vision, however, it is not only women who fulfil roles of subjection in colonial society. White demonstrates that the domination of certain groups over others in Australia continues because of an acceptance of deeply ingrained attitudes which were established during the colony's formative years. Apart from women, the other major deprived groups in colonial society are the convicts and the Aborigines. In his characterisation of Ellen, and in his narration of her tribulations and liberation, White tacitly acknowledges that attitudes to all three groups are linked in the minds of the oppressors.

Just as the convicts are treated as indentured servants to the colonial gentry, so Ellen in her early life is portrayed as a servant sentenced because of her sex and her economic standing, to a life-sentence of drudgery. Her "escape" is possible only through the merciful intervention of a powerful "superior", Austin Roxburgh. The connection between convicts and women is established most patently in the relationship which develops between Ellen and Jack Chance. Ironically, on first encountering Jack, Ellen seeks to dominate him by appealing to vestiges of a class system which might have been relevant at Birdlip House, Cheltenham, but which is simply absurd in the Aboriginal society. Cossetting her aches and luxuriating in having Jack wait upon her with clay-baked pigeon, Ellen "would have liked her assigned slave to entertain her" (p.263), but her fantasies are violently upset as it becomes obvious that *she* is the slave in this Aboriginal group and that she is subjected, potentially, even to convict Jack. Gradually, as Ellen and Jack understand their common predicament, they encounter each other as equals and cooperate in working toward each other's liberation. Ellen and Jack — woman and convict — are equals in involuntary degradation because each has experienced a type of slavery — she as servant girl and Aboriginal woman, and he as transported convict.

From the viewpoint of genteel society, Ellen might also be regarded as equal to "savages", most obviously because of her involvement with the island tribe after the shipwreck. Less explicitly, Ellen is portrayed from adolescence as temperamentally amenable to an instinctive, "savage" world-view: the young Ellen Gluyas "was drawn to nature as she would not have been in different circumstances; she depended on it for sustenance, and legend for hope" (p.45).

Jack Chance can also be equated with the Aborigines, first by virtue of his long exile among the mainland tribe, and secondly because, by consensus of English prejudices, a convict is just another species of savage. Mr Pilcher explains to Ellen quite early that the interior of the continent is populated only with "dirty blacks. . .and a few poor beggars in stripes who've bolted from one hell to another" (pp.134-35). To similar effect Ellen herself reacts with automatic prejudice on first encountering Jack amongst his adoptive tribe: she is "convinced that the man was some escaped prisoner who had taken up with a black tribe and probably acquired their more horrid ways to add to his natural propensities" (p.251). Moreover, Jack's scars, the legacy of a cruelty more barbaric than any aspect of Aboriginal life, are similar to the "tribal incisions" (p.250) which adorn the warriors' bodies.

So, now that it is apparent that both Ellen and Jack are equated to some extent with the Aborigines, we discern in the novel a pattern of connections emerging that is similar to those which occurred in English writers' accounts of Australia before 1850. The pattern might be expressed as a "formula": "woman is to convict as convict is to 'savage', as 'savage' is to woman".

In practical terms, this formula indicates that because all three of these groups are "trapped together" as objects of the prejudice of the dominant (white, non-convict, male) faction of colonial society, attitudes which apply to Aborigines, for example, "spill over" to apply implicitly to convicts and women; and so on for the attitudes bearing explicitly on convicts and on women. Furthermore, as the colonial society has become modern, the convicts have been eliminated. It is perhaps not merely glib to state that with their disappearance prejudice has been thrust onto the Aborigines and women with increased intensity.

As if his exposure of the systems of male dominance in Australian society was not sufficiently "subversive", White throws one more bomb when he demonstrates that the assertive role with which the colonial male is "privileged" can in fact be injurious to the man himself. For example, even the "self-subjected" Miss Scrimshaw and Mrs Merivale are aware that there is "so much that [Mr Merivale's] sex and nature must always prevent him understanding" (p.8); and somewhat more earnestly, the death of Austin Roxburgh is attributable to his faintly ridiculous attempt to fulfil his assigned sexual role as he blunders to the aid of the impaled Captain Purdew: "it was Mr Roxburgh who ran forth, to do what only God could know. Here he was, bestirring himself at least, in the manner expected of the male sex. Into action!" (p.214).

White's concern to reassess the way people relate to each other in civilised society is intended to benefit both sexes. The process must begin with the debunking of some injurious myths.

A Savage Society

There is an obvious alternative to the flawed colonial civilisation, and that is the Aboriginal society, which, after all, has existed in the continent for as long as human beings have occupied it. White's fascination with the Aborigines places him in a long line of writers — English and Australian — who have turned to them for inspiration (at best) or for local colour or confirmation of Anglo-Saxon self-esteem (at worst). White's treatment of the natives in *A Fringe of Leaves* is far more complex than can be accommodated by an appeal to the stereotypes which have strait-jacketed Aborigines through the decades. White is concerned to examine the Aborigines as an actual society living in an actual environment. He is seeking to play the myths of "savagery" against the mundane realities of "savage" existence. He seeks to discredit those myths which hinder a fuller understanding both of the Aborigines themselves and of how an Australian society should function in Australia.

In *A Fringe of Leaves* White can be seen to be writing within a tradition established by the explorer-authors whose works brought literature out of the pastoral fantasies which had been applied to Australia particularly during the 1820s and the early 1830s. Far from being simply historical romance, *A Fringe of Leaves* is, in part, a realist's call to face up to actualities about Aboriginal society and to consider how people might effect significant changes to their attitudes toward Aborigines, and concomitantly toward convicts (and the broader category of "outsiders" whom they can represent) and women.

At the beginning of the novel, the Roxburghs are *returning* to the Old World. The voyage out to Australia had been suggested by Austin, whose preoccupations with the imaginary worlds of literature generally, and with Virgil specifically, should never have been measured against experience outside the library of Birdlip House. For, once the Roxburghs arrive in this colony which had been the subject of so much optimistic fantasy on the part of Austin's contemporaries, he is forced to admit, sadly, that Australia is merely a "real" world which does not conform to the standards of the *Georgics*. As Charles Lamb had pronounced to Barron Field a half-century earlier, it is a "land of d. . .d realities"[23], and while he is in Australia Austin is forced to acknowledge that "his experience of life, like his attitude to death, had been of a predominantly literary nature" (p.186).

Accordingly, with his arcadian illusions discredited in Australia, he is returning to the sanctuary of Cheltenham when the *Bristol Maid* lurches on a coral reef. With his Elzevir Virgil tucked into his waistcoat, Mr Roxburgh initially regards the shipwreck as a mere caprice of actuality from which he will be freed in good time, when his "real, sustaining, and sustained life would only begin again on his return to the library at 'Birdlip House'" (p.211). Brought to earth, literally as well as metaphorically, off the coast of Queensland, the inevitable final reality overtakes him in this region where "of vegetation or shade there was little: nothing of that pastoral green Mr Roxburgh had hoped to find, in which to re-live the pleasures of the *Georgics*" (p.183).

He is slain by the Aborigines, as is the captain of the *Bristol Maid*. The implication is obvious that not only the land but also its native society is far from beneficent. This point is emphasised by the irony of Captain Purdew's fate after he has instructed his crew not to fire on the Aborigines whom he regards as "natural innocents": "Christian advances should meet with Christian results", he advises, "unless our sins are so heavy they will weigh against us" (p.211).

White is concerned to "de-romanticise" "savage" life. Although civilisation definitely has a great deal to learn from the Aborigines (*Voss* is testimony enough to this assertion), there are aspects of native society which cannot be condoned. Especially perturbing is the Aboriginal women's status as slaves, counterpointed by the males' aristocratic bearing as a "superior sex" (p.224). The situation is explicable, if not justifiable, because native society is still organised around the practice of the survival of the fittest, which means in the Australian environment, dominance by the physically strongest:

> As superior beings the men set about gorging themselves with appropriate solemnity. Without doubt the physical splendour, both of the mature males and more slender youths, was worthy of celebration. Occasional morsels were thrown to the wretched females, who grovelled in keeping with their humble station, and scooped up the scraps, and shook off the dust before devouring them. [p.221]

The physical appearances of the sexes reinforce their assigned roles. And these very roles *cause* the physical appearances:

> Contrasting with the women's irregular stubble, curly manes of well-greased hair hung to their [the men's] shoulders. Where the women slouched, grown slommacky from bearing children and carrying loads, the males were for the most part still personable in old age, disfigured only by the welts from incisions deliberately inflicted in patterns on their chests, backs, and often handsome faces. [p.224]

As White indicates, to Anglo-Australian society's shame, there is a distinct parallel between the treatment of women in both the Aboriginal and the civilised Australian societies. If the treatment of women is repugnant even in a situation where the injustices can at least be explained because survival and dominance depend largely on physical strength, it is absurd not to be outraged at the comparable treatment of women in a more sophisticated society where the brute force of an individual ought not to be crucial to her or his survival. In the novel the "savage" society becomes a simplified model of the society which is structured according to the dominance of one group over others. The portrayal of the Aboriginal society which enslaves Ellen Roxburgh serves to highlight, by means of comparison, the more "barbarous" aspects of the "civilised" society which also enslaves her rather more surreptitiously. The similarities between the two societies are as instructive as they are disquieting.

A New Society?

The *differences* between the two societies are also instructive. White is concerned also to examine the positive aspects of the myths and facts about the Aborigines in order to point the way to a better civilisation. As Ellen progresses through several societies it becomes apparent that she achieves enlightenment only during her sojourn with the Aborigines. Out of the suffering experienced with the tribe Ellen comes to understand both her enforced subjection and her capabilities as a woman. From the passion which she discovers with Jack and the Aborigines, away from the rational rectitude of civilisation, Ellen points a way forward to personal liberation in a compassionate society which does not yet exist.

In the relatively young and unformed colony of Australia it is still possible for Ellen to "escape" from the character-roles assigned to her (as servant-woman, convict-slave and "savage"), to get "back to zero" so to speak, and to begin a new life founded on individual dignity and compassionate passion. And as Ellen moves toward liberation she takes with her the readers, who are also "immured" (p.237) in a stultifying civilisation.

The "prison" in which Ellen is initially incarcerated is the highly formalised, kid-gloved society which is represented in chapter one by the trio (of Mr and Mrs Merivale and Miss Scrimshaw) in the carriage which draws away from 'Circular Wharf" after the leave-taking of the *Bristol Maid*. While all three characters manage to ignore the intimacies of physical contact caused inevitably by the rocking of the vehicle over Sydney cobblestones, a clinically formalised ritual of conversation is observed. Characters answer "as expected", according to the codes defined by sexual role-playing: "Mr Merivale being a man, there was no question but that [Mrs Merivale's] remark was intended for Miss Scrimshaw" (p.7). Moreover, it is specifically an *English* code of conduct which is being observed in this markedly non-English environment. It is an etiquette which endures because it can be supported by such genteel capabilities as Mr Merivale's "capacity for enduring boredom" and Mrs Merivale's ability to "[overlook] the possibility of a relationship with a landscape" (p.8). The Merivales are like the Bonners inasmuch as they are not concerned to understand the new land. They simply occupy it, graft their Old World society onto it, and then "retire to a villa at the Glebe, and have the girl draw its curtains almost as at Winchester" (p.9). The foolishness of their mannered behaviour in this untamed land is emphasised by the brilliant cameo performance of Mr Delaney, the emancipist farmer whom Mr Merivale visits on the return journey from "Circular Wharf". Delaney's gruff honesty and relaxed colloquial language imbue him with a depth of character which impresses the reader who compares this more "indigenous" Australian personality with the smug propriety and the "flatness" of the characters who insist on smirking covertly at the emancipist's mannerless manner while they remain determinedly ensconced in their own prejudices.

Ellen must escape the society of role-players wherein one suppresses one's immediate emotions and intuitions. Her liberation in Australia can begin only through direct experience of the new, uncivilised land. As Austin Roxburgh notes in his journal, Ellen does not share his disdain (similar to Mrs Merivale's) for the empty and hostile country (p.61). And as even Austin soon realises, this is an environment in which "the trappings of wealth and station, the pride in ethical and intellectual aspirations" are "stripped" from people, "with a ruthlessness reserved for those who accept their importance" (p.185). Hence, when the *Bristol Maid* strikes the reef, and it becomes apparent that everyone aboard is about to be subjected equally to the rigours of the environment, Ellen experiences a sense of liberation when she is left alone while Austin scurries off to collect his precious Virgil:

> It was the greatest luxury to be sitting alone, to give up the many-faceted role she had been playing, it now seemed, with mounting intensity in recent months — of loyal wife, tireless nurse, courageous woman, and more unreal than any of the

> superficial, taken-for-granted components of this character — expectant mother. [p.156]

She can now escape the servile duties which have been imposed upon her because of her sex. After the lifeboat pulls away from the sinking *Bristol Maid,* Ellen can lie back and muse: "We shall awake, she promised herself in leaving her body, and find we have arrived, *and begin afresh*" (p.181, emphasis mine).

Ellen's subjection and subsequent emancipation are assessed throughout the novel by constant reference to clothing as a multivalent symbol of the constrictions of duty and propriety which trammel her while she is a "civilised" woman. When the reader is introduced to Ellen she is seen mending one of her husband's shirts, which she has brought with her from the claustrophobic ship-cabin. At this stage before the shipwreck the menial chore defines her role in life: "This is *my* occupaation", she proclaims to her husband, "and I thought you would have approved of it. To keep you clothed, my dear, during a long voyage" (p.23). Then, no sooner does she lay down this motif of servitude than she constricts herself anew by clasping her wollen shawl about her (p.24). Given the extent of Ellen's subjugation at this stage, Austin is right to observe that Ellen "would dress. . .up. . .for a breakfast of yams and opossum with savages in the bush" (p.35). While she is servile to her husband she cannot contemplate the freedom from restriction which nakedness amongst the Aborigines might imply. Accordingly she immediately replies corroboratively: "I would dress up for my husband. . .if he was there" (p.35).

The status of clothing as a symbol of an ill-adapted mentality which has grafted to the Australian environment is emphasised in the image which White presents of Ellen when she and the sailors attempt initially to maintain civilised decorum in the wild. As she crawls out of the makeshift tent (constructed for her, for modesty's sake), Ellen is rendered grotesque, in the setting, by her apparel: "her heavy skirt dragged behind her, ploughing a track through the sand such as the tail of some giant lizard might leave" (p.195). Now that she is about to experience the land without the protection of the colonial society, the trappings of that society are ludicrous in the new situation.

In contrast to the excessively clad Ellen, there are the Aborigines, whose nakedness signifies a certain freedom and compatibility in relation to their environment. The role of the native women as instructors in Ellen's emancipation is emphasised by their action in setting upon her and stripping her, first, of the lizard-tail skirt, and then of her ridiculous corsets, until "She was finally unhooked. Then the shift, and *she was entirely liberated*" (p.218, emphasis mine).

At this early stage of her Aboriginal experience, however, she is not prepared for such nakedness, and she immediately covers herself partially with the fringe of leaves, in which she conceals her wedding ring, that final symbol of her civilised servitude. Not until she achieves complete nakedness will she have freed herself entirely from her old English-womanly roles.

The liberation of the "naked" self is not achieved without suffering. As was demonstrated in *Voss*, the centre of experience — personal as well as national — must be approached through erosion of the old self. Appropriately in *A Fringe of Leaves* Ellen feels herself virtually flayed, as life with Jack and the Aborigines strips away civilised affectations:

> There was an occasion when she fell down, scattering skywards a cloud of ashen parrots. She would have continued lying on the ground and perhaps become her true self: once the flesh melts, and the skeleton inside it is blessed with its final articulate white, amongst the stones, beneath the hard sky, in this country in which it can at last belong. [p.281]

It is only through such attrition that a person can become part of the environment. Even the joyful self-discovery which develops out of her naked passion with Jack involves an image of abrasion: "She lay stropping a cheek against an arm, hoping to arrive at layers of experience deeper still" (p.270).

The deprivation and cruelty which Ellen experiences with the Aborigines heighten her senses so that she rediscovers her most basic hungers and desires. Civilised notions of modesty have effectively stunted her personal growth by preventing her from discovering the true scope of her sexuality, which is in fact a power so liberative as to be "subversive" in the civilised society where women are persuaded to accept their place and "lean on" men for support of (imposed) frailty (see p.364 for example).

By rediscovering such drives as, first, hunger, and later, sexuality, Ellen sheds the subservience which had been ascribed to Mrs Roxburgh. It is with Jack Chance that she comprehends all the benefits arising from such "passion discovered only in a country of thorns, whips, murderers, thieves, shipwreck and adulteresses" (p.280). (White indirectly invokes the convention of Australian inversion here. Out of suffering comes joy, out of degeneration, regeneration. As Mrs Roxburgh is informed elsewhere, "There's a lot in this part of the world that looks alive when it's dead, and vicey versy" [p.35].) At last, with this convict who is also an Aborigine (temporarily), this woman who is also an Aborigine (temporarily) attains complete equality with a man. These two people on the lowest rung of the colonial social hierarchy cooperate to liberate each other from their own conditions of servitude. As Ellen realises, Jack depends on her for love and understanding (p.285), and Ellen relies on Jack to "save her" from several fates, the most mundane of which is, being lost in the unfamiliar bush (p.269). Each is the other's saviour. It is not merely fortuitous that the convict's initials are "J.C.". This is in addition to Jack's surname which refers to the Louis Aragon epigraph of the novel, in which love is extolled as our "last chance". Jack does not treat Ellen as a married woman whose existence is defined in terms of a husband. "And ringless didn't prevent you an' me becomin' what we are to each other", he declares to Ellen when she discovers that she has lost her wedding ring and is now completely naked (p.297). For her part, Ellen can shed her "Roxburgh mentality" and acknowledge that she sees in Jack "a nobility transcending the convict's origins and fall from grace", a nobility which contradicts Garnet Roxburgh's opinion of "these miscreants, the sweepings of the London streets" (p.284).

After her associations with this convict and these native Australians, Ellen and the readers can understand that a new, liberative set of values is possible in this new world. White has developed here two major themes from the early English literature about Australia: first the implication that women, Aborigines and convicts were equal and interchangeable in their status as the most lowly classes in the social hierarchy; and secondly, the grand Utopian dream which had always been essential to the image of the diminishing paradise and which is still influencing White in his vision of Australia as a place where radical social changes are yet possible.

White's concentration on the Aborigines provides a focus for his concern with the issues arising from the early colonial experience. In *Voss* the Aborigines are mentors to the alien white people and introduce them to the spirit of the land. To a degree they perform the same function in *A Fringe of Leaves* inasmuch as Ellen's experience with them alerts her to the facts that Australia "is a country designed for human torment, where even beauty flaunted a hostile radiance" (p.222) and that such "purgatorial" torment is prerequisite to any personal progress. But, as mentioned earlier, White's representation of Ellen's island tribe is more complex than the depiction of Jackie and Dugald in *Voss*. In *A Fringe of Leaves* Ellen must transcend the limitations of "savage" life just as she must progress past "civilisation". The Aborigines are afflicted with their own shortcomings (they are human beings, after all): the males enslave the women; they are fearfully superstitious (p.246); and their cannibalism nourishes a "darker need" (p.245) of a humanity which is stripped too far to the "ultimate nakedness" (p.322). In analysing the Aborigines White is not espousing a simplistic romanticism, just as he has no single formula for the development of a more "native" white society in Australia.

As Ellen comes within sight of the Oakes's farm and Jack retreats fearfully to the bush, it becomes obvious that the lessons which each has learned by progressing through Aboriginal status will not be applied simply and directly in the dominant colonial society. The final section of the novel demonstrates how impenetrable that society can be and how improvement of it will be a long and frustrating process. From the detachment enjoyed by the reader, one observes Ellen being drawn back ineluctably into the patronising systems of the colonial society.

At the instant when Ellen panics at the edge of the Oakes's clearing, as she chooses between "the known perils, and the nakedness" of the bush and the "shame disguised" of society (p.354), one senses that the struggle to remain her complete, metaphorically naked self has only just begun. The old civilised tenets begin to restrict her immediately. The well-meaning Mrs Oakes spurs her husband to aid Ellen by reminding him of "our duty" (p.304); and she later advises Ellen on a woman's role: "A woman, as I see, is more like moss or lichen, that takes to some rock or tree as she takes to her husband. An' that is where we belong" (p.313). At this stage, also, Ellen is referred to as "Mrs Roxburgh", nominal appendage of her late husband.

As Ellen is slowly acclimatised back into civilisation she

receives further instructions for correct role-playing. As an alternative to Mrs Oakes's willing subservience to a rock-solid man, there is the competitive mentality of Mrs Lovell, who confides surreptitiously to her peer while her husband is out of the room: "A woman can look to the future, don't you see? However unimportant we are, it is only in unimportant ways. They will always depend on us because we are the source of renewal" (p.345). Neither in the case of Mrs Oakes nor of Mrs Lovell is there an advocacy of the political equality between the sexes which characterised the brief involvement of Ellen and Jack.

The reader senses that a superhuman effort will be required for Ellen to remain uncompromised in her one-person resistance of the dominant society. One begins to fear for her as the pressures to conform intensify. Dressed once again in constricting clothing, Ellen goes walking independently around the Moreton Bay compound, and is immediately accosted and pursued by embittered convicts, and is finally reprimanded by Miss Scrimshaw — still the paragon of propriety — for venturing out alone (pp.334-37). In fact, with the society such as it is, Miss Scrimshaw's advice is sound.

By the time Ellen conducts her interview with fellow-survivor Pilcher, she is assuming the mien of the gentlewoman, dangling a wrist demurely over the arm of the chair and willing to do her "duty by society" by engaging Pilcher in introductory platitudes (p.339). Moreover, her response to the man's conversation is disquietingly familiar:

> "Yes," she agreed, while thinking that only a man could be so self-absorbed and boring.
>
> But because her mother-in-law had taught her that a lady's role in life is to listen, she leaned sideways and propped her chin on a receptive hand. [p.340]

Eventually Ellen herself seems to toll the knell for her liberated self during a conversation with Miss Scrimshaw while they are on board the packet which is taking them back to Sydney. In response to Miss Scrimshaw's spurious aspiration to "soar", eagle-like, to "reach the heights", to be "elevated, and at last free", Mrs Roxburgh can only echo the sentiments of Mrs Oakes:

> *Somewhat to her own surprise, Mrs Roxburgh remained ineluctably earthbound.* "I was slashed and gashed too often," she tried to explain. *"O no, the crags are not for me!"* She might have been at a loss had not the words of her humbler friend Mrs Oakes found their way into her mouth. "A woman, as I see, is more like moss or lichen that takes to some trees or rock as she takes to her husband." [p.363, emphasis mine]

This conversation is discontinued when, with all the meekness of "proper" feminine modesty, the ladies fall silent at the approach of Mr Jevons, Ellen's bumbling (yet affectionately drawn) new suitor.

It can be argued, of course, that all through the final section of the novel Ellen is merely playing at her assigned role, consciously and ironically, in order to survive within the patronising society. However, White implies that any personal autonomy which Ellen might be concealing is ultimately doomed. In the final scene during which Jevons becomes preoccupied with Ellen, she is described as a "smouldering figure in garnet silk" (p.365). From Mr Jevons's point of view Ellen may seem a passionate woman about to ignite with warmth and brilliance, but from the reader's informed perspective, this smouldering fire seems about to be suffocated completely. The role must subsume the individual. The woman who had shed the personalities of Ellen Gluyas and Mrs Roxburgh is now immured once again in the dominant society, this time as the widow Mrs Roxburgh who is in need of the support of a good man.

One senses that the new society is still generations away as White depicts Ellen clinging lichen-like to the basaltic Mr Jevons as they stroll off to dinner on the ship which is sailing away from the Aborigines' bush, back toward Sydney: "The merchant was at liberty to offer Mrs Roxburgh his support, and she to accept. 'Thank you,' she murmured, taking his arm (*what else could she have done*?)" (p.364, emphasis mine). "What else?" indeed. Ellen is simply *not* "at liberty".

In examining the progress toward emancipation of "woman-savage" Ellen and of "convict-savage" Jack, White points the way to a more liberal Australian society at the same time as he is warning that the struggle for human liberation will be long and difficult. The point of so much of White's writing, like the point of the English accounts of Australia during the 1830s and 1840s, is that many of the optimistic Australian myths have now been discredited. The land of freedom and unlimited prosperity does not exist at present. What are now required are myths which do actually stand the test of experience.

Suffering is essential to Australian experience, and no people know that better than the traditional "pariahs" of Australian society. Even so, in *A Fringe of Leaves*, as in *Voss*, the legacy of arcadian myths about Australia prevails, and the rewards of Purgatory are also glimpsed as a possibility. If the readers of *A Fringe of Leaves* last see Ellen strolling back into servitude beside Mr Jevons, they also remember the "age of gold" (p.270) which she shared so briefly yet so intensely with Jack Chance. A new society, though improbable on a mass scale, is still possible, to a smaller extent. Many more survivors like Ellen and Jack (and Laura Trevelyan) need to infiltrate the dominant society so that the resistance need not be as futile as it appears at the conclusion of *A Fringe of Leaves*. The "new Rome" will not be built in a day.

Epilogue

The country grows
into the image of the people,
and the people grow
into the likeness of the country
till the soul's geographer
each becomes the symbol of the other.

Max Dunn, *Portrait of a Country* (1951)

In dealing with *Voss* and *A Fringe of Leaves* I have attempted to demonstrate that our insights into modern Australian literature can be enhanced by an awareness of the issues which preoccupied the earliest English writers who were concerned with Australia. It has been established already that questions such as the evolution of language, the image of the diminishing paradise at the heart of the continent, and the conflict between Australian dreams and actualities are all concerns which date back to writers' earliest attempts to understand and portray the new land.

This knowledge can lead us to a better understanding of

recurrent regional themes. For example, we are able to pinpoint as major such topics as the interrelation of the images of convicts, Aborigines and women, or the interest in the centre of the country and its exploration as metaphors of more universal themes; and we can trace the derivation of such preoccupations while highlighting any significant changes that a modern author might ring on such "traditional" themes. In short we come to understand some of the myths upon which a national literature is built.

Because of the creative and interpretive work performed by earlier English writers who gradually came to comprehend the peculiar qualities of the continent, contemporary writers now have a coherent past and a "well-tested" system of myths through which to interpret their environment and experience. Over the years the land and the white people's culture have been growing together, shaping each other. The images which English writers originally presented of Australia have been embellished almost beyond immediate recognition, but they are fundamental to a culture which is always growing into the country even as the country is changed to accommodate the society.

Chapter Notes

Introduction

1. T. S. Eliot (ed.), *Selected Essays*, Faber and Faber, London, 1934, p.15.
2. Russel Ward, *The Australian Legend*, Oxford University Press, Melbourne, 1958, p.v.
3. F. W. Hegel, anthologised under the "Aesthetics", in E. F. Carritt (ed.), *Philosophies of Beauty*, Clarendon, Oxford, 1931, pp.161-62, and quoted in V. Vallis, "Artist and Environment. An Australian Study", in *British Journal of Aesthetics* 2, 1962, p.332.

Chapter One

1. John Callander (ed.), *Terra Australis Cognita: Or, Voyages to the Terra Australis, or Southern Hemisphere, during the Sixteenth, Seventeenth, and Eighteenth Centuries*, 3 vols, Edinburgh, 1766, vol.I, p.10.

2. Robert Burton, *Anatomy of Melancholy*, 3 vols, G. Bell and Sons, London, 1923, vol.II, p.42.

3. Gabriel de Foigny, *A New Discovery of Terra Incognita Australis, or the Southern World, by James Sadeur a Frenchman*, London, 1693, p.ii.

4. G. A. Wood, "Ancient and Medieval Conceptions of Terra Australis", Royal Australian Historical Society, *Journal and Proceedings* 3, 1916, p.461.

5. Lactantius, *The Works*, translated by William Fletcher, Clark, Edinburgh, 1871, p.122.

6. Saint Augustine, *De Civitate Dei*, xvi. 9, quoted in Ernest Scott, *Australian Discovery by Sea*, J. M. Dent, London, 1927, vol.I, p.vii.

7. Richard Brome, *The Antipodes*, edited by Ann Haaker, Edward Arnold, London, 1967, Act I, sc. vi, ll.116-19, p.30. The play was first performed in 1638.

8. Peter Heylyn, *Cosmographie in foure Bookes Contayning the Chorographie and Historie of the whole World*, 2nd edn, London, 1657, p.1901 (*sic*), misprint for p.1091.

9. James McCauley, "The True Discovery of Australia", *Collected Poems 1936-1970*, Angus and Robertson, Sydney, 1971, p.29.

10. William Dampier, *A New Voyage Round the World*, James Knapton, London, 1697, p.463. All future references to *A New Voyage Round the World* will be to this edition, and will be cited parenthetically in the text.

11. William Dampier, *A Voyage to New Holland, & C. In the Year 1699*, James Knapton, London, 1703, p.148. All future references to *A Voyage to New Holland* will be to this edition and will be cited parenthetically in the text.

12. William Dampier, *A Continuation of A Voyage to New Holland & C. In the Year 1699*, James Knapton, London, 1709, pp.9-10. All future references to *A Continuation* will be to this edition and will be cited parenthetically in the text.

13. See W. H. Bonner, *Captain William Dampier: Buccaneer-Author*, Stanford University Press, Stanford University, 1934, ch. VIII.

14. Daniel Defoe, *A New Voyage Round the World by a Course never sailed before*, London, 1725, pt I, pp.6-7. All future references to Defoe's *New Voyage* will be to this edition and will be cited parenthetically in the text.

15. Daniel Defoe, *Captain Singleton*, Oxford University Press, London, 1969, p.206.

16. Harold Williams, *Dean Swift's Library*, The University Press, Cambridge, 1931, p.91.
17. Jonathan Swift, *Travels Into Several Remote Nations of the World. In Four Parts. By Lemuel Gulliver*, 2 vols, London, 1726, vol.I, pt 1, p.5. All future references to *Gulliver's Travels* will be to this edition and will be cited parenthetically in the text.
18. See Arthur E. Case, *Four Essays on Gulliver's Travels*, Princeton University Press, Princeton, 1945, p.50; W. P. Friederich, *Australia in Western Imaginative Prose Writings, 1600-1960*, University of North Carolina Press, Chapel Hill, 1967, pp.25-27; and John R. Moore, "The Geography of *Gulliver's Travels*", *Journal of English and Germanic Philology* 40, 1941, pp.214-28.
19. John Campbell (ed.), *Navigantium atque Itinerantium Bibliotheca. Or, A Complete Collection of Voyages and Travels*, 2nd edn, 2 vols, London, 1744-48, vol.I, p.270. All future references to *Navigantium* will be to this edition and will be cited parenthetically in the text.
20. Celsus Kelly (ed. and trs.), *La Austrialia del Espiritu Santo. The Journal of Fray Martin de Munilla*, 2 vols, Cambridge University Press, Cambridge, 1966, vol.I, p.vii, fn.1.
21. Bernard McGinn, *Visions of the End. Apocalyptic Traditions in the Middle Ages*, Columbia University Press, New York, 1979, p.284.
22. Samuel Purchas, *Hakluytus Posthumus or Purchas His Pilgrimes Contayning a History of the World in Sea Voyages and Lande Travells by Englishmen and Others*, 20 vols, MacLehose, Glasgow, 1906, vol.XVII, p.217. All future references to *Purchas His Pilgrimes* will be to this edition and will be cited parenthetically in the text.
23. Celsus Kelly, *Pedro Fernandez de Quiros, The Last Great Portuguese Navigator*, Lisbon, 1961, p.4.
24. John Callander (ed.), *Terra Australis Cognita: or, Voyages to the Terra Australis, or Southern Hemisphere during the Sixteenth, Seventeenth and Eighteenth Centuries*, 3 vols, Edinburgh, 1766-68. All future references to Callander's work will be to this edition and will be cited parenthetically in the text.
25. Alexander Dalrymple, *An Account of the Discoveries Made in the South Pacifick Ocean, Previous to 1764*, London, 1767, p.ii.

Chapter Two

1. Sydney Parkinson, *A Journal of a Voyage to the South Seas, in his Majesty's Ship, The Endeavour*, London, 1773, p.133. All future references to Parkinson's *Journal* will be to this edition and will be cited parenthetically in the text.
2. John Hawkesworth (ed.), *An Account of the Voyages Undertaken by the Order of his Present Majesty for Making Discoveries in the Southern Hemisphere*, 3 vols, Strahan and Cadell, London, 1773, vol.III, p.506. All future references to Hawkesworth's *Voyages* will be to this edition and will be cited parenthetically in the text.
3. Bishop Thomas Sprat, *The History of the Royal Society of London*, 3rd edn, London, 1722, p.113. All future references to Sprat's *History* will be to this edition and will be cited parenthetically in the text.
4. F. W. Hegel, anthologised under the "Aesthetics" in E. F. Carritt (ed.), *Philosophies of Beauty*, Clarendon, Oxford, 1931, p.161.
5. Ellen Semple, *Influences of Geographic Environment*, Constable, London, 1911, p.1.
6. Sydney Smith, "Botany Bay" (from *Edinburgh Review*, 1819), in *The Works of the Rev. Sydney Smith*, Longman, Brown, Green, and Longmans, London, 1850, p.254.
7. Barron Field, "The Kangaroo", in his *First Fruits of Australian Poetry*, Sydney, 1819, p.9.
8. T. Bewick, *A General History of Quadrupeds*, Newcastle, 1790, p.315.
9. George Barrington, *The History of New South Wales, including Botany Bay, Port Jackson, Pamaratta* [sic], *Sydney and all its Dependencies*, Jones, London, 1802, p.95.
10. E. W. Landor, *The Bushman: or, Life in a New Country*, Bentley, London, 1847, p.70.
11. Hayden White, "The Forms of Wildness: Archaeology of an Idea", in Edward Dudley and Maximillian E. Novak (eds), *The Wild Man Within. An Image in Western Thought from the Renaissance to Romanticism*, University of Pittsburgh Press, Pittsburgh, 1972, p.12.
12. Arthur Phillip, *The Voyage of Governor Phillip to Botany Bay*, Stockdale, London, 1789, p.75.
13. William Sotheby, "On the Ships sailing for Botany Bay", in his

A Tour Through Parts of Wales, Sonnets, Odes and Other Poems, London, 1794, p.45.

14. T. C. Croker (ed.), *Memoirs of Joseph Holt, General of the Irish Rebels, in 1798*, 2 vols, Henry Colburn, London, 1838, vol.II, pp.56-57.
15. John White, *Journal of a Voyage to new* [sic] *South Wales*, Debrett, London, 1790, pp.129-31. All future references to White's *Journal* will be to this edition and will be cited parenthetically in the text.
16. David Collins, *An Account of the English Colony in New South Wales: with Remarks on the Dispositions, Customs, Manners, etc. of the Native Inhabitants of that Country*, Cadell and Davies, London, 1798, p.69. A continuation of the *Account* was published in 1802 under the title *An Account of the English Colony in New South Wales, From its First Settlement, in January 1788, to August 1801*, Cadell and Davies, London, 1802.

    All future references to Collins' *Account* will be to these editions and will be cited parenthetically in the text. The 1798 edition and the 1802 continuation will be called vol.I and vol.II respectively.
17. Sydney Smith, "New South Wales" [Review of Collins's *Account*], *Edinburgh Review* 2, 1803, p.34.
18. H. M. Green, *A History of Australian Literature. Volume One: 1789-1923*, Angus and Robertson, Sydney, 1961, p.12.
19. Watkin Tench, *A Complete Account of the Settlement at Port Jackson in New South Wales*, London, 1793, pp.95-96. All future references to Tench's *Complete Account* will be to this edition and will be cited parenthetically in the text.
20. Thomas Watling, *Letters from an Exile at Botany-Bay, to his Aunt in Dumfries: Giving a Particular Account of the Settlement of New South Wales, With the Customs and Manners of the Inhabitants*, Penrith, 1794?, p.15. All future references to *Letters* will be to this edition and will be cited parenthetically in the text.
21. Alexander Pope, "An Essay on Criticism", 1.89, in A. W. Ward (ed.), *The Poetical Works of Alexander Pope*, Macmillan, London, 1879, p.52.
22. Watkin Tench, *A Narrative of the Expedition to Botany Bay*, Debrett, London, 1789, p.45. All future references to Tench's *Narrative* will be to this edition and will be cited parenthetically in the text.
23. Bernard Smith, *Documents on Art and Taste in Australia. The*

Colonial Period 1770-1914, Oxford University Press, Melbourne, 1975, p.2.

24. George Dyer, "Preliminary Remarks", in George Thomson, *Slavery and Famine, Punishments for Sedition; or an Account of the Miseries and Starvation of Botany Bay*, Ridgeway, London, 1794, p.48.
25. George Hamilton, *The Telegraph; A Consolatory Epistle from Thomas Muir, Esq. of Botany Bay, to the Hon. Henry Erskine*, Late Dean of Faculty, n.d., n.p., p.3. The date of publication is most likely 1796; for, in January of that year a pamphlet of satirical verse was published anonymously, entitled *The Telegraph Inverted, or Lauderdale's Peep at the Author and Adherents of the Telegraph*. This was a specific reply to Hamilton's poem. All future references to Hamilton's *Telegraph* will be to this edition and will be cited parenthetically in the text.
26. All references are to *Botany-Bay Eclogues* (first published 1794) in *The Poetical Works of Robert Southey*, Galignani, Paris, 1839, pp.611-14.

Chapter Three

1. Coral Lansbury, *Arcady in Australia: The Evocation of Australia in Nineteenth-Century English Literature*, Melbourne University Press, Melbourne, 1970, p.31.
2. Henry Erskine, "The Emigrant", n.d., n.p., Pamphlet ca 1785-95, British Museum, Catalogue No. C58cc 36(6), p.6.
3. George Loveless, *A Narrative of the Sufferings of Jas. Loveless, Jas. Brine, and John Standfield. . . With a Brief Description of New South Wales*, London, 1838, p.16.
4. Anon., *The Farmers; or, Tales for the Times, addressed to the Yeomanry of England*, London, 1823, pp.87-88.
5. Alaric A. Watts (ed.), *Scenes of Life and Shades of Character*, 2 vols, Colburn and Bentley, London, 1831, vol.II, p.83.
6. Watts, vol.II, p.80.
7. Edward Gibbon Wakefield, *A Letter from Sydney, The Principal Town of Australia*, in E. Lloyd Prichard (ed.), *The Collected Works of Edward Gibbon Wakefield*, Collins, London, 1968, p.113. All future references to *A Letter* will be to this edition and will be cited parenthetically in the text.

8. F. G. Clarke, *The Land of Contrarieties. British Attitudes to the Australian Colonies 1828-1855*, Melbourne University Press, Melbourne, 1977, pp.124-25.
9. T. Horton James, *Six Months in South Australia, with some account of Port Philip and Portland Bay, in Australia Felix*, London, 1838, pp.37-38.
10. Thomas Bartlett, *New Holland: Its Colonization, Productions and Resources, with Observations on the Relations Subsisting with Great Britain*, Longman, Brown, Green and Longmans, London, 1843, p.37. All future references to Bartlett's *New Holland* will be to this edition and will be cited parenthetically in the text.
11. Thomas K. Hervey, "Australia", in his *Australia; With Other Poems*, Hurst, Robinson, and Co., London, 1824, p.12.
12. Michael Drayton, "Ode to the Virginian Voyage", in J. Buxton (ed.), *Poems of Michael Drayton*, 2 vols, Routledge and Kegan Paul, London, 1953, vol.I, p.123.
13. Alexander Whittaker, "Virginia's Natural Beauty" (1613), in L. B. Wright (ed.), *The Elizabethans' America: A Collection of Early Reports by Englishmen on the New World*, Harvard University Press, Cambridge (Mass.), 1965, p.222.
14. Robert Thorne, "A Declaration of the Indies", in Richard Hakluyt's *Divers Voyages Touching the Discovery of America and the Islands Adjacent*, edited by J. W. Jones, Franklin, New York, n.d., pp.31-32.
15. Harry Levin, *The Myth of the Golden Age in the Renaissance*, Faber and Faber, London, 1970, p.60.
16. Paul Fussell, *The Great War and Modern Memory*, Oxford University Press, London, 1975, p.174.
17. Bernard Smith, *European Vision and the South Pacific 1768-1850. A Study in the History of Art and Ideas*, Clarendon, Oxford 1960, p.6.
18. Bernard Smith, *The Antipodean Manifesto. Essays in Art and History*, Oxford University Press, Melbourne, 1976, p.161.
19. J. H. Tuckey, *An Account of a Voyage to Establish a Colony at Port Philip*, Longman, London, 1805, pp.185-86.
20. Thomas Campbell, "Lines on the Departure of Emigrants for New South Wales" (1828), in J. L. Robertson (ed.), *The Complete Poetical Works of Thomas Campbell*, Oxford University Press, London 1907, p.283.
21. Arthur Golding's translation of Ovid's *Metamorphoses*, in John

Hollander and Frank Kermode (eds), *The Literature of Renaissance England,* Oxford University Press, London, 1973, p.21.

22. James Montgomery, "The Pelican Island", in *The Pelican Island and Other Poems,* Longman, London, 1828, p.39. As Montgomery explains in the "Preface", p.v, "the subject of 'The Pelican Island' was suggested by a passage in Captain Flinders's Voyage to Terra Australis [*sic*]". The passage cited above concerns Kangaroo Island, just off the coast of South Australia.
23. Hervey, p.20.
24. William Wickenden, "Australasia", in his *Poems. By The Bard of the Forest,* Sherborne, London, 1827, p.21.
25. Peter Miller Cunningham, *Two Years in New South Wales,* 2 vols, London, 1827, vol.I, p.183.
26. Robert Montgomery Martin, *History of Austral-asia,*Whittaker and Co., London, 1839 (first published 1836), p.120.
27. Cunningham, vol.I, pp.171-72.
28. Cunningham, vol.I, p.272.
29. Golding's Ovid in Hollander and Kermode, *The Literature of Renaissance England,* p.21.
30. John Henderson, *Observations on the Colonies of New South Wales and Van Diemen's Land,* Baptist Mission Press, Calcutta, 1832, p.21.
31. Martin, p.129.
32. Anon., *The Farmers; or, Tales for the Times,* pp.105-6.
33. D. D. Mann, *Present Picture of New South Wales,* London, 1811, p.10.
34. Lady Mary Fox, *An Account of an Expedition to the Interior of New Holland,* Bentley, London, 1837, p.15. All future references will be to this edition and will be cited parenthetically in the text.
35. Francis Bacon, *The Essayes or Counsels, Civill and Morall,* London, 1625, p.199.
36. G. H. Haydon, *Five Years' Experience in Australia Felix,* Hamilton, Adams and Co., London 1846, pp.24-25.
37. Alexander Harris, *Settlers and Convicts, or Recollections of Sixteen Years' Labour in the Australian Backwoods, by An Emigrant Mechanic,* London, 1847, p.105. All future references to Harris's *Settlers and Convicts* will be to this edition and will be cited parenthetically in the text.

38. W. S. Ramson, "*The Emigrant Family*: The delineation of actual life", in W. S. Ramson (ed.), *The Australian Experience: Critical Essays on Australian Novels*, Australian National University, Canberra, 1974, p.6.
39. Alexander Harris, *The Emigrant Family: or, The Story of an Australian Settler*, 3 vols, Smith, Elder and Co., London, 1849, vol. I, p.3. For more details about Harris and his attitudes to bush life, see chapter five of this book.
40. Martin, p.369.
41. Edward Bulwer Lytton, *The Caxtons. A Family Picture*, 3 vols, William Blackwood and Sons, Edinburgh, 1849, vol.3, p.244.
42. W. T. Moncrieff, "General Preface", in *Selection from the Dramatic Works of William T. Moncrieff*, Hailes Lacy, London, 1851, p.iii.
43. Moncrieff, "General Preface", in *Selection*, p.iii.
44. W. T. Moncrieff, "Remarks" on *Van Diemen's Land!*, in *Richardson's New Minor Drama*, 4 vols, T. Richardson, London, 1831, vol. 4, p.v. All future references to *Van Diemen's Land!*, will be to this edition, and will be cited parenthetically in the text.
45. Barron Field, "On Reading the Controversy Between Lord Byron and Mr. Bowles", in his *First Fruits of Australian Poetry*, 2nd edn, Sydney, 1823, pp.14-15.
46. Barron Field, "Journal of an Excursion Across the Blue Mountains of New South Wales", in Barron Field (ed.), *Geographical Memoirs on New South Wales*, John Murray, London, 1825, p.422.
47. Field, "Journal of an Excursion Across the Blue Mountains", p.422.
48. Field, "On Reading the Controversy Between Lord Byron and Mr. Bowles", 2nd edn, p.15.

Chapter Four

1. John Hood, *Australia and the East*, John Murray, London, 1843, p.209.
2. Barron Field, "The Kangaroo", in his *First Fruits of Australian Poetry*, Sydney, 1819, p.7.
3. Jonathan Swift, *The Tale of a Tub; with the Fragments, & the Battel of the Books; with considerable additions, & explanatory*

Notes, never before printed, in *Miscellaneous Works, Comical and Diverting: By T.R.D.J.S.D.O.P.I.I.*, London, 1720, p.79.

4. Swift, pp.264-65.
5. Swift, p.264.
6. Peter Miller Cunningham, *Two Years in New South Wales*, 2 vols, London, 1827, vol.II, pp.210-11.
7. W. H. Leigh, *The Emigrant: A Tale of Australia*, Simmonds, London, 1847, p.2.
8. T. J. Maslen, *The Friend of Australia: or, A Plan for Exploring the Interior*, Hurst, Chance and Co., London, 1830, p.15.
9. Maslen, p.12.
10. Anon., "Mitchell's Second and Third Expeditions", *Blackwood's Edinburgh Magazine* 45, 1839, p.125.
11. Anon., "Oxley's Tour in Botany Bay", *Edinburgh Review* 34, 1820, p.422.
12. Charles Darwin, *Journal and Remarks 1832-1836*, in R. Fitz-roy (ed.), *Narrative of the Surveying Voyages of His Majesty's Ships Adventure and Beagle Between the Years 1826 and 1836*, 3 vols, Henry Colburn, London, 1839, vol.III, p.532.
13. John Lort Stokes, *Discoveries in Australia. . .during the Voyage of H.M.S. Beagle*, 2 vols, T. & W. Boone, London, 1846, vol.II, pp.20-21.
14. Anon., "New South Wales", *Blackwood's Edinburgh Magazine* 44, 1838, p.692.
15. H. Rogers, "The Destinies of England", in William Ellis (ed.), *The Missionary's or Christian's New Year's Gift*, Seely and Sons, London, 1833, p.206.
16. Cunningham, vol.II, p.54.
17. E. G. Wakefield, *"A Letter from Sydney"*, in E. L. Prichard (ed.), *The Collected Works of Edward Gibbon Wakefield*, Collins, London, 1968, pp.145-6.
18. Cunningham, vol.II, p.54.
19. John Thomas Bigge, "Report of the Commissioner of Inquiry on the State of Agriculture and Trade in the Colony of New South Wales", *Parliamentary Papers*, 1823, X, 136, p.81.
20. James Tuckey, *An Account of a Voyage to Establish a Colony at Port Philip*, London, 1805, p.190.
21. John Callander (ed.), *Terra Australis Cognita: Or Voyages to*

the Terra Australis, or Southern Hemisphere during the Sixteenth, Seventeenth and Eighteenth Centuries, 3 vols, Edinburgh, 1766-68, vol.I, p.22. The parallel passage in de Brosses is in Tome I, p.35.

22. Anon., "Journal of an Excursion to the Five Islands and Shoal Haven, on the Coast of New South Wales", *London Magazine* 10, 1824, p.181. This article also appears in Barron Field's *Geographical Memoirs*; see note 29.
23. Barron Field, "Sonnet on Affixing a Tablet to the Memory of Captain Cook and Sir Joseph Banks", in *First Fruits of Australian Poetry*, 2nd edn, Sydney, 1823, p.17.
24. See John Fisher, *The Australians. From 1788 to Modern Times*, Robert Hale, London, 1968, p.74; and also, Roderick Cameron, *Australia. History and Horizons*, Weidenfeld and Nicolson, London, 1971, p.151.
25. Letter from Sturt to George Macleay, 27 April 1844, in The Rhodes House "Sturt Papers", vol.II.
26. Thomas Livingstone Mitchell, *Journal of an Expedition, into the Interior of Tropical Australia*, Longman, Brown, Green and Longmans, London, 1848, p.v.
27. Val Vallis, "Artist and Environment. An Australian Study", in *British Journal of Aesthetics* 2, 1962, p.332.
28. Mark Twain, *Following the Equator. A Journey Around the World*, 2 vols, Harper, New York, 1925, vol.I, p.150.
29. Barron Field, "Journal of an Excursion across the Blue Mountains of New South Wales", in *Geographical Memoirs on New South Wales*, edited by Field, John Murray, London, 1825. All future references to Field's "Journal" will be to this edition and will be cited parenthetically in the text.
30. Charles Sturt, *Two Expeditions into the Interior of Southern Australia, during the years 1828, 1829, 1830 and 1831*, 2 vols, Smith, Elder and Co., London, 1833, vol.I, p.xv. All future references to *Two Expeditions* will be to this edition and will be cited parenthetically in the text.
31. Michael Langley, *Sturt of the Murray. Father of Australian Exploration*, Robert Hale, London, 1969, p.199.
32. Langley, p.81.
33. Anon., "Review", *Athenaeum Journal*, 1838, p.707.
34. J. H. L. Cumpston, *Thomas Mitchell: Surveyor General and Explorer*, Oxford University Press, London, 1954, p.205.

35. J. H. L. Cumpston, *The Inland Sea and the Great River. The Story of Australian Exploration*, Angus and Robertson, Sydney, 1965, p.112.
36. Thomas Livingstone Mitchell, *Three Expeditions into the Interior of Eastern Australia, with Descriptions of the Recently Explored Region of Australia Felix, and the Present Colony of New South Wales*, 2 vols, T. & W. Boone, London, 1838, vol.I, p.iii. All future references to *Three Expeditions* will be cited parenthetically in the text and will refer to this edition.
37. Thomas Livingstone Mitchell, *Journal of an Expedition into the Interior of Tropical Australia*, Longman, Brown, Green and Longmans, London, 1848, p.v.
38. Langley, p.225.
39. Charles Sturt, *Narrative of an Expedition into Central Australia*, 2 vols, T. & W. Boone, London, 1849, vol.I, p.134. All future references to *Narrative* will be noted parenthetically in the text and will refer to this edition.
40. Ellen Semple, *Influences of Geographical Environment*, Constable, London, 1911, p.1.
41. Edward John Eyre, *Journals of Expeditions of Discovery in Central Australia, and Overland from Adelaide to King George's Sound, in the years 1840-41*, 2 vols, T. & W. Boone, London, 1845, vol. I, p.23. All future references to *Journals* will be to this edition and will be cited parenthetically in the text.
42. John L. Allen, "Lands of Myth, Waters of Wonder: The Place of Imagination in the History of Geographical Exploration", in David Lowenthal and Martyn J. Bowden (eds), *Geographies of the Mind. Essays in Historical Geosophy*, Oxford University Press, New York, 1976, p.46.
43. Anon., "Review", *Athenaeum Journal* 1845, p.868.
44. Anon., "Australia", *North British Review* 4, 1846, p.312.
45. Patrick White, "Flaws in the glass: Sketches for a self-portrait", in *Bulletin*, Australia, 29 January, 1980, p.152.
46. Edward Bulwer Lytton, *The Caxtons. A Family Picture*, 3 vols, William Blackwood and Sons, Edinburgh, 1849, vol.III, p.211.
47. Thomas McCombie, *Adventures of a Colonist; or, Godfrey Arabin the Settler*, London, 1845, p.200.
48. McCombie, p.200.
49. Marcus Clarke, "Preface" to *Poems of the late Adam Lindsay*

Gordon, edited by M. Clarke, Samuel Mullen, London, 1887, pp.v-vi.

Chapter Five

1. Samuel Purchas, *Hakluytus Posthumus or Purchas His Pilgrimes Contayning a History of the World in Sea Voyages and Land Travells by Englishmen and Others*, 20 vols, MacLehose, Glasgow, 1906, vol.XVII, p.220.
2. William Dampier, *A New Voyage Round the World*, James Knapton, London, 1967, p.464.
3. Erasmus Darwin, *Zoonomia; or, the Laws of Organic Life*, 2 vols, London, 1794, vol.I, p.498.
4. Darwin, vol.I, p.499.
5. Geoffrey Symcox, "The Wild Man's Return: The Enclosed Vision of Rousseau's *Discourses*", in Edward Dudley and Maximillian E. Novak (eds), *The Wild Man Within. An Image in Western Thought from the Renaissance to Romanticism*, University of Pittsburgh Press, Pittsburgh, 1972, p.230.
6. Arthur O. Lovejoy, *The Great Chain of Being. A Study of the History of an Idea*, Harvard University Press, Cambridge (Mass.), 1936, p.296.
7. Symcox, p.242.
8. Jean-Jacques Rousseau, "The General Society of the Human Race", in G. D. H. Cole (tr. and ed.), *The Social Contract and Discourses*, Dent, London, 1972, p.156.
9. Peter L. Thorslev, Jr., "The Wild Man's Revenge", in Dudley and Novak, p.282.
10. John Dryden, *The Conquest of Granada by the Spaniards: In Two Parts*, London, 1672, Part I, p.7.
11. Richard Payne Knight, *The Progress of Civil Society. A Didactic Poem in Six Books*, London, 1796, pp.12-13.
12. Sydney Parkinson, *A Journal of a Voyage to the South Seas, in his Majesty's Ship, The Endeavour*, London, 1773, pp.134-35.
13. J. C. Beaglehole (ed.), *The Journals of Captain James Cook on His Voyages of Discovery*, 4 vols, *The Voyage of the Endeavour, 1768-1771*, Cambridge University Press, Cambridge, 1968, vol.I, p.399.

14. Beaglehole, vol.I, p.312.
15. John Hawkesworth (ed.), *An Account of the Voyages Undertaken by the Order of his Present Majesty for Making Discoveries in the Southern Hemisphere*, 3 vols, Strahan and Cadell, London, 1773, vol.III, p.506.
16. Bernard Smith, *European Vision of the South Pacific 1768-1850, Oxford University Press*, London, 1960, p.128, fn. 2.
17. Hawkesworth, vol.III, p.631.
18. D. J. Mulvaney, "The Australian Aborigines 1606-1929: Opinion and Fieldwork. Part I, 1606-1859", *Historical Studies: Australia and New Zealand* 8, 1958, p.136.
19. George Grey, *Journals of Two Expeditions of Discovery in North-West and Western Australia, During the Years 1837, 38 and 39*, 2 vols, T. & W. Boone, London, 1841, vol.II, pp.219-220.
20. Anon., *The Picture of Australia, Exhibiting New Holland, Van Diemen's Land, And All the Settlements, From the First at Sydney, to the Last at the Swan River*, Whittaker, Treacher & Co., London, 1829, p.228.
21. Mrs Augustus Prinsep, *The Journal of a Voyage from Calcutta to Van Diemen's Land, Comprising a Description of that Country*, London, 1833, p.79.
22. Bernard Smith, *Australian Painting 1788-1970*, Oxford University Press, Melbourne, 1971, p.28.
23. Anon., "On the Aborigines of New Holland", *Alexander's East India Magazine, and Colonial. . . Journal* 8, 1834, p.329.
24. Anon., "Flinders' Voyage to Terra Australis", *Quarterly Review* 12, 1814, pp.21-22.
25. Jeremy Bentham, *Letter to Lord Pelham*, pamphlet circular, Westminster, 1802.
26. Anon., *The History of New Holland, From its First Discovery*, London, 1787, p.70. In 1808 this pamphlet was republished, with the authorship falsely attributed to George Barrington.
27. George Osborne Morgan, "Settlers in Australia: A Prize Poem, recited in the Theatre Oxford; June 24, 1846", Oxford, 1846.
28. John Turnbull, *A Voyage Round the World in the Years 1800, 1801, 1802, 1803 and 1804*, 2 vols, Richard Phillips, London, 1805, vol.I, pp.74-75.

29. Anon., "The *Beagle*'s Discoveries in Australia", *Fraser's Magazine* 34, 1846, p.108.
30. Anon., "On the Aborigines of New Holland", 8, 1834, pp.330-31.
31. Knight, pp.11-12.
32. James Burnet (Lord Monboddo), *Of the Origin and Progress of Language*, 6 vols, T. Cadell, London, 1773-1793, vol.I, p.285.
33. Barron Field, "On the Aborigines of New Holland and Van Diemen's Land", in Barron Field (ed.), *Geographical Memoirs on New South Wales*, John Murray, London, 1825, p.210.
34. William Wickenden, "Australasia", in his *Poems by the Bard of the Forest*, Sherborne, London, 1827, p.17.
35. Robert Montgomery Martin, *History of Austral-asia*, Whittaker and Co., London, 2nd edn, 1839, first published 1836, p.159.
36. Watkin Tench, *A Complete Account of the Settlement of Port Jackson*, London, 1793, p.200. Tench's opinions about the Aborigine stand despite his liberalism about other issues such as the humanitarian treatment of convicts.
37. Winthrop Mackworth Praed, *Australasia. A Poem which obtained the Chancellor's Medal at the Cambridge Commencement, July, 1823*, Cambridge, 1823, p.10.
38. J. C. Byrne, *Twelve Years' Wanderings in the British Colonies from 1835 to 1847*, 2 vols, Richard Bentley, London, 1848, vol.I, p.277.
39. George French Angas, *Savage Life and Scenes in Australia and New Zealand*, 2 vols, Smith, Elder & Co., London, 1847, vol.I, p.73.
40. Martin, pp.149-150.
41. Richard Howitt, *Impressions of Australia Felix During Four Years Residence in that Colony*, Longman, Brown, Green and Longmans, London, 1845, p.204.
42. G. H. Haydon, *Five Years' Experience in Australia Felix*, Hamilton, Adams and Co., London, 1846, p.106.
43. Joseph Lycett, *Views in Australia*, J. Souter, London, 1824, p.2.
44. Anon., "The Poor Transport's Lamentation", in Anon., *The History of Botany Bay in New Holland*, London, n.d. (ca 1800), p.8.
45. Coral Lansbury, *Arcady in Australia: The Evocation of*

Australia in Nineteenth Century English Literature, Melbourne University Press, Melbourne, 1970, p.130.

46. Hayden White, "The Forms of Wildness", in Dudley and Novak, pp.20-21.
47. White, p.20.
48. Charles Darwin, *Journal and Remarks, 1832-1836*, in R. Fitz-Roy (ed.), *Narrative of the Surveying Voyages of his Majesty's Ships Adventure and Beagle, Between the Years 1826 and 1836*, 3 vols, London, 1839, vol.III, p.520.
49. Barron Field, "Journal of an Excursion Across the Blue Mountains of New South Wales", in Barron Field (ed.), *Geographical Memoirs on New South Wales*, John Murray, London, 1825, p.435.
50. Howitt, p.286.
51. Tench, p.179.
52. Patrick Matthew, *Emigration Fields. North America, The Cape, Australia, and New Zealand*, Adam and Charles Black, Edinburgh, 1839, p.11.
53. Alexander Harris, *Settlers and Convicts, or Recollections of Sixteen Years' Labour in the Australian Backwoods, by An Emigrant Mechanic*, London, 1837, p.417.
54. Harris, *Settlers and Convicts*, p.342.
55. T. Richards, "Van Diemen's Land", *Westminster Review* 21, 1834, p.26.
56. Anon., "The *Beagle's* Discoveries in Australia", *Fraser's Magazine* 34, 1846, p.108.
57. William Thomas Moncrieff, *Van Diemen's Land! An Operatic Drama, in Three Acts*, in W. T. Moncrieff (ed.), *Richardson's New Minor Drama*, 4 vols, T. Richardson, London, 1831, vol.IV, p.39. All future references to *Van Diemen's Land!* will be to this edition and will be cited parenthetically in the text.
58. Thomas Bartlett, *New Holland: Its Colonization, Productions and Resources, with Observations on the Relations Subsisting with Great Britain*, Longman, Brown, Green and Longmans, London, 1843, pp.78-79.
59. Edward John Eyre, *Journals of Expeditions of Discovery into Central Australia*, 2 vols., T. & W. Boone, London, 1845, vol.II, p.156.
60. Eyre, vol.II, pp.157-58.
61. Geoffrey Dutton, *The Hero as Murderer. The Life of Edward*

John Eyre, Australian Explorer and Governor of Jamaica, Collins, London, 1967, p.14.

62. Sir Joshua Reynolds, "Discourse IV", 1771, in *The Discourses,* James Carpenter, London, 1842, p.53.
63. Smith, *European Vision and the South Pacific,* p.128.
64. Hawkesworth, vol.III, p.493. See also, the engraving taken from Sydney Parkinson's drawing of "Two of the Natives of New Holland advancing to combat".
65. David Collins, *An Account of the English Colony in New South Wales,* Cadell and Davies, London, 1798, p.329.
66. Tench, p.35.
67. Moncrieff, p.37.
68. Anon., "On the Aborigines of New Holland", 8, 1834, p.330.
69. George Barrington, *The History of New South Wales, including Botany Bay. Port Jackson, Pamaratta [*sic*], Sydney, and all its Dependencies,* Jones, London, 1802, p.24.
70. Thomas Livingstone Mitchell, *Journal of an Expedition into the Interior of Tropical Australia,* Longman, Brown, Green and Longmans, London, 1848, pp.65-66.
71. E. W. Landor, *The Bushman, or, Life in a New Country,* Bentley, London, 1847, p.52.
72. Anon., "Review of Literature", *Monthly Chronicle* 2, 1838, pp.373-74.
73. Tench, p.14.
74. Mitchell, *Journal of an Expedition into the Interior,* p.175.
75. Beaglehole, vol.I, p.399.
76. H. N. Fairchild, *The Noble Savage, A Study in Romantic Naturalism,* Columbia University Press, New York, 1928, p.363.
77. Fairchild, p.364.
78. Smith, *European Vision,* p.202.
79. Mitchell, *Journal of an Expedition into the Interior,* pp.416-17.
80. Thomas Livingstone Mitchell, *Three Expeditions into the Interior of Eastern Australia,* 2 vols., T. & W. Boone, London, 1838, vol.II, p.334.
81. Mitchell, *Three Expeditions,* vol.II, p.334.
82. Alexander Harris, *The Emigrant Family: or, The Story of an*

Australian Settler, 3 vols, Smith, Elder & Co., London, 1849, vol.I, p.64.

83. Smith, *Australian Painting 1788-1970*, p.28.
84. Harris, *Settlers and Convicts*, p.228.
85. Clement Hodgkinson, *Australia from Port Macquarie to Moreton Bay*, T. & W. Boone, London, 1845, pp.144-45, quoted in Russel Ward, *The Australian Legend*, 2nd edn, Oxford University Press, Melbourne, 1966, p.232.
86. Landor, p.3. All future references to Landor's *The Bushman* will be to the previously cited first edition. References will be made parenthetically in the text.
87. H. W. Haygarth, *Recollections of Bush Life in Australia, During a Residence of Eight Years in the Interior*, John Murray, London, 1848, p.22.
88. Anon., "The Pleasures of Bush Life", *London Journal* 8, 1849, p.350.
89. Edward Bulwer Lytton, *The Caxtons. A Family Picture*, 3 vols, William Blackwood and Sons, Edinburgh, 1849, vol.3, p.242.
90. William Wickenden, "Australasia. A Poem", in his *Poems. By the Bard of the Forest*, Sherborne, London, 1827, p.22.
91. Anon., "Pictures of Life in Australia", *Household Words* 1, 1850, p.307.
92. Lansbury, p.164.
93. Peter Miller Cunningham, *Two Years in New South Wales*, 2 vols, London, 1827, vol.II, pp.45-46.
94. Henry Home (Lord Kames), *Sketches of the History of Man*, 2 vols, Edinburgh, 1774, vol.I, p.182.
95. Elizabeth Webby, "The Aboriginal in Early Australian Literature", *Southerly* 40, 1980, p.52. As Elizabeth Webby points out, Mrs Dunlop published other poems when she was in Australia. Examples include "The Eagle Chief" (*Sydney Gazette*, 21 April 1842), "Native Song" (*Sydney Morning Herald*, 11 October 1848) and "Pietta Wollombi" (Isaac Nathan's *The Southern Euphrosyne and Australian Miscellany*, Sydney, 1849).
96. Elizabeth Hamilton Dunlop, "The Aboriginal Mother", *Australian and New Zealand Monthly Magazine* 6, 1842, p.296.
97. Barrington, p.36.
98. Anon., "Manners and Customs of all Nations. The

Australian", *The Mirror of Literature, Amusement, and Instruction* 15, 1830, p.221.

99. Moncrieff, p.40.
100. Martin, p.149.
101. Barrington, pp.34-35.
102. Cunningham, vol.II, p.45.
103. Louisa Anne Meredith (née Twamley), *Notes and Sketches of New South Wales During a Residence in the Colony from 1839 to 1844*, John Murray, London, 1844, p.94.
104. Angas, vol I, p.82.
105. Eyre, vol.II, p.207.
106. Howitt, p.194.
107. Howitt, p.196.
108. Charles Lloyd, "The Slave — An Ode" in his *Poems on Various Subjects*, Carlisle, 1795, p.62.
109. George Loveless, *The Victims of Whiggery*, London, 1837, p.31.
110. Harris, *Settlers and Convicts*, p.238.
111. Anon., "Landed in Botany Bay" (ca 1790), in Hugh Anderson (ed.), *Farewell to Old England. A Broadside History of Early Australia*, Angus and Robertson, London, 1964, p.24.
112. James Backhouse, *A Narrative of a Visit to the Australian Colonies*, Hamilton, Adams and Co., London, 1843, p.162.
113. Robert Southey, "Elinor", in his *Botany Bay Eclogues* (first published 1794), in *The Poetical Works of Robert Southey*, Galignani, Paris, 1829, pp.610-11.
114. Moncrieff, p.3.
115. Byrne, vol.I, p.230.
116. Helen Heney, *Australia's Founding Mothers*, Nelson, Melbourne, 1978, p.16.
117. Leslie Rees, *A History of Australian Drama*, 2 vols, Angus and Robertson, Sydney, 1978, vol.I, p.13.
118. Howitt, p.294.
119. J. Ross, "Savages", *London Journal* 4, 1846, p.24.
120. John Lort Stokes, *Discoveries in Australia...during a Voyage of H.M.S. Beagle*, 2 vols, T. & W. Boone, London, 1846, vol.I, pp.260-61.
121. Byrne, vol.II, p.77.
122. Miriam Dixson, *The Real Matilda. Woman and Identity in*

Australia 1788 to 1975, Penguin, Harmondsworth, 1976, p.123.

123. J. C. Byrne, vol.I, p.232.
124. Dixson, p.222.
125. Anonymous review of "Lang's *Account of New South Wales*", *The Gentleman's Magazine* (new series) 10, 1838, p.359.

Chapter Six

1. Georg Lukacs, "Narrate or Describe", in his *Writer and Critic and other Essays*, Merlin, London, 1978, p.128.
2. Georg Lukacs, "Tolstoy and the Development of Realism", in David Gray (ed.), *Marxists on Literature: An Anthology*, Penguin, Harmondsworth, 1975, p.334.
3. See Patrick White, "Flaws in the Glass", in *Bulletin*, 29 January 1980 (1880-1980 Souvenir Edition), p.152. See also Patrick White, "The Prodigal Son", in *Australian Letters* 1, 1958, No.3, pp.38-39 and *Flaws in the Glass*, Jonathan Cape, London, 1981, p.83 and p.103.
4. J. F. Burrows, "'Voss' and the Explorers", *A.U.M.L.A.* (Australasian Universities Modern Languages Association) 26, 1966, p.238.
5. Patrick White, *Voss*, Penguin, Harmondsworth, 1960, p.189. All future references to *Voss* will be to this edition and will be cited parenthetically in the text.
6. Charles Sturt, *Narrative of an Expedition into Central Australia*, 2 vols, T. & W. Boone, London, 1849, vol.II, p.2.
7. Patrick White, *Riders in the Chariot*, Penguin, Harmondsworth, 1964, p.52.
8. Patrick White, *The Eye of the Storm*, Penguin, Harmondsworth, 1975, pp.409-10.
9. John Docker, *Australian Cultural Elites. Intellectual Traditions in Sydney and Melbourne*, Angus and Robertson, Sydney, 1974, p.60.
10. Peter Beatson, "The Three Stages: Mysticism in Patrick White's *Voss*", *Southerly* 30, 1970, pp.118-19.
11. R. F. Brissenden, *Patrick White*, Longmans, Green and Co., London, 1966, p.32.
12. Judith Wright, "The Upside-down Hut", in John Barnes (ed.),

The Writer in Australia. A Collection of Literary Documents 1856-1966, Oxford University Press, Melbourne, 1969, p.335.

13. John L. Allen, "Lands of Myth, Waters of Wonder: The Place of the imagination in the History of Geographical Exploration", in D. Lowenthal and M. J. Bowden (eds), *Geographies of the Mind. Essays in Historical Geosophy*, Oxford University Press, New York, 1976, p.47.
14. William Wordsworth, *The Prelude*, edited by Ernest de Selincourt, Oxford University Press, London, 1926, Book IV (1805-6 draft), ll.382-83, p.126.
15. Patrick White, "The Prodigal Son", p.39.
16. William Walsh, *Patrick White: Voss*, Edward Arnold, London, 1976, p.33.
17. Patrick White, "The Prodigal Son", p.40.
18. Patrick White, *The Twyborn Affair*, Jonathan Cape, London, 1979, p.337.
19. Veronica Brady, "The Novelist and the New World: Patrick White's *Voss*", *Texas Studies in Literature and Language* 21, 1979, p.176.
20. Patrick White, "The Prodigal Son", p.39.
21. Wilson Harris, *Fossil and Psyche*, Occasional Publication No. 7 of African and Afro-American Studies and Research Center: The University of Texas at Austin, 1974, p.9.
22. Patrick White, *A Fringe of Leaves*, Penguin, Harmondsworth, 1977, p.7. All future references to *A Fringe of Leaves* will be to this edition and will be cited parenthetically in the text.
23. Charles Lamb, "Distant Correspondents", in his *Essays of Elia* edited by N. L. Hallward and S. C. Hill, Macmillan, London, 1960, p.147.

Select Bibliography

General reference material

BARTON, G.B., "Bibliography of Terra Australis, New Holland, and New South Wales to 1820", in his *History of New South Wales from the Records*, 2 vols, Trubner, London, 1889.

COPPELL, W.G. (ed.), *World Catalogue of Theses and Dissertations about the Australian Aborigines and Torres Strait Islanders*, Sydney University Press, Sydney, 1977.

COX, EDWARD G. (ed.), *A Reference Guide to the Literature of Travel*, University of Washington, Seattle, 1935.

FERGUSON, JOHN ALEXANDER, *Bibliography of Australia*, vols I-IV, Angus and Robertson, Sydney, 1941-55.

GREENWAY, JOHN (ed.), *Bibliography of the Australian Aborigines and the Native Peoples of Torres Strait to 1959*, Angus and Robertson, Sydney, 1963.

HEATON, J.H. (ed.), *Australian Dictionary of Dates and Men of the Time*, Silver, London, 1879.

HOLMES, MAURICE (ed.), *Captain James Cook, R.N., F.R.S., A*

Bibliographical Excursion, Francis Edwards, London, 1952.

LAWSON, ALAN (ed.), *Patrick White*, Oxford University Press, Melbourne, 1974.

MILLER, E. MORRIS (ed.), *Australian Literature. A Bibliography to 1938* (Extended to 1950 under the editorship of F. T. Macartney), Angus and Robertson, Sydney, 1956.

PUBLIC LIBRARY OF NEW SOUTH WALES, *Bibliography of Captain James Cook*, 1928.

SERLE, PERCIVAL (ed.), *Dictionary of Australian Biography*, 2 vols., Angus and Robertson, Sydney, 1949.

SHAW, A. G. L., AND C. M. H. CLARK (eds), *Australian Dictionary of Biography 1788-1850*, 2 vols, Melbourne University Press, Melbourne, 1966-67.

Primary material

ANONYMOUS WORKS

Alfred Dudley; or The Australian Settlers, Harvey and Darton, London, 1830.

"Australia" (including a review of E. J. Eyre's *Journals*), *North British Review* 4, 1846, pp.281-312.

"Australia" (including reviews of G. F. Angas's *Savage Life* and G. H. Haydon's *Five Years' Experience in Australia Felix), British Quarterly Review* 5, 1847, pp.29-49.

"Australia", *Emigrants' Penny Magazine* 1, 1850, pp.121-24.

"Australia. A Prize Poem Recited in Rugby School", J. S. Crossley, Rugby, 1843.

"The Australian", *The Mirror of Literature, Amusement and Instruction* 15, 1830, pp.220-21.

"Australian Colonies or Republics", *Fraser's Magazine* 37, 1848, pp.566-78.

"Australian Discovery — Killing Natives by Explorers", *Eclectic Review* 69, 1839, pp.157-85.

"The *Beagle*'s Discoveries in Australia", *Fraser's Magazine* 34, 1846, pp.105-17.

"Cannibalism and Infanticide in Australia", *London Journal* 7, 1848, pp.74-75.

"Colonies and Emigration: South Australia", *Monthly Chronicle* 4, 1839, pp.193-208.

Emigrant Tracts 1-18, The Society for Promoting Christian Knowledge, London, 1850.

Emigrants' Letters: Being Recent Communications from Settlers in the British Colonies, Trelawney Saunders, London, 1850.

Emigration. Who should go; Where to go; How to get there; And what to take, London, 1843.

The Farmers; or, Tales for the Times, addressed to the Yeomanry of England, London, 1823.

An Historical Narrative of the Discovery of New Holland and New South Wales, London, n.d. (1789?).

The History of Botany Bay in New Holland, London, n.d. (ca 1790).

The History of New Holland, from its First Discovery in 1616, to the Present Time, London, 1787. In 1808 this work was republished, with the authorship attributed to George Barrington.

An Impartial Examination of all the Authors on Australia; Official Documents and the Reports of Private Individuals, by "An Intending Emigrant", Smith, Elder and Co., London, 1838.

"Journal of an Excursion to the Five Islands and Shoal Haven on the Coast of New South Wales", *London Magazine* 10, 1824, pp.181-84.

"Mitchell's Second and Third Expeditions", *Blackwood's Edinburgh Magazine* 45, 1839, pp.113-29.

A New History of Botany Bay and Port Jackson, Johnston, Falkirk, 1821.

"New South Wales" (including a review of Thomas Mitchell's *Three Expeditions*), *Blackwood's Edinburgh Magazine* 44, 1838, pp.690-716.

"New South Wales", *Eclectic Review* 32, 1820, pp.131-43.

New South Wales as it was, as it is, and as it will be; or Colonial Dreams, Carnarvon, 1846.

"Notes of a Settler at Swan River", *The Mirror of Literature, Amusement and Instruction* 18, 1831, pp.68-69.

"Notes on Men and Things in the New World of Australia", *New Monthly Magazine* 85, 1849, pp.58-63, pp.159-64; pp.489-95.

"On the Aborigines of New Holland", *Alexander's East India Magazine, and Colonial and Commercial Journal* 8, 1834, pp.329-31.

"Oxley's Tour in Botany Bay", *Edinburgh Review* 34, 1820, pp.422-30.

The Picture of Australia, Whittaker, Treacher and Co., London, 1829.

"Pictures of Life in Australia", *Household Words* 1, 1850, pp.307-10.

"The Pleasures of Bush Life", *London Journal* 8, 1849, pp.350-51.

"Rambles in New South Wales", *New Monthly Magazine* 22, 1828, pp.236-47; pp.419-30; pp.536-44.

"Rambles in New South Wales", *New Monthly Magazine* 23, 1828, pp.216-23.

Review of David Collins's *Account, Eclectic Review* 2, 1805, pp.566-78.

Review of P. M. Cunningham's *Two Years in New South Wales, New Monthly Magazine* 20, 1827, pp.393-400.

Review of P. M. Cunningham's *Two Years in New South Wales, Quarterly Review* 37, 1828, pp.1-32.

Review of E. J. Eyre's *Journals, Athenaeum Journal,* 1845, pp.867-68.

Review of Barron Field's *First Fruits of Australian Poetry, New Monthly Magazine* 1, 1821, pp.682-86.

Review of Matthew Flinders's *A Voyage to Terra Australis, Eclectic Review* 29, 1819, pp.359-76.

Review of Matthew Flinders's *A Voyage to Terra Australis, Quarterly Review* 12, 1814, pp.1-47.

Review of E. W. Landor's *The Bushman, Fraser's Magazine* 37, 1848, pp.343-56.

Review, "Lang's Account of New South Wales", *The Gentleman's Magazine* New Series 10, 1838, pp.347-60.

"Review of Literature", *Monthly Chronicle* 2, 1838, pp.366-80. This article deals largely with travel literature.

Review of Thomas Mitchell's *Three Expeditions, Athenaeum Journal,* 1838, pp.707-10.

Review of W. C. Wentworth's *A Statistical, Historical, and Political Description of New South Wales, Edinburgh Monthly Review* 3, 1820, pp.29-59.

"The Swan River Settlement", *New Monthly Magazine* 25, 1829, pp.497-506.

The Telegraph Inverted or Lauderdale's Peep at the Author and Adherents of the Telegraph, n.p., January 1796.

"The Transport's Return", undated broadside, ca 1832, British Museum catalogue no. 11621 k5 (319).

A True Picture of Australia, by "A Friend to Truth", John Morrison, Glasgow, 1839.

Twenty Years Experience in Australia; being the evidence of. . . residents and travellers in those Colonies, Smith, Elder and Co., London, 1839.

"The Unhappy Transport", undated broadside, ca 1822, British Museum catalogue no. 1875 d13.

"Van Diemen's Land", undated broadside, ca 1850, British Museum catalogue no. 11621 k4 (319).

"Van Diemen's Land", *Westminster Review* 21, 1834, pp.18-54.

A Voice from the Bush in Australia, William Curry, Dublin, 1839.

"Wentworth — Oxley — New South Wales", *Quarterly Review* 24, 1820, pp.55-72.

What is a Pound? or, Waste Lands versus the Australian Settler, Trelawney William Saunders, London, 1848.

AUTHORIAL LISTINGS

ALISON, ARCHIBALD, "The Transportation Question", *Blackwood's Edinburgh Magazine* 66, 1849, pp.519-38.

ANDERSON, HUGH (ed.), *Botany Bay Broadsides*, Ram's Skull Press, Fern Tree Gully, 1956.

—— (ed.), *Colonial Ballads*, Angus and Robertson, London, 1962.

—— (ed.), *Farewell to Old England. A Broadside History of Early Australia*, Angus and Robertson, London, 1964.

ANGAS, GEORGE FRENCH, *Savage Life and Scenes in Australia and New Zealand*, 2 vols, Smith, Elder and Co., London, 1847.

—— *South Australia Illustrated*, Thomas M'Lean, London, 1847.

ASHTON, JOHN (ed.), *Modern Street Ballads*, Chatto and Windus, London, 1888.

ASPIN, JEHOSAPHAT, *Cosmorama; A View of the Costumes and Peculiarities of All Nations*, Harris, London, 1826.

BACKHOUSE, JAMES, *A Narrative of a Visit to the Australian Colonies*, Hamilton, Adams and Co., London, 1843.

BALFOUR, J.O., *A Sketch of New South Wales*, Smith, Elder and Co., London, 1845.

BANKS, JOSEPH, *Journal of the Right Hon. Sir Joseph Banks*, edited by Joseph Hooker, Macmillan, London, 1896.

BARRINGTON, GEORGE, *The History of New South Wales, including Botany Bay, Port Jackson, Pamaratta [sic], Sydney and all its Dependencies*, Jones, London, 1802.

—— *A Voyage to Botany Bay by George Barrington. Together with his life and trial and the sequel to his voyage*, Brummell Press, London, 1969. This is a facsimile edition of the 1795 first edition and the 1800 sequel.

BARTLETT, THOMAS, *New Holland: Its Colonization, Productions and Resources, with Observations on the Relations Subsisting with Great Britain*, Longman, Brown, Green and Longmans, London, 1843.

BENNET, GEORGE, *Wanderings in New South Wales, Batavia, Pedir Coast, Singapore, and China*, Richard Bentley, London, 1834.

BENTHAM, JEREMY, "Letter to Lord Pelham, Giving a Comparative View of the System of Penal Colonization in New South Wales, and the Home Penitentiary System", circular, Westminster, 2 November, 1802.

—— "Second Letter to Lord Pelham, in Continuation of the Comparative View of the System of Penal Colonization in New South Wales and the Home Penitentiary System", circular, Westminster, 17 December 1802.

BEWICK, T., *A General History of Quadrupeds*, Newcastle, 1790.

BIGGE, JOHN THOMAS, *Report of the Commissioner of Inquiry on the State of Agriculture and Trade in the Colony of New South Wales*, Parliamentary Papers, 1823, X, 136.

BISCHOFF, JAMES, *Sketch of the History of Van Diemen's Land*, John Richardson, London, 1832,

BOND, G., *A Brief Account of the Colony of Port-Jackson, in New South Wales; Its Native Inhabitants, Productions*, Southhampton, 1803.

BOWLES, WILLIAM LISLE, *The Spirit of Discovery; or, The Conquest of the Ocean*, Cruttwell, Bath, 1804.

BRAIM, THOMAS HENRY, *A History of New South Wales, from its Settlement to the Close of the year 1844*, Richard Bentley, London, 1846.

BROCK, DANIEL, *To the Desert with Sturt. A Diary of the 1844 Expedition*, Royal Geographical Society of Australia, South Australian Branch, 1975.

BROME, RICHARD, *The Antipodes: A Comedie*, edited by Ann Haaker, Edward Arnold, London, 1967.

DE BROSSES, CHARLES, *Histoire des Navigations aux Terres Australes*, 2 vols, Paris, 1756.

BROWNING, COLIN ARNOTT, *The Convict Ship; A Narrative of the Results of Scriptural Instruction and Moral Discipline*, Smith,

Elder and Co., London, 1844.

BULWER LYTTON, EDWARD, *The Caxtons. A Family Picture*, 3 vols., William Blackwood and Sons, Edinburgh, 1849.

BURN, DAVID, *The Bushrangers*, Manuscript, A1467, Mitchell Library, Sydney.

—— *Vindication of Van Diemen's Land; in Cursory Glance at her Colonists as they are, Not as they have been Represented to be*, J. W. Southgate, London, 1840.

BURNEY, JAMES, *A Chronological History of the Voyages and Discoveries in the South Sea or Pacific Ocean*, 5 vols, London, 1803-1817.

BYRNE, J.C., *Twelve Years' Wanderings in the British Colonies from 1835 to 1847*, 2 vols, Richard Bentley, London, 1848.

—— *Emigrant's Guide to New South Wales Proper, Australia Felix and South Australia*, London, 1848.

CALLANDER, JOHN (ed.), *Terra Australis Cognita: or, Voyages to the Terra Australis, or Southern Hemisphere, during the Sixteenth, Seventeenth, and Eighteenth Centuries*, 3 vols, Edinburgh, 1766.

CAMPBELL, JOHN (ed.), *The Modern Part of the Universal History*, vol.V, London, 1760.

—— *Navigantium Atque Itinerantium Bibliotheca. Or, A Complete Collection of Voyages and Travels*, 2 vols, London, 1744-48. This is a revised and enlarged version of John Harris's 1705 anthology of the same title.

CAMPBELL, THOMAS, "Lines on the Departure of Emigrants for New South Wales" (1828), in J. L. Robertson (ed.), *The Complete Poetical Works of Thomas Campbell*, Oxford University Press, London, 1907.

CAPPER, HENRY, *South Australia. Containing Hints to Emigrants*, 2nd edn, Robert Tyas, London, 1838.

CASWELL, ALFRED, (ed.), *Hints from the Journal of an Australian Squatter*, Smith, Elder and Co., London, 1843.

CHAPMAN, HENRY SAMUEL, "Australia", *Monthly Chronicle* 7, 1841, pp.385-405.

CLARK, JOHN HEAVISIDE, *Field Sports. . . of the Native Inhabitants of New South Wales*, London, 1813.

CLARKE, MARCUS, "Preface" to his edition of *Poems of the Late Adam Lindsay Gordon*, Samuel Mullen, London, 1887.

COBBET, WILLIAM, "Convicts' Bank", *Cobbet's Political Register* 67, 1829, pp.766-67.

COLLINS, DAVID, *An Account of the English Colony in New South Wales, with Remarks on the Dispositions, Customs, Manners, &c of the Native Inhabitants of that Country*, Cadell and Davies, London, 1798.

—— *An Account of the English Colony in New South Wales, from its First Settlement, in January 1788, to August 1801*, Cadell and Davies, London, 1802.

COOK, JAMES, *The Journals of Captain James Cook on his Voyages of Discovery*, 4 vols, edited by J. C. Beaglehole, Cambridge University Press, Cambridge, 1968.

CRAWFURD, JOHN, "New South Australian Colony", *Westminster Review* 21, 1834, pp.441-76.

CROLY, GEORGE, "The Navigation of the Antipodes", *Blackwood's Edinburgh Magazine* 62, 1847, pp.515-33.

CUNNINGHAM, PETER MILLER, *Two Years in New South Wales*, 2 vols, London, 1827.

—— *Hints for Australian Emigrants*, T. and W. Boone, London, 1841.

CURR, EDWARD, *An Account of the Colony of Van Diemen's Land*, London, 1824.

DALRYMPLE, ALEXANDER, *An Account of the Discoveries Made in the South Pacifick Ocean, Previous to 1764*, London, 1767.

—— *An Historical Collection of the Several Voyages and Discoveries in the South Pacific Ocean*, 2 vols, London, 1770.

—— *A Serious Admonition to the Public on the Intended Thief-Colony at Botany Bay*, John Sewell, London, 1786.

DAMPIER, WILLIAM, *A New Voyage Round the World*, James Knapton, London, 1697.

—— *A Voyage to New Holland, & C. In the Year 1699*, James Knapton, London, 1703.

—— *A Continuation of a Voyage to New Holland, & C. in the Year 1699*, James Knapton, London, 1709.

DARWIN, ERASMUS, *Zoonomia; or, The Laws of Organic Life*, 2 vols, London, 1794.

DAWSON, ROBERT, *The Present State of Australia; A Description of the Country, Its Advantages and Prospects with Reference to Emigration*, Smith, Elder and Co., London, 1830.

DEFOE, DANIEL, *The life, adventures and pyracies of the famous Captain Singleton*, edited by K. S. Kumar, Oxford University Press, London, 1969.

—— *A New Voyage Round the World by a Course never sailed before*, in *The Novels and Miscellaneous Works of Daniel Defoe*, George Bell and Sons, London, 1893, vol.VI.

DE FOIGNY, GABRIEL, *A New Discovery of Terra Incognita Australis, or the Southern World. By James Sadeur a Frenchman*, London, 1693.

DIXON, JAMES, *Narrative of a Voyage to New South Wales and Van Diemen's Land*, Edinburgh, 1822.

DUNLOP, ELIZA HAMILTON, "The Aboriginal Mother", *The Australian and New Zealand Monthly Magazine* 6, 1842, p.296.

EYRE, EDWARD JOHN, *Journals of Expeditions of Discovery into Central Australia, and Overland from Adelaide to King George's Sound, in the Years 1840-1*, 2 vols, T. and W. Boone, London, 1845.

ERSKINE, HENRY, *The Emigrant. A Poem*, n.p., n.d.. The British Museum Catalogue approximates the latest publication date as 1795.

FIELD, BARRON, *First Fruits of Australian Poetry*, Sydney, 1819.

—— *First Fruits of Australian Poetry*, 2nd and enlarged edn, Sydney, 1823.

—— (ed.), *Geographical Memoirs on New South Wales*, John Murray, London, 1825.

FITZGERALD, GERALD, *The Injured Islanders; or, the Influence of Art upon the Happiness of Nature*, London, 1779.

FITZ-ROY, ROBERT (ed.), *Narrative of the Surveying Voyages of His Majesty's Ships Adventure and Beagle, Between the Years 1826 and 1836*, 3 vols, Henry Colburn, London, 1839. See especially vol.III, *Charles Darwin's Journal and Remarks 1832-1836*.

FLINDERS, MATTHEW, *A Voyage to Terra Australis*, 2 vols, Nicol, London, 1814.

FOX, MARY, *An Account of an Expedition to the Interior of New Holland*, Bentley, London, 1837.

GLEN, WILLIAM, *The Lonely Isle: A South Sea Island Tale*, Mackenzie, Glasgow, 1816.

GOUGER, ROBERT, *South Australia in 1837*, Harvey and Darton, London, 1838.

GREY, GEORGE, *Journals of Two Expeditions of Discovery in Northwest and Western Australia*, 2 vols, T. and W. Boone, London, 1841.

HAKLUYT, RICHARD, *Divers Voyages Touching the Discovery of*

America and the Islands Adjacent, edited by J. W. Jones, Franklin, New York, n.d.

HAMILTON, GEORGE, *The Telegraph; A Consolatory Epistle from Thomas Muir Esq. of Botany Bay to the Hon. Henry Erskine, Late Dean of Faculty*, n.p., n.d., ca 1796.

—— *A Voyage Round the World in His Majesty's Frigate Pandora*, London, 1793.

HAMILTON, THOMAS, "Cunningham's New South Wales", *Blackwood's Edinburgh Magazine* 22, 1827, pp.602-10.

HARRIS, ALEXANDER, *The Emigrant Family: or, The Story of an Australian Settler*, 3 vols, Smith, Elder and Co., London, 1849.

—— *A Guide to Port Stephens*, W. S. Orr, London, 1849.

—— *Settlers and Convicts, or Recollections of Sixteen Years' Labour in the Australian Backwoods*, London, 1847.

HASLAM, JOHN, *Convict Ships. A Narrative of a Voyage to New South Wales in the Year 1816*, London, 1819.

HAWKESWORTH, JOHN (ed.), *An Account of the Voyages Undertaken by the Order of His Present Majesty for Making Discoveries in the Southern Hemisphere*, 3 vols, Strahan and Cadell, London, 1773.

HAYDON, G.H., *Five Years' Experience in Australia Felix*, Hamilton, Adam and Co., London, 1846.

HAYGARTH, H.W., *Recollections of Bush Life in Australia, During a Residence of Eight Years in the Interior*, John Murray, London, 1848.

HENDERSON, JOHN, *Observations on the Colonies of New South Wales and Van Dieman's Land*, Baptist Mission Press, Calcutta, 1832.

HERVEY, THOMAS K., *Australia; With Other Poems*, London, 1824.

HEYLYN, PETER, *An Appendix. . .Endeavouring a Discovery of the Unknown Parts of the World. Especially of Terra Australis Incognita, or the Southern Continent*, London, 1656.

—— *Cosmographie, in four Bookes Contayning the Chorographie and Historie of the whole World*, rev. edn, Philip Chetwind, London, 1670.

HODGKINSON, CLEMENT, *Australia, From Port Macquarie to Moreton Bay*, T. and W. Boone, London, 1845.

HOLMAN, JAMES, *A Voyage Round the World, Including Travels in Africa, Asia, Australasia, America*, 4 vols, Smith, Elder and Co., London, 1834-35.

HOLT, JOSEPH, *Memoirs of Joseph Holt*, 2 vols, edited by T. C. Croker, Henry Colburn, London, 1838.

HOME, HENRY, *Sketches of the History of Man*, 2 vols, Edinburgh, 1774.

HOOD, JOHN, *Australia and the East*, John Murray, London, 1843.

HOWITT, RICHARD, *Impressions of Australia Felix During Four Years' Residence in that Colony*, Longman, Brown, Green and Longmans, London, 1845.

HOWITT, WILLIAM, *Colonization and Christianity. A Popular History of the Treatment of the Natives by the Europeans in all their Colonies*, Longman, Brown, Green and Longmans, London, 1838.

HUNTER, JOHN, *An Historical Journal of Events at Sydney and at Sea 1788-1792*, Angus and Robertson, Sydney, 1968. Hunter's *Journal* was first published in 1793.

INGLETON, GEOFFREY (ed.), *True Patriots All, or News from Australia as Told in a Collection of Broadsides*, Angus and Robertson, Sydney, 1952.

INNES, FREDERICK MAITLAND, "The Convict System of Van Diemen's Land", *Monthly Chronicle* 5, 1840, pp.431-49.

JAMES, G.P.R., *The Convict*, 3 vols, Smith, Elder and Co., London, 1847.

JAMES, T. HORTON, *Six Months in South Australia*, London, 1838.

JAMESON, R.G., *New Zealand, South Australia and New South Wales: A Record of Recent Travels in these Colonies*, London, 1842.

JEFFREYS, CHARLES, *Van Dieman's Land. Geographical and Descriptive Delineations of the Island of Van Dieman's Land*, J. M. Richardson, London, 1820.

KENEALLY, THOMAS, *Bring Larks and Heroes*, Quartet Books, London, 1973.

KNIGHT, RICHARD PAYNE, *The Progress of Civil Society. A Didactic Poem in Six Books*, London, 1796.

LANDOR, E.W., *The Bushman; or, Life in a New Country*, Bentley, London, 1847.

LEICHHARDT, LUDWIG, *Journal of an Overland Expedition in Australia from Moreton Bay to Port Essington*, London, 1847.

LEIGH, W.H., *The Emigrant: A Tale of Australia*, Simmonds, London, 1847.

—— *Reconnoitering Voyages, Travels and Adventures in the New*

Colonies of South Australia, Smith, Elder and Co., London, 1847.

LLOYD, E., *A Visit to the Antipodes*, London, 1846.

LOVELESS, GEORGE, *A Narrative of the Sufferings of Jas. Brine, and Thomas & John Standfield. . . With a Brief Description of New South Wales*, London, 1838.

—— *The Victims of Whiggery; Being a Statement of the Persecutions experienced by the Dorchester Labourers*, London, 1837.

LYCETT, JOSEPH, *Views in Australia*, J. Souter, London, 1824.

MCAULEY, JAMES, *Collected Poems 1936-1970*, Sydney, Angus and Robertson, 1971.

MCCOMBIE, THOMAS, *Adventures of a Colonist; or Godfrey Arabin the Settler*, London, 1845.

MACKANESS, G. (ed.), *Fourteen Journeys over the Blue Mountains*, 3 vols, D. S. Ford, Sydney, 1950-51.

MACKENZIE, DAVID, *The Emigrant's Guide: or Ten Years' Experience in New South Wales*, London, 1845.

MACQUEEN, T. POTTER, *Australia as She is and as She may be*, London, 1840.

MALTHUS, T.R., *An Essay on the Principle of Population; or, A View on its Past and Present Effect on Human Happiness*, London, 1803.

MANN, D.D., *The Present Picture of New South Wales*, London, 1803.

MARTIN, ROBERT MONTGOMERY, *History of Austral-asia*, Whittaker and Co., London, 1839.

MASLEN, T.J., *The Friend of Australia; or, A Plan for Exploring the Interior*, Hurst, Chance and Co., London, 1830.

MATTHEW, PATRICK, *Emigration Fields, North America, The Cape, Australia, and New Zealand*, Edinburgh, 1839.

MELLISH, T., "A Convict's Recollections of New South Wales", *London Magazine* 2, 1825, pp.49-67.

MEREDITH, LOUISA ANNE, *Notes and Sketches of New South Wales During a Residence in that Colony from 1839 to 1844*, John Murray, London, 1844.

MITCHELL, THOMAS LIVINGSTONE, *Journal of an Expedition into the Interior of Tropical Australia, in Search of a Route from Sydney to the Gulf of Carpentaria*, Longman, Brown, Green and Longmans, London, 1848.

—— *Three Expeditions into the Interior of Eastern Australia, with Descriptions of the Recently Explored Region of Australia Felix, and the Present Colony of New South Wales*, 2 vols, T. and W. Boone, London, 1838.

MONCRIEFF, WILLIAM THOMAS, *Van Diemen's Land! An Operatic Drama in Three Acts*, in T. Richardson (ed.), *Richardson's New Modern Drama Vol.IV*, T. Richardson, London, 1831.

MONTGOMERY, JAMES, *The Pelican Island and Other Poems*, Longman, Brown, Green and Longmans, London, 1828.

MORGAN, GEORGE OSBORNE, *Settlers in Australia: A Prize Poem, recited in the Theatre, Oxford; June 24, 1846*, Oxford, 1846.

MUDIE, JAMES, *The Felonry of New South Wales*, Angus and Robertson, London, 1965. The book was first published in 1837.

NEVILLE, HENRY, *The Isle of Pines. Or a late discovery of a fourth Island, in Terra Australis Incognita*, T. Cadell, London, 1768. The book was first published in 1668.

NICOL, JOHN, *The Life and Adventures of John Nicol, Mariner*, T. Cadell, London, 1822.

OGLE, NATHANIEL, *The Colony of Western Australia: A Manual for Emigrants to that Settlement or its Dependencies*, London, 1839.

O'HARA, JAMES, *History of New South Wales*, Hatchard, London, 1817.

PALMER, THOMAS FYSHE, *A Narrative of the Sufferings of T. F. Palmer and W. Skirving During a Voyage to New South Wales on board the Surprise Transport*, London, 1797.

PARKER, HENRY WALKER, *The Rise, Progress, and Present State of Van Dieman's Land*, J. Cross, London, 1833.

PARKINSON, SYDNEY, *A Journal of a Voyage to the South Seas, in His Majesty's Ship, The Endeavour*, London, 1773.

PATERSON, G., *The History of New South Wales from its First Discovery to the Present Time*, London, 1811.

PENNANT, THOMAS, *The View of the Malayan Isles, New Holland, and the Spicy Islands*, London, 1800.

PHILLIP, ARTHUR, *The Voyage of Governor Phillip to Botany Bay*, Stockdale, London, 1789.

PRAED, WINTHROP MACKWORTH, *Australasia, A Poem which obtained the Chancellor's Medal at the Cambridge Commencement*, Cambridge, 1823.

PRINSEP, MRS AUGUSTUS, *The Journal of a Voyage from Calcutta to Van Diemen's Land*, London, 1833.

PURCHAS, SAMUEL, *Hakluytus Posthumus or Purchas His Pilgrimes*, 20 vols, James MacLehose, Glasgow, 1906.

REYNOLDS, JOHN HAMILTON, *The Eden of the Imagination*, Cawthirn and Martin, London, 1814.

ROBINSON, DAVID, "The Surplus Population of the United Kingdom", *Blackwood's Edinburgh Magazine* 21, 1827, pp.377-91.

ROGERS, H., "The Destinies of England", in William Ellis (ed.), *The Missionary; Christian's New Year Gift*, Seely and Sons, London, 1833, pp.201-19.

ROSS, J.W., "Savages", *London Journal* 4, 1846, pp.23-24.

ROUSSEAU, JEAN-JACQUES, *The Social Contract and Discourses*, translated and edited by G. D. H. Cole, Dent, London, 1973.

ROWCROFT, CHARLES, *The Bushranger of Van Diemen's Land*, 3 vols, Smith, Elder and Co., London, 1848.

—— *Tales of the Colonies, or, The Adventures of an Emigrant*, 3 vols, Saunders and Otley, London, 1843.

SAMWELL, DAVID, *A Narrative of the Death of Captain James Cook*, Robinson, London, 1786.

SCOTT, THEODORE, *Description of South Australia; with sketches of New South Wales, Port Lincoln, Port Philip, and New Zealand*, London, 1839.

SEWARD, ANNA, *Elegy to Captain Cook. To which is added an Ode to the Sun*, Dodsley, London, 1780.

SHAW, GEORGE, *Zoology of New Holland*, Sowerby, London, 1794.

SIDNEY, JOHN ("A Bushman"), *A Voice from the Far Interior of Australia*, Smith, Elder and Co., London, 1847.

SPRAT, THOMAS, *The History of the Royal Society of London*, 3rd edn, London, 1722.

SLESSOR, KENNETH, *Cuckooz Contrey*, Johnson, Sydney, 1932.

SMITH, SYDNEY (?), "Botany bay", *Edinburgh Review* 32, 1819, pp.28-48.

—— "New South Wales", a review of Collins's *Account*, *Edinburgh Review* 2, 1803, pp.30-42.

—— *The Works of the Rev. Sydney Smith*, Longman, Brown, Green and Longmans, London, 1850.

SOTHEBY, WILLIAM, *A Tour Through Parts of Wales, Sonnets, Odes and Other Poems*, London, 1794.

SOUTHERN, HENRY, review of P. M. Cunningham's *Two Years in*

New South Wales, *Westminster Review* 8, 1827, pp.219-24.

SOUTHEY, ROBERT, *Botany-Bay Eclogues* (first published in 1794), in *The Poetical Works of Robert Southey*, Galignani, Paris, 1829.

STEPHENS, JOHN, *The Land of Promise: Being an Authentic and Impartial History of the Rise and Progress of the New British Province of South Australia*, Smith, Elder and Co., London, 1839.

ST JOHN, J.A., "Aboriginal Natives of Australia", *Westminster Review* 12, 1830, pp.166-86.

STOKES, JOHN LORT, *Discoveries in Australia. . .during the Voyage of H.M.S. Beagle*, 2 vols, T. and W. Boone, London, 1846.

STURT, CHARLES, *Narrative of an Expedition into Central Australia*, 2 vols, T. and W. Boone, London, 1849.

—— *Two Expeditions into the Interior of Southern Australia, during the years 1828, 1829, 1830, and 1831*, 2 vols, Smith, Elder and Co., London, 1833.

SWIFT JONATHAN, *Travels into Several Remote Nations of the World. In Four Parts. By Lemuel Gulliver*, 2 vols, London, 1726.

—— *Miscellaneous Works, Comical and Diverting: by T.R.D.J.S.D.O.P.I.I.*, London, 1720.

TENCH, WATKIN, *A Complete Account of the Settlement at Port Jackson, in New South Wales*, London, 1793.

TUCKEY, J. H., *An Account of a Voyage to Establish a Colony at Port Philip*, Longman, London, 1850.

TWAIN, MARK, *Following the Equator. A Journey Around the World*, 2 vols, Harper, New York, 1925.

WATTS, ALARIC A., "Decline and Fall of the English Empire, by an Australasian Statesman, in the Year 2377", in his *Scenes of Life and Shades of Character*, 2 vols, Colburn and Bentley, London, 1831, pp.79-102.

WEBB, FRANCIS, *Collected Poems*, Angus and Robertson, Sydney, 1969.

—— *Socrates and Other Poems*, Angus and Robertson, London, 1969.

WHITE, JOHN, *Journal of a Voyage to New South Wales*, Debrett, London, 1790.

WHITE, PATRICK, *The Eye of the Storm*, Penguin, Harmondsworth, 1975.

—— "Flaws in the Glass. Sketches for a Self-portrait", *Bulletin* (Australia), 29 January 1980, pp.146-54.

—— *Flaws in the Glass*, Jonathan Cape, London, 1981.

—— *A Fringe of Leaves*, Penguin, Harmondsworth, 1977.

—— "The Prodigal Son", *Australian Letters* 1, iii, 1958, pp.37-40.

—— *Voss*, Penguin, Harmondsworth, 1960.

WICKENDEN, WILLIAM, *Poems. By the Bard of the Forest*, Sherborne, London, 1827.

WILLIAM, JOHN, "News from an Exiled Contributor", *Blackwood's Edinburgh Magazine* 55, 1844, pp.184-96.

Secondary material

ADAMS, PERCY G., *Travelers and Travel Liars 1660-1800*, University of California Press, Berkeley, 1962.

AITKEN, JONATHAN, *Land of Fortune. A Study of the New Australia*, Secker and Warburg, London, 1971.

ALEXANDER, MICHAEL, *Mrs Fraser on the Fatal Shore*, Michael Joseph, London, 1971.

ALLEN, H.C., *Bush and Backwoods. A Comparison of the Frontier in Australia and the United States*, Angus and Robertson, Sydney, 1971.

ANDERSON, DON, "A Severed Leg: Anthropophagy and Communion in Patrick White's Fiction", *Southerly* 40, 1980, pp.399-417.

ATKINSON, GEOFFROY, *The Extraordinary Voyage in French Literature Before 1700*, Columbia University Press, New York, 1920.

BAKER, J.N.L., *A History of Geographical Discovery and Exploration*, Harrap, London, 1931.

BARNES, JOHN (ed.), *The Writer in Australia. A Collection of Literary Documents 1856-1964*, Oxford University Press, Melbourne, 1969.

BARTON, G.B., *The History of New South Wales from the Records*, London, 1899.

BAUDET, ERNEST HENRI, *Paradise on Earth. Some Thoughts on European Images of Non-European Man*, Yale University Press, New Haven, 1965.

BEAGLEHOLE, J.C., *Cook the Writer*, Sydney University Press, Sydney, 1970.

BEALE, EDGAR, *Sturt, the Chipped Idol. A Study of Charles Sturt,*

Explorer, Sydney University Press, Sydney, 1979.

BEATSON, PETER, *The Eye in the Mandala. Patrick White: A Vision of Man and God*, Paul Elek, London, 1976.

BESSES, PIERRE, "Du bon sauvage comme sous-homme du Pacifique", *Caliban* 14, 1979, pp.165-83.

BISSELL, BENJAMIN, *The American Indian in English Literature of the Eighteenth Century*, Yale University Press, New Haven, 1925.

BLAINEY, GEOFFREY, *The Tyranny of Distance: How Distance Shaped Australia's History*, Macmillan, Melbourne, 1968.

BOLITHO, HECTOR, AND JOHN MULGAN, *The Emigrants: Early Travellers to the Antipodes*, Selwyn and Blount, London, 1929.

BOLT, CHRISTINE, *Victorian Attitudes to Race*, Routledge and Kegan Paul, London, 1971.

BONNER, WILLIAM, *Captain William Dampier: Buccaneer-Author*, Stanford University Press, Stanford University, 1934.

BRADY, VERONICA, "A Fringe of Leaves: Civilization by the Skin of Our Own Teeth", *Southerly* 37, 1977, pp.123-40.

—— "In My End is My Beginning: Laura as Heroine of *Voss*", *Southerly* 35, 1975, pp.16-32.

—— "The Novelist and the New World: Patrick White's *Voss*", Texas Studies in Literature and Language 21, 1979, pp.169-85.

BREE, GERMAINE, "The Ambiguous Voyage: Mode or Genre", *Genre* 1, 1968, pp.87-96.

BUCKLEY, VINCENT, "Utopianism and Vitalism in Australian Literature", *Quadrant* 3, 1958, pp.39-51.

BURROUGHS, PETER, *Britain and Australia 1831-1855. A Study in Imperial Relations and Crown Lands Administration*, Clarendon Press, Oxford, 1967.

CARNALL, GEOFFREY, *Robert Southey*, Longmans, Green and Co., London, 1964.

CARRITT, E.F. (ed.), *Philosophies of Beauty*, Clarendon Press, Oxford, 1931.

CARROTHERS, W.A., *Emigration from the British Isles*, Augustus M. Kelly, New York, 1969.

CASE, A.E., *Four Essays on Gulliver's Travels*, Princeton University Press, Princeton, 1945.

CHIAPELLI, FREDI (ed.), *First Images of America. The Impact of the New World on the Old*, 2 vols, University of California Press, Berkeley, 1976.

CHISHOLM, ALEC HUGH, "The Odd Case of Alexander Harris", *Meanjin* 19, 1960, pp.411-20.

—— *Strange New World. The Adventures of John Gilbert and Ludwig Leichhardt*, rev. edn, Angus and Robertson, Sydney, 1955.

CLARK, C.M.H., *A History of Australia*, 5 vols, Melbourne University Press, Melbourne, 1962-78.

—— (ed.), *Sources of Australian History*, Oxford University Press, London, 1957.

CLARKE, DONOVAN, "The Image of Australian Man", *Australian Quarterly* 37, 1965, pp.67-78.

CLARKE, F.G., *The Land of Contrarieties. The British Attitudes to the Australian Colonies 1828-1855*, Melbourne University Press, Melbourne, 1977.

CLUNE, FRANK, *The Scottish Martyrs. Their Trials and Transportation to Botany Bay*, Angus and Robertson, Sydney, 1969.

COLLINGRIDGE, GEORGE, *The Discovery of Australia*, Hayes Bros, Sydney, 1895.

COLLINS, C.R., *Saga of Settlement. A Brief Account of the Life and Times of Lieutenant-Colonel David Collins*, Imperial Printing Co., Perth, 1956.

COTTER, MICHAEL, "The Image of the Aboriginal in Three Modern Australian Novels", *Meanjin* 36, 1977, pp.582-92.

COUCH, B.V., *Thomas Livingston Mitchell 1827-1837. A Study of the Man and his Impact on his Contemporaries*, M.A. thesis, University of Sydney, 1963.

CROWLEY, F.K. (ed.), *A New History of Australia*, Heinemann, Melbourne, 1974.

CUMPSTON, J.H.L., *The Inland Sea and the Great River. The Story of Australian Exploration*, Angus and Robertson, Sydney, 1965.

—— *Thomas Mitchell: Surveyor General and Explorer*, Oxford University Press, London, 1954.

CURTIN, PHILIP D., *The Image of Africa. British Ideas and Action 1780-1850*, Macmillan, London, 1965.

DAVIS, DAVID BRIAN, *The Problem of Slavery in Western Culture*, Cornell University Press, Ithaca, 1966.

DIXSON, MIRIAM, *The Real Matilda. Woman and Identity in Australia. 1788 to 1975*, Penguin, Harmondsworth, 1976.

DOCKER, JOHN, *Australian Cultural Elites. Intellectual Traditions in Sydney and Melbourne*, Angus and Robertson, Sydney, 1974.

DUDLEY, EDWARD, AND MAXIMILLIAN E. NOVAK (eds), *The Wild Man Within. An Image in Western Thought from the Renaissance to Romanticism*, University of Pittsburgh Press, Pittsburgh, 1972.

DUTTON, GEOFFREY, *The Hero as Murderer. The Life of Edward John Eyre, Australian Explorer and Governor of Jamaica*, Collins, London, 1967.

—— *White on Black. The Australian Aborigine Portrayed in Art*, Macmillan, Melbourne, 1974.

ELLIOTT, BRIAN, "Antipodes: An Essay in Attitudes", *Australian Letters* 7, 1966, pp.51-75.

—— *James Hardy Vaux. A Literary Rogue in Australia*, Wakefield Press, Adelaide, 1944.

—— *The Landscape of Australian Poetry*, Cheshire, Melbourne, 1967.

ERICKSEN, RAY, *Ernest Giles. Explorer and Traveller, 1835-1897*, Heinemann, Melbourne, 1978.

EXCELL, PATRICIA, "'Eyre All Alone': Francis Webb as Myth-maker", *Australian Literary Studies* 10, 1981, pp.101-105.

FAIRCHILD, HOXIE NEALE, *The Noble Savage. A Study in Romantic Naturalism*, Columbia University Press, New York, 1928.

FAVENC, ERNEST, *The Explorers of Australia and their Lifework*, Whitcombe and Tombs, London, 1908.

—— *The History of Australian Exploration from 1788 to 1888*, Turner and Henderson, Sydney, 1888.

FISHER, JOHN, *The Australians. From 1788 to Modern Times*, Robert Hale, London, 1968.

FITZPATRICK, BRIAN, *British Imperialism and Australia 1788-1833*, Sydney University Press, Sydney, 1971.

FRIEDERICH, W.P. (ed.), *Australia in Western Imaginative Prose Writings 1600-1960. An Anthology and History of Literature*, University of North Carolina Press, Chapel Hill, 1967.

FROST, ALAN, "What Created, What Perceived? Early Responses to New South Wales", *Australian Literary Studies* 7, 1975, pp.185-205.

GAREBIAN, KEITH, "The Desert and the Garden: The Theme of Completeness in *Voss*", *Modern Fiction Studies* 22, 1976, pp.557-69.

GLADSTONE, HUGH, *Thomas Watling, Limner of Dumfries*, privately printed, Dumfries, 1938.

GOODWIN, CRAWFORD, *The Image of Australia: British Perception of the Australian Economy from the Eighteenth to the Twentieth Century*, Duke University Press, Durham, 1974.

GRAY, JANE CAMERON, "The Image of the Aborigine in Literature", *Children's Libraries Newsletter* 9, 1973, pp.35-38.

GREEN, H.M., *A History of Australian Literature*. Volume One: *1789-1921*, Angus and Robertson, Sydney, 1961.

GREENWAY, JOHN, *The Last Frontier: A Study of Cultural Imperatives in the Last Frontiers of America and Australia*, Davis-Poynter, London, 1972.

HACKFORTH-JONES, JOCELYN, *The Convict Artists*, Macmillan, Melbourne, 1978.

HANGER, EUNICE, "David Burn in Sydney, 1844-1845", *Southerly* 24, 1965, pp.232-41.

HARLOW, VINCENT T., *The Founding of the Second British Empire*. Volume I: *Discovery and Revolution*, Longmans, Green and Co., London, 1952.

HARRIS, WILSON, *Fossil and Psyche*, Occasional Publication, no. 7, African and Afro-American Studies and Research Center: The University of Texas, 1974.

HARTZ, LOUIS, *The Founding of New Societies. Studies in the History of the United States, Latin America, South Africa, Canada and Australia*, Harcourt, Brace and World, New York, 1964.

HEALY, JOHN JOSEPH, "The Convict and the Aborigine: The Quest for Freedom in Ralph Rashleigh", *Australian Literary Studies* 3, 1968, pp.243-54.

—— *Literature and the Aborigine in Australia 1770-1975*, University of Queensland Press, Brisbane, 1978.

—— *The Treatment of the Aborigine in Australian Literature from the Beginning to the Present Day*, Ph.D. thesis, University of Texas, 1968.

—— "The Treatment of the Aborigine in Early Australian Fiction, 1840-70", *Australian Literary Studies* 5, 1972, pp.233-52.

HENEY, HELEN, *Australia's Founding Mothers*, Nelson, Melbourne, 1978.

HESELTINE, H.P., "Australian Image: (I) The Literary Heritage", *Meanjin* 21, 1962, pp.35-49.

HONOUR, HUGH, *The New Golden Age. European Images of America from the Discoveries to the Present Time*, Allen Lane, London, 1975.

KELLY, CELSUS, *La Austrialia del Espiritu Santo. The Journal of Fray Martin de Munilla O.F.M. and other documents relating to the Voyage of Pedro Fernandez de Quiros to the South Sea (1605-1606) and the Franciscan Missionary Plan (1617-1627)*, 2 vols, Cambridge University Press, Cambridge, 1966.

—— *Calendar of Documents*, Franciscan Historical Studies, Madrid, 1965.

—— "The Narrative of Pedro Fernandez de Quiros", *Historical Studies Australia and New Zealand*, 9, 1960, pp.186-88.

—— *Pedro Fernandez de Quiros, The Last Great Portuguese Navigator*, Lisbon, 1961.

—— "The Terra Australis — A Franciscan Quest (Part I)", *The Americas* (Washington, D.C.), 4, 1948, pp.429-48.

—— "The Terra Australis — A Franciscan Quest (Part II)", *The Americas* (Washington, D.C.), 5, 1948, pp.68-94.

KENEALLY, THOMAS, "The World's Worse End", *Caliban* 14, 1977, pp.81-89.

KIERNAN, BRIAN, *Images of Society and Nature. Seven Essays on Australian Novels*, Oxford University Press, Melbourne, 1971.

LANGLEY, MICHAEL, *Sturt of the Murray. Father of Australian Exploration*, Robert Hale, London, 1969.

LANSBURY, CORAL, *Arcady in Australia: The Evocation of Australia in Nineteenth-Century English Literature*, Melbourne University Press, Melbourne, 1970.

LEVI, J.S., AND G.F.J. BERGMAN, *Australian Genesis. Jewish Convicts and Settlers 1788-1850*, Robert Hale, London, 1974.

LEVIN, HARRY, *The Myth of the Golden Age in the Renaissance*, Faber and Faber, London, 1970.

LOVEJOY, ARTHUR O., *Essays in the History of Ideas*, Johns Hopkins Press, Baltimore, 1948.

—— *The Great Chain of Being. A Study in the History of an Idea*, Harvard University Press, Cambridge (Mass.), 1936.

LOWENTHAL, DAVID, AND MARTYN J. BOWDEN (eds), *Geographies of the Mind. Essays in Historical Geosophy*, Oxford University Press, New York, 1976.

MCGUIRE, PAUL, *Westward the Course: The New World of Oceania*, Heinemann, London, 1943.

MCINTYRE, KENNETH GORDON, *The Secret Discovery of Australia. Portuguese Ventures 200 Years before Captain Cook*, Souvenir Press, London, 1977.

MACKENZIE, JEANNE, *Australian Paradox*, Macgibbon and Kee, London, 1962.

MCQUEEN, HUMPHREY, *A New Britannia: An Argument Concerning the Social Origins of Australian Radicalism and Nationalism*, Penguin, Harmondsworth, 1975.

MADGWICK, R.B., *Immigration in Eastern Australia 1788-1851*, Sydney University Press, Sydney, 1937.

MARKHAM, CLEMENTS, *The Voyages of Pedro Fernandez de Quiros, 1595 to 1606*, Hakluyt Society, London, 1904.

MASSEY, IRVING, *The Uncreating Word. Romanticism and the Object*, Indiana University Press, Bloomington, 1970.

MATHIESON, WILLIAM LAW, *England in Transition, 1789-1832. A Study of Movements*, Longmans and Co., London, 1920.

MAGROZ, R.L., *The Real Robinson Crusoe; being the life and strange surprising adventures of Alexander Selkirk*, Cresset Press, London, 1939.

MILLS, R.C., "Gibbon Wakefield's 'Letter from Sydney'", *Royal Australian Historical Society. Journal and Proceedings* 15, 1929, pp.121-42.

MOORE, JOHN R., "The Geography of Gulliver's Travels", *Journal of English and Germanic Philology* 40, 1941, pp.214-28.

MOORE, T. INGLIS, *Social Patterns in Australian Literature*, Angus and Robertson, Sydney, 1971.

MULVANEY, D.J., "The Australian Aborigines 1606-1929. Opinion and Fieldwork. Part I 1606-1859", *Historical Studies: Australia and New Zealand* 8, 1958, pp.131-51.

MUSGROVE, S., "The Flowering of New Holland", *Landfall* 4, 1950, pp.324-31.

O'BRIEN, ERIS, *The Foundation of Australia. 1786-1800*, Sheed and Ward, London, 1937.

O'GORMAN, EDMUNDO, *The Invention of America. An inquiry into the historical nature of the New World and the meaning of its history*, Indiana University Press, Bloomington, 1961.

OGUDE, STEPHEN EFE, *Africa (Between the Deserts i.e. The Sahara and the Kalihari) in English Literature between 1660-1807*, Ph.D. thesis, University of London, 1970.

PALMER, VANCE, *The Legend of the Nineties*, Melbourne University

Press, Melbourne, 1954.

PAPPE, H.O., "Wakefield and Marx", *Economic History Review* (second series) 4, 1951, pp.88-97.

PERKINS, ELIZABETH, "Escape with a Convict: Patrick White's *A Fringe of Leaves*", *Meanjin* 36, 1977, pp.265-69.

PIKE, D.H., *Paradise of Dissent: South Australia 1829-1857*, 2nd edn, Melbourne University Press, Melbourne, 1967.

PORTER, H.C., *The Inconstant Savage. England and the North American Indian 1500-1660*, Duckworth, London, 1979.

POTTLE, FREDERICK A., *Boswell and the Girl from Botany Bay*, Heinemann, London, 1938.

PRICE, A. GRENFELL, *Island Continent. Aspects of the Historical Geography of Australia and its Territories*, Angus and Robertson, Sydney, 1972.

RAMSON, W.S. (ed.), *The Australian Experience: Critical Essays on Australian Novels*, Australian National University Press, Canberra, 1974.

—— (ed.), *English Transported: Essays on Australasian English*, Australian National University Press, Canberra, 1970.

REES, LESLIE, *A History of Australian Drama*, rev. edn, 2 vols, Angus and Robertson, Sydney, 1978.

ROBSON, L.L., *The Convict Settlers of Australia*, Melbourne University Press, Melbourne, 1965.

ROSENBERG, SIDNEY, *Black Sheep and Golden Fleece. A Study of Nineteenth Century English Attitudes Toward Australian Colonials*, PhD. thesis, Columbia University, 1970.

RUBIN, GAYLE, "Woman as Nigger", in Betty Roszak and Theodore Roszak (eds), *Masculine/Feminine. Readings in Sexual Mythology and the Liberation of Women*, Harper Colophon, New York, 1969.

SANZ, CARLOS, *Australia. Its Discovery and Name*, Dirreccion General de Relaciones Culturales, Madrid, 1964.

SCOTT, ERNEST, *Australian Discovery by Sea*, J. M. Dent and Sons, London, 1927.

SEMPLE, ELLEN, *Influences of Geographical Environment*, Constable, London, 1911.

SERLE, GEOFFREY, *From Deserts the Prophets Come: The Creative Spirit in Australia 1788-1972*, Melbourne, Heinemann, 1973.

SMITH, BERNARD, *The Antipodean Manifesto. Essays in Art and History*, Melbourne University Press, Melbourne, 1976.

—— *Australian Painting 1788-1970*, Oxford University Press, Melbourne, 1971.

—— *Documents on Art and Taste in Australia. The Colonial Period 1770-1914*, Oxford University Press, Melbourne, 1975.

—— *European Vision and the South Pacific 1768-1850. A Study in the History of Art and Ideas*, Clarendon Press, Oxford, 1960.

SPATE, O.H.K., "Terra Australis — Cognita?", *Historical Studies: Australia and New Zealand* 8, 1857, pp.1-19.

SUMMERS, ANNE, *Damned Whores and God's Police. The Colonization of Women in Australia*, Allen Lane, London, 1975.

TAYLOR, ALAN CAREY, *Le Président de Brosses et l'Australie*, Boivin, Paris, 1937.

TEALE, RUTH (ed.), *Colonial Eve. Sources on Women in Australia 1788-1914*, Oxford University Press, Melbourne, 1978.

TIFFIN, CHRIS (ed.), *South Pacific Images*, South Pacific Association for Commonwealth Literature and Language Studies, 1978.

TINKER, CHAUNCEY B., *Nature's Simple Plan. A Phase of Radical Thought in the Mid-Eighteenth Century*, Princeton University Press, Princeton, 1922.

TRIEBEL, L.A., "Australia's Image in the Literature of the West", *Australian Teacher* 45, 1969, pp.26-32.

TURNER, FREDERICK JACKSON, *The Frontier in American History*, Henry Holt, New York, 1953.

TURNER, IAN (ed.), *The Australian Dream: A Collection of Anticipations about Australia from Captain Cook to the Present Day*, Sun Books, Melbourne, 1968.

UREN, MALCOLM, AND ROBERT STEPHENS, *Waterless Horizons*, Robertson and Mullens, Melbourne, 1945.

VALLIS, VAL, "Artist and Environment. An Australian Study", *British Journal of Aesthetics* 2, 1962, pp.328-36.

WALKER, DON D., "The Western Explorer as a Literary Hero: Jedediah Smith and Ludwig Leichhardt", *Western Humanities Review* 29, 1975, pp.243-59.

WALKER, RONALD C., *Infernal Paradise. Mexico and the Modern English Novel*, University of California Press, Berkeley, 1978.

WARD, RUSSEL, *Australia*, Prentice Hall, Englewood, 1965.

—— *The Australian Legend*, Oxford University Press, Melbourne, 1958.

WARNER, OLIVER, *English Maritime Writing. Hakluyt to Cook*, Longmans, Green, London, 1958.

WEBBY, ELIZABETH, "The Aboriginal in Early Australian Literature", *Southerly* 40, 1980, pp.45-63.

WHITE, PATRICK, "A Conversation with Patrick White", *Southerly* 33, 1973, pp.132-42.

—— "Patrick White speaks on factual writing and fiction", *Australian Literary Studies* 10, 1981, pp.99-101.

WHITE, RICHARD, *Inventing Australia*, George Allen and Unwin, Sydney, 1981.

WHITNEY, LOIS, *Primitivism and the Idea of Progress in English Popular Literature of the Eighteenth Century*, Johns Hopkins Press, Baltimore, 1934.

WILKINSON, CLENELL, *William Dampier*, John Lane, London, 1929.

WILLIAMS, HAROLD, *Dean Swift's Library*, The University Press, Cambridge, 1932.

WOOD, G.A., "Ancient and Mediaeval Conceptions of Terra Australis", *Royal Australian Historical Society. Journal and Proceedings* 3, 1916, pp.455-65.

—— *The Discovery of Australia*, Macmillan and Co., London, 1922.

WRIGHT, JOHN KIRTLAND, *Human Nature in Geography*, Harvard University Press, Cambridge (Mass.), 1966.

WRIGHT, JUDITH, "Australia's Double Aspect", *Literary Criterion* 6, 1946, pp.1-11.

—— *Preoccupations in Australian Poetry*, Oxford University Press, Melbourne, 1965.

—— "The Upside-down Hut", in John Barnes (ed.), *The Writer in Australia. A Collection of Literary Documents 1856-1964*, Oxford University Press, Melbourne, 1953.

WRIGHT, LOUIS B., *The Elizabethans' America: A Collection of Early Reports by Englishmen on the New World*, Harvard University Press, Cambridge (Mass.), 1965.

Index